TI

TICC

GUIDE

INDUSTRIAL HERITAGE

CONSERVATION

INDUSTRIAL HERITAGE RE-TOOLED

The TICCIH guide to Industrial Heritage Conservation

edited by
James Douet

THE INTERNATIONAL COMMITTEE FOR THE
CONSERVATION OF THE INDUSTRIAL HERITAGE

TICCIH

J.M.
KAPLAN
FUND

TICCIH – The International Committee for the Conservation of the Industrial Heritage – is
the international organisation for industrial archaeology and the industrial heritage.
Its aim is to study, protect, conserve and explain the remains of industrialisation.
For further information and how to join, see **www.ticcih.org**

Frontispiece:
The challenge faced by industrial heritage:
empty maltings in Lincolnshire, UK. (Masaaki Okada)

Industrial Heritage Re-tooled: The TICCIH guide to Industrial Heritage Conservation

Text copyright © individual authors, 2012

The moral rights of the respective authors have been asserted by them
in accordance with the Copyright, Designs and Patents Act 1988

First edition published in 2012
in association with
The International Committee for the Conservation of the Industrial Heritage (TICCIH)
by Carnegie Publishing Ltd
Carnegie House
Chatsworth Road, Lancaster LA1 4SL
www.carnegiepublishing.com

ISBN 978-1-85936-218-1

British Library Cataloguing-in-Publication data
A catalogue record for this book is available from the British Library

Designed, typeset and originated by Carnegie Publishing
Printed and bound in China by Latitude Press

Contents

Part IV   Sharing and enjoying

Part V   Teaching and learning

Part VI   TICCIH

List of contributors

PROFESSOR HELMUTH ALBRECHT is head of industrial archaeology and the history of technology and director of the Institute for Industrial Archaeology, History of Science and Technology in Freiberg, Germany. Since 2006, he has been a member of the board of directors of TICCIH and organised the XIV TICCIH Congress in 2009 in Freiberg. His research interests include the industrial archaeology of Germany, world heritage studies as well as the history of technology, of physical sciences and of innovation processes. Helmuth.Albrecht@ iwtg.tu-freiberg.de

PROFESSOR LOUIS BERGERON taught as Directeur d'études at the École des Hautes Études en Sciences Sociales, Paris, from 1971 to 1997. Honorary president of the French National Association for Industrial Archaeology and Heritage (CILAC) and President (1990–2000), Honorary President for life (2000) of TICCIH. He was President of the Eco-museum in Le Creusot-Montceau les Mines (France), 1996–2004, co-founder of Koinetwork e.g.e.i., 2002 and co-publisher of the TICCIH *Journal Patrimoine de l'industrie/Industrial Patrimony*. His research interests cover the industrialization of Europe in the eighteenth and nineteenth centuries. lbergeron@wanadoo.fr

EUSEBI CASANELLES is the founder and director of the Museu Nacional de la Ciència i de la Tècnica de Catalunya (MNACTEC), the Catalan national museum of science and technology. It was set up in 1984 and has developed into a network of over 25 industrial museums, each one dealing with a distinct industrial and technical topic. He was first Executive President and then President of TICCIH from 1997 until 2009 and president of the Spanish Association of Industrial Heritage from 1987 until 1992. ecasanelles@gencat.cat

SIR NEIL COSSONS has been engaged in industrial heritage and archaeology for over fifty years and is a founder of TICCIH. He was the first Director of the Ironbridge Museum, from 1971 to 1983 and Director of the Science Museum, London – the National Museum of Science & Industry – for fourteen years. From 2000 to 2007 he was Chairman of English Heritage, the United Kingdom Government's principal adviser on the historic environment of England. nc@ cossons.org.uk

PROFESSOR MICHEL COTTE is emeritus professor of the history of technology at the University of Nantes. He currently works as ICOMOS' advisor for the implementation of the World Heritage Convention. He pays specific attention to the technical and scientific heritage, editing recently with Clive Ruggles (UAI) a joint thematic study: *Heritage Sites of Astronomy and Archaeoastronomy in the context of the UNESCO World Heritage Convention*. michel.cotte@ univ-nantes.fr

PROFESSOR GRÀCIA DOREL-FERRÉ is a professor of the history of industry and teaching industrial archaeology. She is the founder and president of the Association pour le patrimoine industriel de Champagne-Ardenne (APIC), France. After her thesis on the industrial colonies of Catalonia her main research interests have been the evolution of workers' housing and industrial settlements. Her publications include 'La contribution des indianos à la formation du territoire et du paysage industriel catalans durant la seconde moitié du XIX siècle', and *Atlas du patrimoine industriel de Champagne-Ardenne.* She is secretary of the TICCIH agricultural industry section and organiser of several TICCIH section conferences. gracia.dorel@gmail.com

JAMES DOUET is a historic buildings consultant advising on conservation plans and exhibition projects, and editor of the *TICCIH Bulletin.* He trained in geography and industrial archaeology, and undertook various thematic studies for English Heritage including naval dockyards, pumping stations and military barracks, from which came his principal publication, *British Barracks, 1600–1914.* He teaches heritage management and urban history in Barcelona and is researching a publication on royal manufactories. jdouet@movistar.es

DR WOLFGANG EBERT was the developer of the European Route of Industrial Heritage (ERIH) industrial heritage networks. He is Senior Consultant to MSP Impulsprojekt, a German developing agency dealing with any kind of developments of industrial heritage sites on a global level. ebert@industriekultur.de

KEITH FALCONER was appointed in 1971 to undertake the British Industrial Monuments Survey and became Head of Industrial Archaeology at English Heritage, with general oversight for industrial heritage and helped develop a thematic approach to the UK's industrial World Heritage Sites. He has advised on World Heritage Site proposals in Japan, northern France and Uruguay. He is a founder member of TICCIH and a founder council member of the UK Association for Industrial Archaeology. He has co-authored several books including *Guide to England's Industrial Heritage* (1980), *Swindon: Legacy of a Railway Town* (1995) *Ancoats: cradle of industrialization* (2011). keithfalconer@blueyonder.co.uk

DR BENJAMIN FRAGNER has been the director of the Research Centre for Industrial Heritage (VCPD) at the Faculty of Architecture of the Czech Technical University in Prague since 2002. He is a member of the Czech Ministry of Culture's Permanent Committee for the assessment of sites nominated for cultural heritage status. He is currently coordinating a research project on the Industrial Topography of the Czech Republic – Adaptive Re-use of Industrial Heritage, as Part of National and Cultural Identity, and also organises the popular international biennial Vestiges of Industry. He is a member of the executive board of the Czech National Committee of ICOMOS and TICCIH Board member since 2009. benjamin.fragnercpd.cvut.cz

DR JAN AF GEIJERSTAM (Industrial Heritage studies, Royal Institute of Technology. Stockholm, Sweden) is an independent researcher and author. Chairman of the Swedish Industrial Heritage Association and TICCIH's National Representative for Sweden. Presently guest researcher at Heritage Studies, Dept of Conservation, University of Gothenburg. His most recent publication is *National Atlas of Sweden. Swedish mining and metalworking, past and present* (edited with Marie Nisser). jan@geijerstam.se

JOHANNES GROSSEWINKELMANN is curator at the Weltkulturerbe Erzbergwerk Rammelsberg in Goslar, Germany. He has worked at various German industry museums and has published papers on the treatment of collected objects and on the history of vocational education in the German metals industries in the nineteenth and twentieth centuries. sammlung@ rammelsberg.de

STEPHEN HUGHES is Projects Director at the Royal Commission on the Ancient & Historical Monuments for Wales and Vice-President of ICOMOS-UK. He co-ordinated the TICCIH/ ICOMOS *International Canal Monuments List* and *The International Collieries Study* and is a member of the TICCIH Board. He has advised ICOMOS on World Heritage Sites and has represented TICCIH at UNESCO Meetings. His books include *Copperopolis: Landscapes of the Early Industrial Period in Swansea*; *The Archaeology of an Early Railway System: The Brecon Forest Tramroads* and *The Archaeology of the Montgomeryshire Canal: A Guide and Study in Waterways Archaeology*. stephen.hughes@rcahmw.org.uk

DR HELEN LARDNER, architect, is the director of the award-winning heritage conservation firm HLCD Pty Ltd which specialises in providing strategic advice for conservation and adaptive re-use of complex heritage places and undertaking analysis of cultural significance. She is particularly interested in industrial sites and twentieth-century architecture, works internationally and enjoys examining the transfer of technology and knowledge, and its impact on local cultures. She is a member of the Australian Heritage Council, was formerly Vice President of Australia ICOMOS and is currently the National Representative for TICCIH in Australia.   h.lardner@hlcd.com.au

DR HSIAO-WEI LIN is an assistant professor of architecture at Chung Yuan Christian University. She is a board member of TICCIH and the chairman of the organising committee of the XV TICCIH Congress 2012 in Taiwan. She researches as well as advises practical heritage sites. Her most recent publication is *The Introduction of Taiwan's Industrial Heritage* which is the first English text book of this subject in Taiwan. Her research interests include planning, reuse and management of cultural heritage, cultural landscape and industrial heritage.   linhw23@cycu.edu.tw

PROFESSOR PATRICK MARTIN is Professor of Archaeology and Director of Graduate Studies in the Department of Social Sciences at Michigan State University, US. He is editor of *IA, the Journal of the Society for Industrial Archaeology*, and the Executive Secretary of that organisation. He has been president of TICCIH since 2009.   pemartin@mtu.edu

MIRIAM MCDONALD is Industrial Survey Project Manager at the Royal Commission on the Ancient and Historical Monuments of Scotland, the body responsible for recording and maintaining records of Scotland's historic environment. She is secretary both of TICCIH GB, and of the Scottish Industrial Archaeology Panel.   miriam.mcdonald@rcahms.gov.uk

DR JAIME MIGONE RETTIG, architect, at the Pontifical Catholic University of Chile, Doctor in the Conservation of Architectural Goods, Politecnico di Milan, Italy. Dean, Faculty of Cultural Heritage Studies of the SEK International University and President TICCIH-Chile. He has advised on the UNESCO World Heritage Centre Humberstone and Santa Laura in Chile and the nomination of San Luis Potosi in Mexico, with national and international publications. Heritage buildings restoration projects include cathedral of Santiago, Santiago Post Office, Chilean Historic and Military Museum, Sacramentino Church of Santiago, among others.   jaime.migone@gmail.com

DR TUIJA MIKKONEN is senior adviser at the Ministry of the Environment, in Helsinki, Finland, with issues concerning the built heritage and cultural environment. She is the chair of TICCIH-Finland and has advised ICOMOS in assessing industrial World Heritage Sites. Her research interests include industrial buildings and sites and mining industry. She has written about corporate architecture in Finland in the 1940s and 1950s.   tuija.mikkonen@ymparisto.fi

DR BODE MORIN is the director of Eckley Miners' Village, an historic coal-mining site operated by the Pennsylvania Historic and Museum Commission, and has nearly twenty years' experience in the heritage field. He holds the first Ph.D. in industrial heritage and archaeology from Michigan Technological University, where his work focused on industrial heritage practices and conflicts with environmental remediation at US Superfund sites. He also has a masters degree in Industrial Archaeology from Michigan Tech. and has worked as an historian for the Historic American Engineering Record of the US National Park Service, curator of Sloss Furnaces in Birmingham, Alabama, and as Historic Fort Wayne project manager for the Detroit Historical Museum.   bjmorin@gmail.com

MASSIMO NEGRI was the co-author of the first book published in Italy about industrial archaeology (1978). Founding member of the Italian Society for Industrial Archaeology and then of the Italian Association for the Archaeological Industrial Patrimony (AIPAI). He teaches museology at the Master Course in Industrial Heritage, and industrial archaeology at the TPTI course both at the State University of Padua. He has also founded the Executive Master Course in European Museology at the IULM University of Milan. Director of the European Museum Forum (UK) for ten years, he is currently director of the European Museum Academy Foundation (NL). Frequently engaged in museum projects, has recently directed the museological program of the new Museum of the History of Bologna.   kriterion.negri@libero.it

PROFESSOR GYÖRGYI NÉMETH is associate professor in industrial history and industrial archaeology at the University of Miskolc, Hungary, where she developed the country's first industrial archaeology university programme. She was a member of the TICCIH board between 1993 and 2009, and organised the 1999 regional TICCIH conference in Hungary and Slovakia. Her research interests include the theory and practice of industrial heritage conservation as well as the evolution of heavy industrial landscapes, publishing *Growth, Decline and Recovery: heavy industrial regions in transition*.   nemethgeorgie@freemail.hu

DR MILES OGLETHORPE is Head of International Policy at Historic Scotland, the Scottish Government Agency responsible for protecting and promoting the historic environment. He has been a board member of TICCIH since 2003.   miles.oglethorpe@scotland.gsi.gov.uk

PROFESSOR MASAAKI OKADA is associate professor at Kinki University, Department of Civil and Environmental Engineering, Osaka, and visiting scholar at the University of Cambridge. He is interested in social and aesthetic value of Technoscape (landscape of industry), industrial, civil engineering and defence heritage. He is on the executive committee of ICOHTEC and member of many committees of academic (JSCE) or national and local governments in Japan. His recent publications are *Technoscape – Landscape Theory of Integration and Estrangement* (Kajimashuppankai 2003) and *Civil Engineering Heritage in Japan* (Kodansha, 2012: co-authorship).   okd@orion.ocn. ne.jp

BELEM OVIEDO GAMEZ is director of the Archivo Histórico y Museo de la Minería de Pachuca, Mexico, TICCIH Mexico President (2006–2012) and ICOMOS Mexicano National Vice President (2012–2015). She was elected to the TICCIH Board in 2000.   ahmm@prodigy. net.mx

PROFESSOR MASSIMO PREITE teaches urban planning at the Faculty of Architecture in Florence, Vice-Chairman of the Italian Association for the Industrial Archaeological Heritage (AIPAI), board member of TICCIH. He has coordinated numerous projects for the redevelopment of the mining and industrial heritage, the Park/Mining Museum of Abbadia San Salvatore, the National Mining Park of the Colline Metallifere and the new Steel-Working Museum in Piombino. He advised on the nomination of mining and industrial sites as a UNESCO World Heritage Site. His most recent publications are Paesaggi industriali del Novecento (Florence, 2006) and Masterplan, the Development of the Mining Landscape (Florence, 2009).   preite@unifi.it

GUSTAV ROSSNES trained as an ethnologist and works as senior adviser on Industrial Heritage at the Norwegian Directorate for Cultural Heritage. He has taken part on several field works in Polar areas – documenting mining installations in the Arctic (Svalbard) and shore whaling stations in the South Antarctic Islands.   gr@ra.no

DR PAUL SMITH is an historian who has been working since 1986 at the Direction générale des Patrimoines, the heritage department of the French Ministry of Culture, with a particular interest in the industrial heritage and in the built heritage of transport systems. He has been involved in several European projects, for example on historic airports and on the future of historic industrial cities ('Working Heritage'). He has published widely on the French tobacco and match industries and is a member of the editorial committee of the French industrial archaeology review.   paul. smith@culture.gouv.fr

STUART SMITH OBE was Secretary of TICCIH for 26 years and has attended every General Assembly. Starting at Ironbridge in 1972 as Curator of Technology, he succeeded Neil Cossons as Director and worked there for 20 years. Subsequently he moved to Cornwall to head The Trevithick Trust, which was charged with restoring and creating industrial museums throughout the county to support the successful application for World Heritage Site status for Cornish hard rock mining. He has lectured all over the world on industrial archaeology and TICCIH and since retirement has acted as a consultant on potential world heritage sites, particularly in Asia and Norway.   stuartbsmith@chygarth.co.uk

PETER STOTT, the US representative to TICCIH, was a staff member of the UNESCO World Heritage Centre in Paris between 1996 and 2006. Most recently, for the 50th anniversary of the US National Park Service's Office of International Affairs, he has been engaged in the preparation of a history of the National Park Service and the World Heritage Convention, being published serially in 2011 and 2012 in the *George Wright Forum*. He is currently a Preservation Planner at the Massachusetts Historical Commission in Boston, US. ph.stott@gmail.com

IAIN STUART is an archaeologist and historian based in south-eastern Australia. His company, JCIS Consultants, provides professional consulting services in the areas of history, archaeology, heritage management and cultural landscapes.   iain_stuart@optusnet.com.au

NORBERT TEMPEL trained as a mechanical engineer (Dortmund University of Technology), and is Head of the Engineering and Conservation Department, Westphalian Museum of Industry, Dortmund, the largest museum of industry in Germany managing eight former industrial sites, since 1986. Co-Founder (1995) and Associate Editor of the quarterly *IndustrieKultur Magazine*. Research, publications and lectures in the field of conservation of big industrial sites and the history of railways. Member of TICCIH and ICOMOS (Member of the Scientific Committee of ISC 20C), National Representative of TICCIH Germany. Co-organiser of the international conferences BigStuff 2007 and TICCIH 2009 in Germany. Norbert.Tempel@lwl.org

DR BARRIE TRINDER was closely involved with the Ironbridge Gorge Museum in its formative years, was joint organiser with Neil Cossons of FICCIM in 1973, and taught at the Ironbridge Institute between 1980 and 1995. He has written extensively on the history of industry in Shropshire and nationally, edited the *Blackwell Encyclopedia of Industrial Archaeology* (1992), and contributed substantially to the designation documents for the World Heritage Sites at Ironbridge, Blaenafon and Pontcysyllte. His large-scale study, *Britain's Industrial Revolution: the making of a manufacturing people*, will be published by Carnegie Publishing in 2012.   barrie@trinderhistory.co.uk

MARK WATSON is a buildings and areas conservation professional, experienced in urban regeneration projects, delivering the adaptive re-use of buildings in partnership with others, and evaluating outcomes with a view to their socio-economic and sustainability benefits. Trained in history and in industrial archaeology, he works in Historic Scotland, the government agency for heritage conservation. He has worked on the nomination, assessment and management of world heritage sites, and is British national representative for TICCIH. His research interests include textile mills and landscapes – drafting the international comparative study of these – iron building structures, and impact evaluation.   mark.watson@scotland.gsi.gov.uk

Introduction

James Douet

R*ETOOLING* is an industrial engineer's term; it means reequipping a factory with the latest machinery and the most modern methods in order to keep it up to date and competitive. This book aims to perform a similar function for everyone interested in the heritage left by industry, collecting together the most effective techniques and modern practices, tried and tested around the world, for dealing with this singular cultural legacy.

Singular but challenging, too, for its technical complexity, its economic weight, its scale and magnitude, its social consequences as well as the negative perceptions that sometimes hamper its appreciation. What should we make of the industrial heritage, how can we make the most of it, and the best of it?

Consider its scope. Of the 'cultural goods' that modern societies aim to sustain for their future well-being, few are more universal than the industrial heritage. This, therefore, is not a book just for industrial archaeologists and heritage managers. In any part of the world affected by industrialisation, archaeologists are certain to encounter material from the period, while architects and builders have greater opportunities to adapt and re-use old industrial buildings than any other, for their quantity as well as versatility. Their embodied energy helps environmentalists to deliver sustainable development goals. Adapting and repurposing them are now mainstream strategies for urban planners. As tourism becomes central to the economy of many towns, the potential of the industrial heritage is fast becoming apparent. Similarly, the educational possibilities offered by historical industry are a resource of which schools and teachers must be aware. Meanwhile, the 'challenge of the evidence' – the intrinsic evidential value of the places – continues to confront historians and academics wherever industrialisation had, or is having, its transformational consequences.

This phenomenon is not exclusive to the rust belts or ghost towns of post-industrial decline in northern Europe and America. The most striking examples of factory adaptation, urban regeneration or historic interpretation are no longer in the canonical cradles and birthplaces of the Industrial Revolution but likely to be found in Shanghai, New York or Istanbul.

In 2002 The International Committee for the Conservation of the Industrial Heritage (TICCIH), hammered out a charter, signing it in the great steel-milling and tank-manufacturing town of Nizhny Tagil in the Russian Urals. International charters are a way of formulating key concepts and fundamental methodologies, which the Nizhny Tagil Charter does for industrial archaeology. It proposes some basic definitions

The High Line park in New York is an elevated railway that passes through Manhattan's West Side. It is owned by the City of New York and maintained and operated by a non-profit conservancy, the Friends of the High Line. The linear park is credited with revitalising a swathe of the city, generating $2 billion in private investment alongside the park and contributing to 12,000 jobs in the area. (Jim Henderson – Creative Commons)

for the scope and period of the subject, while advising on the best ways to understand, maintain and share what is especially meaningful about the remains of industrial culture. In 2011 a further framework document was signed, this time by TICCIH and the International Council for Monuments and Sites (ICOMOS), their *Joint Principles for the Conservation of Industrial Heritage Sites, Structures, Areas and Landscapes*. This took place in Dublin, hence the name 'Dublin Charter'.

To get the most from these skeletal 'doctrinal texts' they need to be fleshed out and clothed, which is the idea behind this book. *Industrial Heritage Retooled* started as a 'glossed' version of the Nizhny Tagil Charter. Specialist authors would be invited to elucidate and expand the sparse text of the Charter's main clauses, illustrating them with examples drawn from outstanding heritage sites around the world.

The title of the book comes from a 2010 symposium held in Tarrytown, New York, co-sponsored by the J M Kaplan Fund. The assembled experts explored the present and future of America's industrial heritage, and asked some tough questions about how the heritage of industry gets treated alongside other more familiar or amenable remains of our past, and what sort of tools and resources can and should be applied to keep it in good shape both for now and in the future.

The symposium was intended as a launching pad for new ideas and this is one of them. Patrick Martin forged the link between the symposium and TICCIH, of which he is President. *Industrial Heritage Retooled* – the book – was also made possible by the open-handed financial support of the J M Kaplan Fund, and the backing of a key member of the Fund's staff, Ken Lustbader. It was he who framed the specific goal that it be a definitive international guide to contemporary best practices. The book was to be presented in an accessible and approachable format and written for a wide audience of enthusiasts, preservationists, community-based not-for-profits and private-sector developers, industrial archaeologists, teachers and scholars.

Through TICCIH's international network, more than thirty expert authors were identified and brought together, each kindly agreeing to contribute a chapter on a subject with which they were intimate through many years of research, reflection and professional experience.

The book opens with four reflective essays which set out the essential values and meanings associated with the Industrial Revolution, industrialisation and its material and cultural heritage. Part II examines the methodological and technical options that we have available to interrogate the raw material, the physical evidence for industrialisation and the societies that developed within it: artefacts, structures, sites, processes and landscapes as well as documents and images.

Part III presents the procedures by which the abundant resources of *industrial archaeology* are transformed into the valued but vulnerable material we try to capture and conserve as *industrial heritage*: what is to be selected and why; how to protect and to manage change while ensuring that historic value is sustained; how conservation can also be an economic catalyst; all the modern techniques for adapting or repurposing sites without disproportionate sacrifice; profiting from the in-built energy in existing buildings; letting nature conserve the industrial ruin; the benefits that community participation inspires; and finally the dynamic of World Heritage and the spin-off and trickle-down effects that nomination and designation can prompt.

The industrial heritage identified, understood, protected … Part IV examines how it can be shared and enjoyed. The industrial museums and the conserved production sites which have opened to visitors in recent years have brought a sometimes difficult and unapproachable subject to a wide public, including disproportionate numbers of the young. The success of innovative techniques for preserving and interpreting working machinery and for presenting complex processes is evident in their unprecedented visitor figures, as well as in the growing number of people, loosely categorised as tourists, who set out to discover places once thought inimical to tourism.

The fifth section of the book discusses the part education has to play, not only by traditional methods but also through the internet, in making sure that public heritage agencies, non-profit groups, archaeological contractors, architectural practices, consultancies or owners, are suitably equipped to treat the historic material of industry in an informed way.

This publication is an important step for TICCIH and part of a determined effort to reach beyond the organisation's habitual constituency. Patrick Martin takes much of the credit for giving definitive form to the original idea. Neil Cossons' support and advice contributed greatly to the final shape and style of the book. The Nizhny Tagil Charter around which it is structured is one of Eusebi Casanelles' major achievements. All three, together with Terry Reynolds, Benjamin Fragner, Barry Gamble, Massimo Preite, Iain Stuart and Alison Wain made valuable comments on the texts, and thanks are also due to Myrick Howard, Marie-Noëlle Polino and Hans-Peter Bärtschi. All the photographic credits are in the text, but particular thanks to Billy Hustace for permission to reproduce his photograph on the cover. Finally, special recognition is owed to all the authors, each connected with TICCIH over many years, who have tapped an immense reserve of professional experience and personal enthusiasm to produce perceptive and illuminating chapters.

Part I

Values and meanings

1

Why preserve the industrial heritage?

Neil Cossons

The world order is changing. Inexorably, the economic centre of gravity is moving east. That progression is driven in the main by the industrial revolution taking place in China. For some three centuries industrialisation has been the crucial prime mover of global economic and social change as one country after another has lifted itself from agrarian dependency to some new form of prosperity. Only industrialisation enables nations to make that transition. The effects have been wide-ranging and profound. For some, industrialisation has become the central engine of their economies. For others, moving successively from primary commodity producers to adding value through processing has enabled them to achieve increased economic self-determination.

Historically, the effects of industrialisation have been challenging and far-reaching. The legacy is prolific and overwhelming. In most industrial countries urbanisation has been one of the more significant of the social and economic consequences. Today, for the first time in human history, more people live in towns and cities than in rural environments. Far-reaching improvements in the standard of living and per-capita GDP, and advances in national power and enhanced global status, are all qualities reserved for industrial nations. Capitalism as we know it is also a product of nineteenth-century industrialisation; so too are socialism and communism. And, although globalisation has its roots well before the age of industry, it has been the development of the extraordinary commercial and trading empires of the industrial world that has given real meaning to the term. Out of this has grown the most fundamental change in the human condition and the human habitat.

Today, flourishing trade and industrial investment among emerging countries represents a further dramatic shift in how the world economy has worked for over two hundred years, replacing the traditional flow of natural resources into the industrial West, which in return exported textiles and other factory-made goods to the developing world. The United States is no longer India's largest trading partner; China has assumed that position. And India and Brazil both export more manufactured goods to fellow emerging markets than to the developed world. China is the largest foreign investor in Brazil, challenging the historical dominance of the United States in South America; and, Russia's Rusal, the world's largest aluminium producer, launched its first public offering not in London or New York but on the Hong Kong stock exchange.

There is abundant evidence too that existing industrial nations that neglect their manufacturing capability, and the technological innovation that underscores it, and that fail to adapt to these seismic global transmutations, will fall back in terms of national and per-capita GDP and long-term economic sustainability. As new nations industrialise so older ones have to consider their position in the changing world order. Where does their future lie? And what, if anything, do they do with their past?

In the second half of the eighteenth century, the early stirrings of what by the 1840s had come to be called the 'Industrial Revolution' could be found, first in Great Britain and increasingly across Western Europe; new technologies, new methods of organising labour, new means of applying the power of water or steam to manufacture, in new forms of buildings that we now call mills or factories and, crucially, new models of settlement. And in these new industrial communities grew up a new industrial culture with patterns and conditions of work that were novel, replacing the thousand-year traditions of seasonality and uncertainty that had characterised pre-industrial agricultural economies. The industrial heritage is a complex amalgam of places and people, processes and practices, which continues to defy explanation of its origins and astounds in the effects of its subsequent development and decay.

Values

All this raises the question of whether, given the overwhelming magnitude of the three hundred-year-old industrial experience, it has a history and heritage that matters and, if so, why and to whom? It is only in the last fifty years or so that industrial heritage – recognition and valuing of the material evidence of industrialisation – has begun to figure in our consciousness. There are several reasons for this. Most of the initial interest

Ditherington Flax Mill, Shrewsbury, England, built in 1796/97, is the world's first iron-framed building. It was converted to a maltings in the 1880s. This c.1970 photograph shows one of the malt floors shortly before closure. Now empty, it is in the ownership of English Heritage but its future remains uncertain. Too precious to lose, too fragile to use, the flax mill illustrates the dilemma of buildings of high evidential value but low utility. (Brian Bracegirdle/Ironbridge Gorge Museum Trust)

in what is today called heritage grew out of curiosity about and study of the history and archaeology of the medieval age and earlier. Indeed, in Europe the desire to preserve the past was in some senses a consequence of industrialisation and its cataclysmic effects on pre-industrial communities and landscapes.

So, when we contemplate the values attaching to the industrial heritage we need to understand that, despite the overwhelming impact of industrialisation on the lives of us all – and in part because of it – the public's perceptions of heritage derive from roots, sentiments and attitudes that lie elsewhere, in an earlier age and a different aesthetic. Industrial heritage is a new, novel and challenging arrival in the heritage arena. Defining why it matters is important not just for the public at large but for many heritage organisations and professionals. For these reasons it is crucial to understand what we mean by value and importance and, at the same time, recognise that the techniques of preservation and conservation built up over many years in the wider historic environment sector do not necessarily meet the demands of industrial heritage. Just as industrialisation has been a new and unique economic and social phenomenon, so too the challenges posed by the conservation of its remains require innovative new approaches. Often, legislation defined for one purpose may not fit the new demands posed by the industrial heritage. All these factors impact on the approach to determining value. Indeed, having a clear understanding of value is the more important in an environment where levels of understanding and acceptability may be low. The context – social, economic, environmental and political – all need to be taken into account. So too do the skills and predilections of those who have a stake in the future, as public or practitioners, developers or heritage professionals. Industrial heritage is, arguably, a unique cultural discourse; it brings challenges found nowhere else in the heritage sector and requires new answers, for there are few precedents. It is not for the faint-hearted.

Dramatic as the arrival of industrialisation may have been, as the most significant engine of change in human history, the effects of its decline have often been equally cataclysmic, reflected in decay, dereliction and despair. Here again, the heritage of the post-industrial poses unique challenges; to find a future for industrial places in the context of economic fragility and the social issues that so frequently stem from it. To advocate preservation of a redundant industrial site, basing the arguments on traditional heritage values, does not always look attractive to a community afflicted by economic collapse or high levels of unemployment. Or, alternatively, while the community may find the notion appealing, offering as it might the chance of capturing something of their former spirit and pride, harsh economic circumstances make realisation by conventional means an impossibility. It is in these contexts that one might legitimately ask, 'why preserve the industrial heritage?' Finding answers often poses challenges beyond the ordinary.

Consider some of the basic principles. First, the material heritage has intrinsic value as evidence of a past. This evidential value may derive from its archaeology; the remains are the means of our understanding a past and a people. In this respect industrial remains enjoy common currency with other archaeological verification. Often, documentary evidence, unavailable to those who study earlier periods of history, can provide additional – and sometimes the most substantive – information. But it is rare that documentary sources can wholly replace the physical. Increasingly, as industrial studies have matured over recent years, the real contribution that material evidence can make to understanding has become apparent. This evidential value reflects activities that had and continue to have profound historical consequences, and the motives for protecting the industrial heritage are based on the universal value of this evidence.

But evidential importance in the archaeological sense is not the only value attaching to industrial sites and landscapes, nor is it necessarily the most significant. The industrial heritage is of wider social and cultural significance as part of the record of people's lives, and as such provides an important sense of history and identity. That may relate to an industry, a specific company, an industrial community, or a particular trade or skill. Or, the industrial heritage may have technological and scientific value in the history of manufacturing, engineering and construction, or have aesthetic qualities deriving from its architecture, design or planning. These values are intrinsic to the site itself, its fabric, components, machinery and setting in the industrial landscape, in written documentation, and also in the intangible records of industry contained in human memories, traditions and customs. Industrial heritage may offer identity for a community or provide the signature for a place, recognised externally.

Evidential value can extend further, to embrace places where significant innovations took place. Care needs to be exercised here as technological innovation, even more than pioneering entrepreneurial enterprise, can rarely be ascribed to one place or person. 'World firsts' are temptingly attractive but often raise more questions than they answer. But taking a less deterministic view there are undoubtedly places that for legitimate historical reasons have taken on a primary significance in terms of scholarly acceptance and public perception that justifies their veneration – for the purposes of history. Some are World Heritage Sites and, as such, they have had to meet UNESCO's criteria of Outstanding Universal Value.

The Ironbridge Gorge in England was one of the first, inscribed as a World Heritage Site in 1987. Here was a landscape rich in the remains of early industry, ranging from icons such as the Old Furnace where in 1709 iron was first smelted with coke instead of charcoal, to the 1779 Iron Bridge across the River Severn, and set in a river valley that both defined context and offered prolific evidence of an evolving community, from pre-industrial roots to post-industrial decay. Significant in realising the intrinsic heritage value of the Ironbridge Gorge was the impact of prolonged economic decline. This had two effects; first, to slow the rate of change, as new investment was largely absent. This is the ossification factor so frequently encountered in areas of industrial relapse; survival through benign decay. Second, conditions had become bad enough to prompt outside intervention in the form of a government-funded regeneration agency – Telford Development Corporation – with a remit to revive the economic and social fortunes of the wider East Shropshire coalfield area. The Corporation saw Ironbridge as an asset and an opportunity, with history and conservation as the keys to reviving its fortunes. Out of this grew a not-for-profit management body, the Ironbridge Gorge Museum Trust, which since 1968 has managed the key sites.

In ascribing value to historic industrial environments it is easy to forget that these were places of work. Empty mills once contained manufacturing machinery and the prime movers that powered it. Almost invariably, both will have disappeared soon after closure. Most of the industrial buildings that feature in the heritage debate on value, and subsequent discussions on their future, are thus empty husks, devoid of the life and activity that went on in them and which were the reasons for their existence. The consequence is that the perpetuation of machinery *in situ*, and especially in working

Queen Street Mill, Burnley, England. This once-typical weaving shed from 1894, its looms powered by a Lancashire steam mill engine through line-shafting and belt-wheels, is now unique and preserved as a working cotton mill. The accident of survival has made this a site of outstanding importance. (Neil Cossons)

condition, is a rare attribute that can confer exceptional value simply by virtue of the accident of survival.

In 1900 there were some 100,000 looms in and around Burnley in Lancashire, England. The town was the world's largest single manufacturer of cotton cloth; the industry is today extinct there. But one mill survives substantially intact, Queen Street Mill, Harle Syke, opened in 1894 for the manufacture of grey cloth, cotton fabric that was bleached and dyed elsewhere (see illustration). The co-operative multiple-ownership financial structure of the company inhibited change, and when the mill closed in 1982 the original looms and steam engine were still in place and in use. It was at this point that its extraordinary importance was recognised, and it reopened in 1986 as a working museum where cotton fabric is still woven on some of the 308 remaining looms. Sale of the cloth makes a modest contribution towards running costs. Here is an example of something typical and commonplace that by virtue of serendipity survived into an era where its extraordinary rarity gave it a value beyond the ordinary. Today, it is thought to be the only steam-powered weaving shed in the world.

Queen Street Mill epitomises the issues faced when ascribing value to industrial sites and landscapes. Value may be sensed and articulated at a very local level, often by people who have no background in heritage or understanding of the methods of protest or advocacy. These are often people with passion but no voice, and time and again the industrial heritage is the subject of their concerns. These are the people directly affected by industrial change. Their arguments may be easily dismissed as emotional attachment to jobs lost or communities destroyed, or simply as fear of the future, whatever that might hold. Here can be found industrial strength dedication combined with an innocence of how to campaign for a different future.

Not far from Burnley, also in Pennine Lancashire, is the Whitefield area of Nelson, another former cotton town where the mills had closed. Demolition of the terraced houses of the former industrial community, still occupied and generally in sound condition, was seen by the local authority as an opportunity for the regeneration of Whitefield's economic fortunes. But the people of Whitefield did not want to move. Nor did they know how to protest. They appealed to the outside world. Help came from English Heritage and other agencies to support them in their cause and today their houses and their futures in them are secure. The lesson here is that national agencies need to be aware of local priorities and be prepared to step in to support them.

The case of Nelson highlights another of the issues presented by the industrial heritage. When the mill has closed or the seam runs out and the mine shuts down, it is communities that survive. Industrial housing represents in many cases the most prolific evidence of former industrialisation. These are the houses that litter the rust-belt landscapes of old industrial regions and that are often all that is left when the rest has gone. But the people are still there, with their memories, their friendships, and what is left of their pride. Time and again the claim is made that these are the people who want to see the back of old industrial plant and the hardship and anguish that attended it. Almost invariably the opposite is the case; some of the greatest commitment to supporting the cause of industrial heritage comes from communities whose history it was. In terms of values, these are some of the most difficult to capture but most powerfully expressed.

An example is the abandoned Chesapeake & Ohio Canal, which was purchased in 1938 by the United States government and placed under the care of the National Park Service to be restored as a recreation area. As a result the lower 35 kilometres (22 miles) of the full 292-kilometre length (182 miles) were repaired and re-watered. After the war the idea of turning the remaining route over to automobiles was vigorously opposed by numerous communities along the route. Their initiative was championed by United States Supreme Court Associate Justice William O. Douglas who in 1954 led an eight-day hike along the full length of the towpath from Cumberland to Washington DC. Popular support was galvanised, and in January 1971 the canal was designated as a National Historic Park. Here national and community interests coalesced around a common cause but the timescale involved – despite the intervention of the Second World War – was not untypical of projects of this nature and magnitude.

Another United States initiative has put community groups in the driving seat of conservation projects, some of great scale and complexity. National Heritage Areas are sites designated by Congress to encourage historic preservation of an area and an appreciation of its heritage. Several have industrial heritage as their central theme. They are not National Park Service sites, nor are they federally owned or managed, but are administered by state governments, not-for-profit organisations or private corporations. There are currently 49 – some using an alternative title, such as National Heritage Corridor. Rivers of Steel Heritage Corporation is one, dedicated to capturing something of the history of south-west Pennsylvania's industrial communities. Another is the Delaware and Lehigh National Heritage Corridor, which stretches 265 kilometres (165 miles) across five counties and some hundred municipalities in eastern Pennsylvania, following the historic routes of the Lehigh & Susquehanna Railroad, the Lehigh Valley Railroad and the Lehigh Navigation, Lehigh Canal and Delaware Canal from Wilkes-Barre to Bristol. Included is the industrial heritage of Bethlehem Steel.

This raises the issue of the relationship between national and local agencies, between academic and community interests, between those who seek certainty based on defined and quantifiable value measures and others driven by more emotional imperatives. It is easy for head and heart to be in conflict when the future of industrial places is in debate. There has to be room for both. Industrial heritage demands knowledge, great judgement and real understanding. From understanding grows valuing; from valuing grows caring; and from caring grows enjoyment and inspiration. Industrial heritage is often a bottom-up business, struggling to survive in a top-down world. The best results come from a symbiotic relationship between the two. But, it is crucial that value is understood and that it is expressed in language that non-believers can understand. One of the weaknesses of the wider heritage community in recent years is that its carefully honed mores mean little to the outside world. Grandiloquence can be a fatal flaw. If this is a public heritage then the public deserves to be accorded the respect of understanding the nature and content of the arguments. Equally, for the heritage sector to indulge in academic casuistry is a recipe for losing the confidence of the people.

The values that underscore these initiatives are complex and multi-layered and do not sit easily with conventional conservation legislation. What the industrial heritage demonstrates repeatedly in many countries is that its values need to be articulated powerfully and forcefully, and that determination is needed to shape the bureaucratic system, and often the legislation, to meet the needs of this new heritage challenge. And industrial heritage often involves the collision of principles on the one hand and the scale and challenge of practicality on the other.

Sustainability

This is manifest in the movement, worldwide, to recycle industrial buildings which, having enjoyed one life, are now redundant. For long seen as liabilities these are increasingly appreciated as assets-in-waiting, ready to be adapted to another perhaps quite alien purpose unconnected with, or quite alien to, their history. Adaptive re-use has blossomed in recent years and is often seen as the only means of retaining old industrial buildings or areas. The roots of this movement can be found in the United States in the 1960s, with celebrated examples in economically buoyant cities such as San Francisco and Boston. The conversion between 1964 and 1968 by architects Wurster, Bernadi and Emmons of the Ghirardelli chocolate factory into shops, restaurants, galleries, and offices at a cost of some US $12 million, followed by the conversion of nearby ice-houses into offices and showrooms, is widely credited with starting the trend for waterfront rehabilitation based on recycled historic buildings. It set a style that has evolved on similar lines worldwide. And it has turned historic industrial waterfronts into hot property. Retail, residential and leisure-based waterfront schemes now abound in, for example, St Katharine Docks, London; Albert Dock, Liverpool; Darling Harbour, Sydney; Victoria & Alfred, Cape Town and Granville Island, Vancouver.

Equally influential has been the transformation of the great textile mill complex of Lowell, Massachusetts, into a National Historical Park. Here one of the largest industrial textile communities in the world was faced with future decay unless a new and radical solution could be found; the result, a combination of federal, state and city investment, in an historic area that has become the engine not only of Lowell's regeneration but hugely influential in shaping attitudes internationally.

Such is the power and attractiveness of the re-use formula and so commercially successful can be the results, that the value and intrinsic importance of the historic buildings themselves can easily be easily overlooked. Here again understanding is the key. It requires good architects and historians with the right level of understanding of intrinsic quality to effect an economically viable transformation that reinforces rather than erodes the fundamental values of the place – the buildings externally and internally, their context and setting. That these are not simply structures with structural and aesthetic qualities that make them attractive for re-use, but places where the memories of the world were formed, is an elusive attribute easily overlooked. Definition of value as a prelude to regeneration is critical.

Regeneration of whole post-industrial regions offers still bigger challenges, driven by different motives. Here the scale of dereliction demands an answer; to do nothing is not an option. The role of public-sector driver as a means of mitigating environmental and social dislocation, and thus creating opportunity for private-sector investment, has been a thread that runs through much of the heritage- and culturally-led industrial regeneration schemes across Europe. A prime example has been Emscher Park, where the vast brownfield landscape of the Ruhr valley in north-west Germany, once the heartland of Europe's coal and steel industries, has been revitalised. Here a top-down and carefully integrated development plan backed with huge funds from the state government of North Rhine-Westphalia, the German Federal Government, European Union and private sector, has enabled nearly 800 square kilometres (more than 300 square miles) of industrial dereliction to be rehabilitated within a carefully defined framework of ecological principles. Within this macro-structure individual sites were then targeted for redevelopment and local private and public initiatives encouraged.

Removal of the polluted remnants of mine tailings, coke ovens, gas and chemical plants, has been followed by landscaping to create linear green spaces interspersed with development areas in which old industrial housing has been renovated and new residential property built. Four fundamental principles characterise the approach at Emscher:

- re-use of brownfield land as a means of making good dereliction and preventing exploitation of previously undeveloped 'greenfields';

- extending the life of existing buildings that can be saved, in preference to building new;

- using ecologically sound building practices for new build and for adaptive re-use;

- transforming the region's production and employment structure towards environmentally friendly methods.

As Emscher's visionary planner, Karl Ganser, states, 'Even the best planned new buildings are no match against the preservation, modernisation, conversion and re-use of existing buildings when it comes down to the consumption of resources'. And re-use makes sense in terms of infrastructure costs, as these sites are usually well endowed with services such as roads and sewers.

One of the striking aspects of Emscher Park is the profusion of mammoth steel plants, gasholders and mine headframes. These have, where possible, been retained, often as monuments in the landscape. The great gasholder in Oberhausen is now a cultural centre for conventions, theatre and concerts, while the celebrated Zollverein pithead frame in Essen, designed in 1928 by Fritz Schupp and Martin Kremer, forms the heart of a cultural complex that is now a World Heritage property. It was designated European Capital of Culture for 2010.

In France some 100 square kilometres (40 square miles) of the Nord-Pas-de-Calais offers an outstanding diversity of coal-mining remains; five generations of winding engines, some 200 waste tips, transport systems, and numerous areas of miners' housing. All this illustrates the impact of a 300-year industry on a huge area, reflecting its vivid industrial culture and traditions. Mining ended in 1990, but since 2000 the Mission Bassin Minier has been promoting the candidacy of the coalfield for World Heritage status.

Similarly, in Kyushu and Yamaguchi, the evidence of the extraordinary transition, from the end of the Tokugawa era through the period of the Meiji restoration, which built the foundation for Japan's industrial revolution, forms the basis for a World Heritage nomination embracing the coal, iron and steel and ship-building industries. Here is first-hand material evidence, captured in sites and landscapes of intrinsic archaeological and historic value, of the birth of a modern nation, the first Asian country to industrialise.

Conclusion

The industrial landscape is a misunderstood heritage: at worst, urban rustbelt, dangerous, a toxic wilderness; at best, an outstanding historical resource to be re-used, regenerating communities, offering real richness and opportunity, reinforcing cultural identity and creating new commercial prospects. But it can also be a vivid reminder of how today's world came to be the way it is, when industry employed whole communities and provided the heartbeat for many towns and cities. In this respect these historic industrial landscapes deserve our closest attention.

Today in many post-industrial societies, industrial culture is no longer central to people's lives; ensuring its past matters to new generations poses new dilemmas. The narrow economic arguments – tourism and cultural renaissance, adaptive re-use and expanded retail opportunities – are challenged by the sheer scale of Liverpool's or Detroit's predicament. And yet the fate and future of these places is of interest to us all because as world cities they belong to us all. In a global society this is an even more persuasive argument than we might at first imagine. We have an opportunity to recalibrate our view of the past and the values we place on its heritage by acknowledging

Pithead baths, preserved coal mine, Kladno, Czech Republic. The presence of absence: miners' clothing from the last shift hanging in the pithead baths. (Neil Cossons)

the democracy of the meanings and metaphors that attach to it. These are whole places, and they deserve to be treated as such.

That means ditching some of our heritage predilections and comfortable traditions; move away from individual sites, structures and buildings to see landscapes in the round as places to be re-ordered for people and where an understanding of the past can liberate a resource for the future. The new urbanism, a growing recognition that human habitats and the web of history afford creative synergies, the innovative philosophies of new-generation architect planners, are all responses to the challenge of reviving the fortunes of what for many communities can be a daunting prospect.

And the world's post-industrial landscapes are littered with outstanding places that have an intrinsic value, in terms of their history and archaeology. This transcends any usefulness that adapting them for new purposes might afford, even supposing that to be possible. Here we need to preserve for history's sake. The origins of the industrial age, the first great global empire, stand with those of ancient Egypt, Athens or Rome. Capturing these industrial landscapes and their futures for posterity is increasingly seen as an obligation by nations proud of their industrial roots and keen to retain symbols of a distinguished past.

The future of these working places is in our hands; to preserve for posterity, to recycle for tomorrow, or here and there to leave alone as unmanaged ruins so that future generations can make choices for themselves based on our prudence and their values and judgements.

Further reading

BLUESTONE, Daniel: *Buildings, Landscape and Memory: case studies in historic preservation*. New York: W W Norton, 2011

CLARK, Kate (ed.): *Capturing the Public Value of Heritage: the proceedings of the London conference, 25–26 January 2006*. English Heritage: Swindon, on behalf of the conference sponsors, the Department for Culture, Media and Sport, English Heritage, the Heritage Lottery Fund and the National Trust, 2006

COSSONS, Neil (ed.): *Perspectives on Industrial Archaeology*. London: Science Museum, 2000

COSSONS, Neil: 'Industrial Archaeology, the challenge of the evidence'. *Antiquaries Journal 87*, 2007, pp. 1–52

DRURY, Paul and MCPHERSON, Anna (eds): *Conservation Principles, Policies and Guidance – for the sustainable management of the historic environment*. Swindon: English Heritage, 2008

'Inherited Infrastructure'. *Conservation Bulletin* (Winter 2010), Issue 65, English Heritage, Swindon, 2010

'Saving the Age of Industry'. *Conservation Bulletin* (Autumn 2011), Issue 67, English Heritage, Swindon, 2011

2

What does the
Industrial Revolution signify?

Helmuth Albrecht

Introduction

Today, the uses and the meanings of the term 'industrial revolution' are quite diverse. For example, 'industrial revolutions' are postulated for Europe in the Middle Ages, associated with the diffusion of waterwheel technology in the thirteenth century, or for the western world with the introduction of semiconductor technology and the rise of the age of computers in the second half of the twentieth century. Moreover, for the public and most historians the term 'revolution' stands for a radical change within a short time – such as occurred during the French Revolution in 1789, or the Russian in 1918 – and not for long-lasting evolutionary, and still on-going, processes like the industrialization of our world since its beginnings in Great Britain around 1760. On the other hand, no one can deny that exactly the process of industrialization caused, in history and continuing today, one of the most radical changes in human history all over the world: the transformation of an agricultural society into an industrial society with radical changes in all aspects of human, social, political and economic life. Even nature and the global environment have been deeply influenced and changed by this process during the last 250 years.

Without a doubt the industrialization of our world is a revolutionary process, and its 250-year history is a very short time compared to other radical changes in the history of mankind, such as the Neolithic Revolution in food production and settled communities between 7,000 and 10,000 years ago. Today, industrial archaeologists as well as historians of economics or technology use the term 'industrial revolution' within the broader concept of industrialization as a *terminus technicus* for the starting period of the process of industrialization followed by the periods of 'high industrialization' and 'post-industrialization'. Thus the 'industrial revolution' is the take-off phase of industrialization, during which the change from an agricultural society to an industrialized society occurred. In the field of technology and production, this means the change from *hand-tool technology* to *machine-tool technology* with the introduction of machines into manufacturing and the birth of factory production, and is centralization within one building or a central complex of buildings – the so-called *factory*. The systematic adoption of machines in the production process for the generation of operating power and the production of all kinds of goods – last but not least of machines themselves – revolutionized the means of production. It allowed division of labour and with this a radical increase of productivity. Furthermore it allowed mass-production and the development of standardized tools, machine parts, machines and all kinds of goods.

The implementation of the factory system with its machine production led to far-reaching consequences within society. The social structure of traditional rural society changed with the emergence of new social groups such as the industrial bourgeoisie and the industrial proletariat. The rapid growth of population, the migration of people from the countryside into the new industrial regions, and the development of fast-growing urban industrial centres with their new social and infrastructural problems and challenges, led to the birth of the modern industrial society, along with its new social classes, its new political system of parties, parliamentarianism, democracy and communism, and the economic systems of capitalism and socialism. But the process of industrialization did not only change the life of all human beings, of social groups and whole societies. It also changed our environment, the landscape and our whole planet with increasing velocity. Within this on-going process, the 'industrial revolution' was only the starting point and the transition period from the old traditional rural society into the new industrial society.

Despite a widespread, commonly held opinion, the technological activator of the Industrial Revolution was not the invention of the steam engine. The first useful steam engine had been built in 1711 by Thomas Newcomen, years before the process of industrialization started in Great Britain around 1760. The early motivating power of industrialization was the use of water power by waterwheels that were used to drive the first modern production machines for spinning cotton in centralized production sites. Both the first spinning machine, called the *water frame* (patented in 1769), and the first modern factory, the Cromford cotton mill (built 1771) near Derby in England, were built by Richard Arkwright, who became one of the most successful inventors and entrepreneurs at the beginning of the Industrial Revolution in Great Britain. Both as an inventor and as an entrepreneur he opened the way to mass production of textiles by the mechanization of the whole cotton spinning process and by the creation of the prototype of an industrial production site. Other inventors such as Samuel Crompton (*spinning mule*, 1779), Edmond Cartwright (*power loom*, 1785) or Richard Roberts (*self-acting mule*, 1830) followed Arkwright's example and laid the technical foundations for a fully mechanized production process of spinning and weaving. Thus the Industrial Revolution and the process of industrialization in Great Britain started with the mechanization of the spinning process of cotton and the foundation of water-powered spinning mills around 1770. Other and more advanced spinning technologies followed as well as the mechanization of weaving so that by 1830 the whole process of textile production had been mechanized and industrialized.

With the growing number of textile mills the demand for special and more efficient machines for the spinning and weaving process increased. This demand laid the foundation for the development of other industries, including textile machine production, the production of machine tools, or the production of chemicals and dyes for bleaching and colouring of the textiles. Timber as the traditional main construction material of pre-industrial machines, and still used for the construction of the first spinning and weaving machines of Arkwright and Cartwright, was now replaced by cast iron and steel. The development of larger, faster and more efficient machinery advanced

Robert Stephenson's *Rocket* locomotive, built in 1829, is conserved in the Science Museum, London. Railway construction was spurred by industrialisation and fed it with increased consumption of coal and iron while providing tremendous scope for territorial development. *Rocket* is rich evidence for the progress of technology and a museum object of unfading interest. (Les Chatfield – Creative Commons)

the development of iron and steel technology and these technologies in turn fostered the development of machine construction. The mass-production of cast iron was possible since the invention of the coke blast furnace process by Abraham Darby in 1709 in Coalbrookdale, England, and its further development by Darby's son and grandson until its breakthrough as a widely used iron production technology in England in the 1760s. Two decades later, the invention of the puddle-process for refining of pig iron, and the rolling mill in 1783 by the English ironmaster Henry Cort, opened the way for the large-scale production of wrought-iron and its further mechanical processing. The Scottish inventor James Watt developed a new type of steam engine, patented in 1769, which was much more fuel efficient than the Newcomen engine. Together with the entrepreneur Matthew Boulton, Watt founded the company Boulton and Watt in 1775 in Soho near Birmingham which produced and sold steam engines not only in Great Britain but into many parts of the world. Watt's first steam engine was installed in 1776 at the machine-tool factory of John Wilkinson, who had developed a new technology for the precise boring of iron cannon and which now was used for the production of cylinders for Boulton & Watt.

The development of Watt's steam engine made factory production independent from water power. Factories could now be built wherever they were needed and with almost no limit to size and productivity. Moreover, the development of more effective and lighter steam engines led to the construction of steam locomotives. In 1825, the world's first public railway – the *Stockton and Darlington Railway*, with Stephenson's *Locomotion No. 1* – was opened. For Britain, the 1830s and 1840s brought a period of railway mania with its zenith in 1846 when in one year 272 new railway companies were set up.

The development of railway systems in Britain, Europe and North America as well as the invention of Bessemer steel, which made the mass-production of steel possible, led to an acceleration of the process of industrialization from the 1860s – a period sometimes referred to as the Second Industrial Revolution. By the beginning of the twentieth century it led to mass production and production lines and to the birth of new sectors such as the chemical, electrical and automobile industries. It was also the period of accelerated urbanization, of the rise of workers' unions and the fight for better working and living conditions for the working class, of the mechanization of warfare, and of imperialism and colonialism by the leading industrial countries of the time. Britain lost its position as the world's leading industrial nation to Germany which was itself overtaken by the United States of America at the end of the period.

The inventions and innovations of British engineers in the century between 1750 and 1850 formed the technological basis for the rapid development of textile, coal, iron and steel, machine-tool and engine-building industries in Great Britain, which became the first and leading industrialized country in the world.

Why Britain? The answer to this question is as complex as those relating to the technological, economic, political and social background and the outcome of the Industrial Revolution. Factors included the political, economic and social structure of Great Britain in the eighteenth and early nineteenth century, with its parliamentary monarchy and its relatively open social structures; the presence of a politically and economically active middle class as well as a substantial labour force; the British Empire and the possibilities it provided for a world-wide source of raw materials and a market place for British products; the nation's great navy and merchant fleets, as well as the world's financial centre in its capital, London; its national patent law as a strong protection for early nineteenth-century inventors and their inventions; the country's highly developed transportation system of canals, harbours, roads and bridges. All of these aspects together provided a unique set of conditions for the birth of the Industrial Revolution in this country. Britain thus became the first and for many years the leading industrial society in the world. Its transformation process – known as the Industrial Revolution – started around 1750–60 and reached its climax around 1850, represented for the whole world by the first Great Exhibition in London the following year. This exhibition was an imposing expression of the world-wide British leadership in technology and industry. But it also showed that other nations were following the British example. Industrialization had started to become a global phenomenon.

Throughout the nineteenth and twentieth centuries, the Industrial Revolution and the process of industrialization spread all over the world, beginning in each country with a characteristic time-delay to Britain depending upon the political, social, economic and technological conditions of each one. The first impulses for an industrial take-off could be found in Europe and North America around the turn from the eighteenth to the nineteenth century. The process started first in France and in Belgium, followed by Germany and the United States. In all these countries, the transfer of British technology and know-how played a major role for the launch of industrialization. This transfer happened by different ways and means: official visits and spying, copying and reproduction of ideas and technology, legal and illegal export of technology as well as the migration of British experts. The different political, social and economic environment of each country also played a major role for the success and the timing of the process. The political background of the French Revolution and the following Napoleonic wars, with the blockade of all British trade to continental Europe and North America between 1806 and 181, played a crucial role in the growth of factory production in these early industrializing countries: in the wind-shadow of the blockade, without the overwhelming competition of Britain's technology and goods, it was possible to go the first steps towards the development of independent national industries.

Belgium with its provinces of Flanders and Wallonia was the first country on the European continent influenced by the Industrial Revolution coming from Britain. Its long tradition of textile and iron production, its large coal deposits in the north and south as well as its strong and self-confident middle classes with close connections to Britain, formed the basis for an early industrialization. The first Newcomen engine outside Britain was erected in the coal mines of Liège in 1720. In 1799 the British entrepreneur William Cockerill built the first wool spinning machine on the European continent in Verviers, where he set up his own textile factory in 1807. Ten years later he founded the largest European iron foundry and machine workshop near Liège. Cockerill's industrial activities, together with the development of a modern transportation network of canals and from 1830 of a light railway system, led Belgium into the Industrial Revolution and the age of industry.

Two other early examples for the adoption of British technology and industrial proficiency could be found in Germany and the United States. The first cotton spinning mills of Germany in Ratingen/Rhineland (1784) or in Chemnitz-Harthau/Saxony (1798) used British technology and the expertise of British engineers. Both the first steam engine of the Watt type in Germany at the copper mine of Hettstedt/Prussia (1785), and the first German coke blast furnace in Upper Silesia/Prussia (1797), followed the example of British prototypes. Around 1800, regional clusters of early coal, iron and steel in Prussia (Westphalia and Silesia) or textile industry (Saxony) developed. The Ruhr Valley in Westphalia was at that time known as *Miniature England* despite the fact that a lot of influences for the early industrialization of this region came from nearby Belgium.

In the United States, Samuel Slater, an immigrant from Britain and former co-worker of Richard Arkwright, founded the Slater Mill on the Blackstone River in Rhode Island in 1793 and more than ten textile mills were built in the following years. With Slater Mill and numerous other mills, the Blackstone River became the birthplace of the Industrial Revolution in the United States. In 1813–14, Francis Cabot Lowell established the Boston Manufacturing Company on the Charles River in Waltham, Massachusetts, the first 'integrated' textile mill in America. Lowell had previously spent two years in Britain secretly studying the textile industries of Lancashire and Scotland. America's first planned factory town, Lowell, Massachusetts, was founded in the 1820s as a manufacturing centre for textiles; by the 1850s it had become the largest industrial complex in the United States.

In Belgium, Germany and in the United States early industrialization was concentrated in regions with ideal conditions in respect of manufacturing traditions, skilled and cheap labour forces, the availability of water power or the necessary raw materials such as cotton and mineral resources such as coal or iron. In addition, in

Boott Cotton Mills on the Merrimack River, Lowell, US, recorded by the Historic American Engineering Record (HAER). Thirty years after the first textile mill opened, Lowell was the largest industrial complex in the country. The town is now a National Historical Park after a pioneering heritage-based regeneration strategy combining federal, state and city investment reactivated the town from the 1970s. (Library of Congress, Prints & Photographs Division, HAER MASS,9-LOW,7--66 (CT))

Belgium and Germany – like later on in Russia or Japan – financial and administrative support by the state played a major role in the industrialization process. Outstandingly, the rise of German industry in the nineteenth century was fostered by an active policy of the state in the fields of settling industry, infrastructural development (railways) and scientific and technological education with a state financed and controlled system of schools, universities and technical high schools. This engagement of the state was important and necessary for the development of the Industrial Revolution in Germany. At the beginning of this process the country was still split into more than thirty independent and autocratically ruled states with no unified national market, no suitable infrastructure and no developed, self-confident middle class. With the long process of political and economic unification of Germany under Prussian leadership between 1815 and 1870, this situation changed only slowly. Therefore the final breakthrough of the Industrial Revolution in Germany was delayed until the period of the German Empire

(1871–1918), when Germany finally changed from an agricultural into an industrial society. Shortly before the outbreak of World War I, Germany was the leading industrial nation in Europe.

Technical, economic, social and political changes similar to those in Britain or Germany in the eighteenth and nineteenth centuries can be found in all countries which passed or are still passing through the process of industrialization. Of course there are differences too, depending on the particular conditions and circumstances in each country and society as well as on the time and period when the process of industrialization was begun. This process – the setup of the Industrial Revolution – is dated for Britain to 1750/60, for France to 1780, for Belgium to 1790, for Germany to 1795, for the United States to 1800, for Russia to 1850, for Japan to 1860, for Brazil to 1929, for India to 1947 and for China to 1953. From a global perspective, industrialization spread out from west to east and north in Europe and America during the nineteenth century and then from the north-western hemisphere during the twentieth century to the east and the south of Europe, to South America, to Asia and Africa. From this point of view it is an on-going process in the twentieth century, especially in China, India, South-East Asia and Africa.

Further reading

BRAUN, Rudolf, FISCHER, Wolfram, GROSSKREUTZ, Helmut, VOLKMANN, Heinrich (eds): *Industrielle Revolution*. Köln: Wirtschaftliche Aspekte, Kiepenheuer & Witsch, 1976

BUCHANAN, Ralph Angus: *The Power of the Machine. The impact of technology from 1700 to the present day*. Harmondsworth: Penguin Books, 1992

O'BRIEN, Patrick (ed.): *The Industrial Revolution in Europe*. Vols 1 and 2. Oxford: Blackwell, 1994

PAULINYI, Akos: *Industrielle Revolution. Vom Ursprung der modernen Technik*. Reinbek: Rowohlt Taschenbuch Verlag, 1989

STERNS, Peter N.: *The Industrial Revolution in World History*. 2nd edn, Boulder, Colorado: Westview Press, 1998

3

Industrial archaeology: a discipline?

Barrie Trinder

'There is no substitute in the writing of military history for going to see for oneself.'
John Keegan, *Warpaths: travels of a military historian in North America* (2004 edn), p. 228

Historians and archaeologists gain many insights from observing the methodology employed by specialists in sub-disciplines other than their own. It is enlightening to read the thoughts of the late Sir John Keegan, the distinguished military historian, as, in 1992, he observed the sites of the Seven Days Battles fought in Virginia in 1862. He realised that when he taught Sandhurst students about the battle he had not grasped the relationships between the places that had featured in the fighting, even though he had based his teaching upon one of the classics of military cartography. It was not always obvious to earlier military historians that they should study battle sites or the ways in which weapons work, nor that they should analyse the social structure of armies, as Keegan did in *Six Armies in Normandy*. Similarly much of the history of industry written in Britain before 1960 is ridden with misunderstandings of technology – such as an inability to distinguish between a forge, a furnace and a foundry, for example – and with topographical confusions revealing that authors had not understood what Keegan called 'the special relationship between one place and another'. The task of industrial archaeologists might be defined as remedying that situation.

Six decades have passed since the term 'industrial archaeology' came into currency in the English language. The self-styled 'industrial archaeologists' of the 1950s and early 1960s had several distinct objectives. The first was advocacy, to argue that some of the remaining structures of the industrial age were beautiful, that all were historically important, and that consequently they were as worthy of legislative protection and of state-funded recording as the monuments of the middle ages or prehistory. It is significant that the international assembly in England in 1973 from which TICCIH developed was concerned with the conservation of industrial *monuments*. While it is necessary to be aware that conservation gains of the recent past can be nullified in a changed economic climate, and it would be hazardous to be complacent about the long-term future of the smaller industrial sites, it is broadly true that in most of the countries represented in TICCIH the most important monuments of industry, broadly conceived, are subject to legislative protection, and that threatened sites are given consideration for such protection. The industrial monuments and landscapes designated by UNESCO as World Heritage Sites provide evidence of broad change in attitudes internationally.

A second objective was interpretation, to explain to a broad public the significance of mining and manufacturing in our past, and in particular to use the evidence that remains in artefacts, images, structures, sites and landscapes to throw light on the history of the industrial period. Again, it is possible modestly to record some success. Industrial heritage is popular in a tourist context and can no longer be dismissed as a minority interest. The implications of this success across the world are discussed elsewhere in this volume, and are can be studied in detail on the website of the European Route of Industrial Heritage (http://www.erih.net).

A third objective, where rather less has been achieved, was to establish the academic credentials of a new academic discipline. Few courses in industrial archaeology appear in university prospectuses, and information about those few will probably be out-of-date within a few years. Universities in the West are no longer expanding, the nature of undergraduate teaching is changing, and in England there is uncertainty about the consequences of charging substantial fees to students. The mid-twentieth century in the United Kingdom was a time of increasing historical specialisation, of the creation of many sub-disciplines, such as economic history, social history, urban history, local history, the study of vernacular architecture, oral history, business history, historical metallurgy, the history of agriculture, and so on. In a contracting academic environment such specialisms are threatened as individuals retire or move on and courses are terminated.

Attempts to establish postgraduate courses have been scarcely more successful. The study of industrial archaeology flourished at the Ironbridge Institute in the 1980s when some graduate students could still gain public funding, but it has been displaced by courses providing students with a broad measure of employability in the heritage sector by teaching elements of other disciplines, the ability to understand balance sheets and draw up budgets, to hold meaningful conversations with software engineers or graphic designers, or to understand the mechanisms of the planning system. Similar courses in Heritage Management have proliferated in other universities at both undergraduate and postgraduate levels.

While industrial archaeology has made only fitful appearances in academia, there is plentiful evidence that it is widely practised. The current English Heritage publications list includes books on the warehouses of Manchester and the planned industrial suburb of Ancoats, on the Bradford suburb of Manningham, on the buildings of the Sheffield metal trades, the Northamptonshire boot and shoe industry, furniture manufacturing in the Shoreditch area of London, the flax and hemp industry in Bridport, the Birmingham Jewellery Quarter and the canal town of Stourport-on-Severn. Similar publications have emerged from other conservation bodies in the United Kingdom, and their websites show that the industrial heritage is far from neglected. Legislation in the United Kingdom now requires the archaeological assessment of many sites prior to development, which, as in other countries, has stimulated the growth of archaeological consultancies, much of whose work relates to former industrial premises. They continue to produce an extensive 'grey literature' of reports on sites and desktop assessments. It is paradoxical that while academic provision for industrial archaeology has diminished the demand for practitioners of the discipline has increased.

That paradox may in part be explained by the varied nature of practical industrial archaeology. The discipline can be defined in theoretical terms, as, for example, 'a means of allowing the study of artefacts, images, structures, sites and landscapes to stimulate new questions and new hypotheses'. When compiling the syllabus of a lecture series, defining the scope of a journal or setting out the contents of a book, it is necessary to go further and take decisions about content, methodology and chronological scope. Such decisions can readily be challenged, which over several decades has prompted debate. Many have been tempted to make 'ought' statements about industrial archaeology in general, that it should *always* be centred on measured drawings, that it *'should not be concerned with'* prisons or chapels, that it relate *only* to the period between 1700 and 1914.

In practice industrial archaeology has developed a network of sub-sectors, some of which are only ever likely to be practised by a few specialists, surveyors of buildings, explorers of disused mines, or interpreters of aerial photographs.

The study of machines, loftily dismissed by some as 'rivet counting', provides illuminating examples. Many adherents of industrial archaeology have asserted that familiarity with particular machines gained during long careers has provided them with an element of understanding superior to that of historians or archaeologists who lacked

The diversity of industrial archaeology: Bedlam or Madeley Wood Furnaces, near the Iron Bridge, the only works from the period of rapid expansion in iron-making in Shropshire in the 1750s of which there are substantial remains. Measured drawings, excavation, documentary research and the interpretation of paintings have contributed to our understanding of the site, but much remains to be discovered by future generations. (Barrie Trinder)

Industry in a complex landscape: the mining village of New Bolsover, Nottinghamshire, a community of about 200 houses built in the early 1890s to accommodate miners from a nearby colliery. It is viewed from the ramparts of a medieval castle which had been rebuilt as a mansion fit to entertain royalty in the early seventeenth century. (Barrie Trinder)

that experience, which, of course, in a narrow sense it does. Relatively few have actually used that understanding in the investigation of historic machines. Michael Bailey and John Glithero have shown over the past two decades that detailed study, in effect forensic mechanical engineering, involving the scientific stripping-down of historic locomotives, can provide insights into the manufacture and operating life of early locomotives. They have demonstrated that practical experience of engineering can be combined with archaeological discipline, and have established that 'rivet-counting' can be rewarding. Other projects have shown that much can be learnt from the evidence-based replication of locomotives and other machines. It is unlikely that forensic mechanical engineering will ever be widely practised, nor can it readily be taught in the narrow confines of a university course. Nevertheless, everyone with a concern for the industrial past can draw enlightenment from the work of Bailey and Glithero. We can gain more understanding by appreciating the skills and insights of those who work in different ways from our own than by erecting barriers between our work and theirs, whether such barriers relate to archaeological practice or time-period limits.

The same applies to many archaeological skills displayed in research centred on the industrial past, to excavation, the phasing and recording of buildings, the classification of artefacts, the study of landscapes, the laboratory analysis of slag and slimes, the interpretation of aerial photographs, the practice of oral history. Mastery of such skills is usually learned 'on the job', or sometimes through experience gained through adolescent enthusiasm, rather than in university lecture rooms or laboratories. University courses can draw attention to the varied approaches that can illuminate our understanding of the past. They cannot produce individuals fully equipped with the skills to practise from graduation every form of archaeological investigation.

Few of these specialised approaches to the past are unique to the industrial period. Aerial photographs are as likely to provide evidence of prehistoric settlements as of the water-power systems of eighteenth-century ironworks. The understanding of structures necessary for the effective recording of textile mills is equally applicable to the analysis of the roofs of cathedrals or tithe barns. 'Forensic mechanical engineering' can be practised on Renaissance astronomical clocks as well as on early railway locomotives or spinning frames. The study of the industrial past cannot be wholly isolated from other periods. The analysis of particular technologies over long periods of time, of weaving or working copper, is enlightening and worthwhile, whether or not it is called industrial archaeology. Linear archaeology, the study of transport features pioneered in the United States by Schlereth in his analysis of roads, and carried forward in Wales in studies of the Montgomeryshire Canal, the Brecon Forest Tramroads and the Holyhead Road, must necessarily take account of features of all historical periods, as well as the transport systems upon which it is focused.

When examining any question about the past it is enlightening to ask what we would understand if we had only archaeological evidence, with no documentation or any inheritance of written history to shape our thinking. If we are concerned with recent centuries we ask such questions, ponder the answers and move towards synthesising our conclusion with what we know from other sources. The prehistorian, practitioner of the 'purest' form of archaeology, has no 'other sources' to throw light on his question, other than the sometimes dubious legacy of whatever other people may have written about it, and his/her predicament can in many respects aid our understanding of the industrial past. Distribution maps can be applied to eighteenth-century tobacco pipes as well as to flint axe-heads. Kate Clark showed at Ironbridge that it is possible to understand the development of a series of limestone quarries by creating a Harris matrix.

The study of urban 'brownfield' sites, dictated by the requirement for archaeological assessments prior to development, has led some scholars to analyse the remains of eighteenth- or early nineteenth-century working-class housing in the same way that prehistorians would approach the site of a Bronze Age settlement, asking what the traces of structures and the remaining artefacts tell us about material culture, about living standards and the roles of women and children in society. In this and in other contexts the analysis of diaries, directories, census returns and account books is essential to take forward our understanding of an industrial community, alongside whatever archaeological techniques that may be appropriate, and the same applies, with variations in the types of document, to medieval monasteries or sixteenth-century fortifications. It is difficult therefore to claim either that industrial archaeology can be isolated from the archaeology of other periods, or that its methodology is distinctive.

The use of models, as commonly practised by prehistorians, is also enlightening. Michael Lewis's portrayal of the two distinct forms of railway that evolved in British coalfields from the early seventeenth century has been the foundation of much broader studies of early railways. Michael Nevell's interpretation of the development of domestic textile production around Manchester as a twin-mode process – one where manufacturing was combined with farming and organised on a family basis, where the archaeological expression of growth was the addition of workshops to farmstead; the other a merchant capital process of production, under which clothiers put out work to spinners, weavers and finishers working in their own homes – has proved similarly enlightening. David Worth's application of network theory to explain the growth of public utilities in Cape Town has proved valuable in the analysis of English suburbs.

Arguments can be advanced for more profound studies of the British 'industrial revolution' of the eighteenth and nineteenth centuries, but it is increasingly difficult to accord a special place for that phenomenon within industrial archaeology as a discipline. The establishment of TICCIH has helped to disperse the fog of parochialism. The contributions of Russian scholars to the Canadian conference in 1994, describing the sixteenth- and seventeenth-century ironworks and saltworks of the Urals, raised profound new questions about the place of mining and manufacturing in the history of Europe. Some scholars have come to interpret British technology in a global context by examining railways, ironworks or jute mills in India, or assessing the impact of technology from the United States on Britain in the decades after the Great Exhibition.

Arthur Young on his tour of France in 1789 progressed from Lorraine to Savern in Alsace and reflected on changes in material culture, in heating stoves and kitchen hearths. He concluded that crossing a great range of mountains and entering a level plain inhabited by a people totally distinct and different from France, gave him an understanding of Louis XIV's seizure of Alsace, 'more forcible than ever reading had done: *so much more powerful are things than words*'.

The evidence of things may be more powerful than that of words, but while observation is enlightening, a discipline should be based on scientific recording and evaluation. If it is difficult to justify industrial archaeology as a distinct methodology, the value of sound archaeological practice cannot be discounted. Nevertheless, there is a need for a vision that can be shared by all those practising archaeological research that concerns the industrial past, whatever methods they are employing, and by those working principally with documents, images or oral testimonies. For all that has been achieved in conservation, interpretation and publication there remains a need for innovative thinking, for productive methodologies and enlightening models that can only come from academic discipline. The significance of the industrial past needs to be asserted against those scholars of other periods who regard it with lofty disdain. There is a need for a constant re-thinking of the process of industrialisation. In 2000 Linsley suggested that Beamish presents a sanitised, integrated, ordered, harmonious view of a period, of which 'disorder, disharmony, disintegration, sacrifice, degradation and split blood' were features [Cossons, 2000], and the same is true of other industrial museums in the United Kingdom and elsewhere. Scholars should be prepared to challenge museum directors who ask them to provide 'what visitors expect' (unless those expectations relate to lavatories or refreshments) and point out that concepts change, that industrialisation, like the Renaissance, the French Revolution, Slavery or the Holocaust, will have different meanings for succeeding generations.

This essay began with a sage observation from a military historian and ends with another excursion in that direction. Some have suggested that the study of 'industrial archaeology' should terminate with the onset of the First World War. It is reasonable to make 1914 the *terminus ad quem* of a lecture course, or to determine that a journal should only publish contributions relating to the period before that date, but to suggest that the disciplined study of the physical evidence of the industrial past should be so confined is ludicrous and ultimately meaningless. We can consider some of the artefacts of the Second World War, the Supermarine Spitfire, the V2 rocket, the Boeing B-17 Flying Fortress, the T-34 tank. Military historians would sensibly consider them weapons. They are also artefacts, products of the engineering industries of the countries that produced them, and, like the munitions plants of that war – the Royal Ordnance Factory at Bridgend, the rocket establishment at Peenemünde, the Chrysler Tank Arsenal at Warren, Michigan, the Uralskiy Tankovyj Zawod No. 183 which produced T-34 tanks at Nizhny Tagil – their history reflects much about those countries' economies and social structures. It seems absurd to suggest that those who study them should necessarily come out of a different pigeon-hole from those concerned with Richard Arkwright's cotton mills. 'When I use a word,' said Humpty Dumpty scornfully to Alice in *Through the Looking Glass*, 'it means just what I choose it to mean, neither more nor less.' We can all try to define industrial archaeology, but if a scholar researching fourteenth-century copper smelting, the Dounreay nuclear reactor, or school buildings in nineteenth-century Bradford wishes to call himself or herself an industrial archaeologist there is nothing in a relatively democratic society that can be done to prevent it. Trying to put limits on industrial archaeology simply causes confusion. It is more helpful to regard an industrial archaeologist as one who affirms that mining and manufacturing are a significant part of our history, and that the study of artefacts, images, structures, sites and landscapes is essential in the formulation of hypotheses that will increase our understanding of the industrial past. 'Industrial archaeology' should perhaps be regarded as a creed, a set of beliefs, a faith, rather than a catechism or a monastic rule.

Further reading

ALFREY, Judith, and CLARK, Kate: *The Landscape of Industry: patterns of change in the Ironbridge Gorge*. London: Routledge, 1993

COSSONS, Neil (ed.): *Perspectives on Industrial Archaeology*. London: Science Museum, 2000

NEVELL, Michael (ed.): *From Farmer to Factory Owner: models, methodology and industrialisation*. Manchester: Council for British Archaeology, North West, 2003

QUARTERMAINE, Jamie, TRINDER, Barrie, and TURNER, Rick: *Thomas Telford's Holyhead Road: the A5 in North Wales*. York: Council for British Archaeology, 2003

TRINDER, Barrie (ed.): *The Blackwell Encyclopedia of Industrial Archaeology*. Oxford: Blackwell, 1992

4

The heritage of
the industrial society

Louis Bergeron

Introduction

When reading the word *heritage* at the head of this chapter, one could be right in thinking immediately of a list of the numerous kinds of goods or elements embraced by the label *industrial heritage*, tangible or intangible. That is not, in fact, what is intended, but rather to help the reader to think of some selected values we have inherited from the kind of society which has been shaped by industrialization, in particular during the two past centuries, and which we are at present either enjoying or trying to convey to coming generations. And, further, to evaluate briefly to what extent these values are … valuable.

Mastering the space

Setting aside thousands of other easily recognizable remains – which are mainly related to production, trade and consumption, needs and habits – it can be argued that the heaviest mark of industrialization has been in the field of the relationship of human communities with one another and with respect to the planet Earth and to the passage of time. Contracting distances and travel times, mastering the space inside the continents, across the seas and finally over the world has, for more than two hundred years, been an uninterrupted obsession of advanced countries, resulting, for instance, in China's as well as Spain's passion for Japanese, French or German types of high-speed trains and connections. Within industrial heritage, railway history and its physical monuments (stations, tunnels under the Alps and so on) have helped to provoke widespread public interest, as has the more recent curiosity for cars and aircraft. But what about all that has existed behind that façade?

Practical means of transport and the various types of vehicles are just the thin layer on top of the history of infrastructures (and of power sources). And that history is the triumph, in the history of the human mind, of engineering genius and of knowledge and improvement or discovery of construction and building materials. This is not, of course, to deny an analogous relevance to the history of research, experimentation and discovery in other sectors of an industrialized economy. Canals, roads, bridges and railway tracks have been the cradle of industrialization and remain tools of the utmost importance for encompassing the earth in a single network. The long-term progress of engineering appears to be an exceptional illustration of an individual's or a national capacity for innovation. Now this last is the key word for the successful future of the industrialized economies – just as the search for unknown, synthetic and composite materials is a remedy to the exhaustion of natural resources.

A number of powerful engineers' associations have lived up to our key responsibilities of increased knowledge and awareness by tirelessly researching their predecessors, their training, careers, achievements, and inventions. In the United States, several associations have been instrumental in supporting the growth of industrial archaeology and heritage knowledge, and the first steps of TICCIH itself: the American Society of Civil Engineers (1852), the Mechanical Engineers, even of military and naval engineers. In Washington, the American Society for Industrial Archaeology (SIA) was promoted by Robert M Vogel, curator of the Division of Mechanical and Civil Engineering at the Smithsonian Institution. In Washington, the National Park Service created the Historic American Engineering Record (HAER), of which Eric DeLony was head for some thirty years.

In fact, the territorial expansion of the United States owes a great deal to the construction of bridges, from east to west. Emory Kemp, one of the SIA builders from the Department of Civil Engineering at the University of West Virginia, has precisely assessed the role of Wheeling Bridge, across the Ohio River, in opening the doors to the Mid-West. Crossing the Mississippi in Saint-Louis by means of Eads Bridge was another significant step, not to mention the symbolism attached to the crossing of the Hudson River by means of the George Washington Bridge.

Bridges – in particular suspension bridges – have also provided a wide range of exciting opportunities for builders to experiment with successive generations of materials, from metal to concrete. Different materials and techniques had to be deployed to suit the physical characteristics of each location, in some cases spanning extremely wide voids between the two main anchor points.

Does one need to remind the reader, in this context, of the pivotal role of British engineers in providing so many countries, as well as the United Kingdom itself, with the most inventive networks of land communication systems, prerequisites to the growth of an industrial capitalistic economy? This was a story that began with Scottish architect and engineer Thomas Telford (1757–1834), president of the Institute of Civil Engineers (1820), who built, among others, the Conway Bridge, forty bridges in Shropshire, and the St Katharine Docks in London. In England, Wales and Scotland, British Waterways clearly enhanced hundreds of works which are viewed as having been as fundamental as coal to the building of the long-term industrial prominence of the nation, or as characteristic of the national genius as was the command of the oceans. In the same years, French engineer Marc Seguin was busy realising the first suspension bridge in Tournon, on the river Rhône, and one of the first railways designed for steam power traction and service of industrial areas, between Lyons and Saint-Etienne. One may view communication as the key instrument for enabling the building of industrial societies as well as, apparently, for new forms of sustainable development.

Building for industry

On the other hand, in the heritage of industrial societies one can discern a major change in the composition of the leading social groups: traditional hierarchies were disturbed and constrained to open their ranks to growing cohorts of indispensable engineers, bearers of new talents and promoters of a new culture. Industry has been the theatre of that social rise, for several reasons.

In particular, constant expansion in the size and complexity of industry from the end of the eighteenth century required recourse to an unprecedented number of specific human capacities. The time had gone when entrepreneurs or companies – in creating new factories along watercourses, in opening new pits for the exploitation of underground resources, or in developing ironworks – could be satisfied by hiring the services of millwrights, iron masters or other qualified craftsmen from renowned regions or countries for the purpose of establishing and maintaining their installations. Engineers became permanent members of the staff, some of them relatively modest but definitely useful engineers of production, others very close to the head of the business and possible heirs.

Increasingly, the leading industrialized countries could boast of a wide range of schools at different levels of training, as well as an increasing specialization according to evolving stages of technologies. No longer could engineers belong exclusively to the closest circles of a sovereign, or to some *delegates* of the state military schools entering the creation or management of businesses or public works – as was the case in France for the École Polytechnique or the École d'Artillerie, or in the United States for West Point. Henceforth, engineers began to form a special social cadre that was strongly structured by networks of alumni (in France, for instance, from the prestigious École des Ponts et Chaussées or the École Centrale, down to the Écoles des Arts et Métiers) and of professional associations. Not only did this constitute an important mechanism for the renewal and reinvigoration of social elites, it was without doubt a most important legacy of the industrial societies, and a future asset, for these nations to have access to such channels for training and for the transmission of such technological traditions and consolidated results.

Of particular relevance was the social challenge now presented by the new engineers corps to the previously dominant representatives of the humanistic and more precisely of the beaux arts culture; that is, the development of the well-known rivalry between architects and engineers, embodied, for instance, towards the end of the nineteenth century by the quarrel around and against the Eiffel Tower in Paris. Prior to modern industrialization, architects used to be invited mainly for the purpose of enhancing industrial initiatives and activities, directly or indirectly supported by the political power in the interest of the state. Consequently, their plans and the elevations they realized had little connection either with the products or with the related production processes, but rather with the dignity of the principals who were eager to show the excellence of their industrial policy and to demonstrate their power. This was common behaviour among many European kings in the epoch of the *manufactures royales* of the seventeenth and eighteenth centuries.

Things changed radically when entrepreneurs and businessmen of the Industrial Revolution and afterwards ordered the construction of buildings intended to meet all the requirements of the new industrial economy, in terms of size and height, of dimensions of the machinery, in distribution of power (water or steam, and later electricity), of the organization of production, the circulation of goods or the workforce … and in terms of cost. Brick and metal were rapidly substituted for stone and wood, while scientific calculations were now brought to bear in the construction of multi-storey buildings, including the provision of wall openings to maximize natural light for all that required it, the division of internal space into standard cells of a determined volume, and the determination of weight limits of floors, while appropriate materials were carefully selected according to the different elements of the building.

For the major part these requirements were alien to the classical culture and training of architects. Many deemed it scandalous to use building materials as common or lowly-regarded as brick or metal, and considered as barbarians those engineers who were not first and foremost preoccupied by stylistic and ornamental references. Around 1850, the American inventor James Bogardus called himself an 'architect in iron' (in fact, in cast iron). The second half of the nineteenth century, however, was marked by

The Pontcysyllte Aqueduct, Wales, UK (1805) by Thomas Telford and William Jessop. 'It is,' Eric DeLony writes, 'one of the world's most renowned and spectacular achievements of waterway engineering. The structure was a pioneer of cast-iron construction and is the highest canal aqueduct ever built. It is one of the heroic monuments which symbolize the world's first industrial revolution and its transformation of technology.' (Crown copyright RCAHMW)

A view of part of the skyline generated by the waste tips in the Nord-Pas-de-Calais coal basin, France. In the forefront, one of the very many types of workers' colonies found in the western part of that area. (Marie Patou)

the success of 'architecture for industry', and even by examples of co-operation between architects and engineers.

A remarkable example is that of the different phases of the construction of the modern and highly rationalized chocolate factory of Menier in Noisiel (France). A prominent part in the wide diffusion of that new art of building, and in its standardization, was played by agencies who specialized in offering to industrial companies an on-demand planning and execution service. Examples include Stott of Oldham (United Kingdom), who equipped a number of textile factories in northern Germany, or Greene from Boston and Roebling from Trenton who were so active in New England. However, the greatest triumph occurred with Albert Kahn from Detroit, between the 1900s and the 1940s. He was particularly successful in forging a new aesthetic of the industrial age that was drawn directly from an exceptionally bold technical combination of glass and steel. Yet much should be said equally, in the same period, of another novelty combining brick in-filling and concrete framework in the construction of huge factory halls in America and later in Germany and other countries.

This all too brief overview concludes that from Pontcysyllte Aqueduct on the Ellesmere Canal in Britain to the Millau Viaduct in France, from the textile factories of Manchester and Oldham to Zollverein XII mine in Essen or the FIAT car factory in Turin, the industrial society has accumulated a heritage of a technical, architectural and social value which is today recognized all around the world. The names of the great engineers – Nervi, Hennebique, Freyssinet – are those of peaceful defenders of human creativity.

Creating landscapes

Industrialization such as it developed since the eighteenth century has noticeably altered the living environment in the areas it which it has occurred, and has been extremely space-consuming with respect to earlier periods. In some rural or hilly valleys, exploiting hydraulic power developed up to the limits of the streams' capacities while, elsewhere, industrial needs have relied heavily on forest resources. Above all, such needs have resulted in exploiting on a large scale the below-ground wealth (metal mines, coal seams) or of resources available in the open air or at a little depth, including brown coal in Lausitz, Germany, iron or copper ore near Nizhny Tagil (Middle Urals, Russia), in Rio Tinto (Andalusia, Spain), or Anaconda (Montana, United States).

Ancient and modern maps, or recent aerial or satellite photography, can demonstrate such evolutions. Large-scale landscape changes are easy to spot. Less immediately obvious, being more diffuse and scattered, are features to be found within economically powerful towns and cities such as evidence for a variety of wage earners' or craftsmen's housing, or in boroughs and villages where one can see, for instance, the influence of textile companies.

On the other hand, the actors of industrialization have assumed the role of new partners and decision makers in the urban fabric and in the growth of urban agglomerations. Within the limits of pre-existing cities, these forces have swallowed all the still-vacant space which was suitable for their activities. Beyond these limits, they have more or less extensively colonized the nearest well-served suburbs, enforcing their control over the real estate with regard to future utilisation of their productive locations. See, for instance, the process of settlement of industrial businesses in Manchester or in Lille-Roubaix-Tourcoing, or in the ironworks district of Longwy (Lorraine, France), as it has been investigated in the last twenty-five years by French researchers, starting from cadastral, notarial and company archives. Still more directly, a number of sizeable companies have created new settlements. After de-industrialization, these remain available for housing, albeit often with different populations, as well as being worthy testimonies of various styles of labour-force economic management and sometimes of philanthropic thought on the part of broad-minded entrepreneurs.

Once again, engineers played a central role in that kind of achievement, as designers and builders on behalf of the companies. Some of them, as early as the mid-nineteenth century, acted as 'social engineers' and claimed to stand at the core of contemporary societies, being best qualified for pointing the way of improving incomes, health, education and social rank of the salaried workers, due to a re-distribution of the global wealth created by industry.

Rather suddenly, de-industrialization has drawn attention to vast forgotten areas inside or near historic cities – sites of production, living spaces, symbolic places – which few people have been ready to qualify as 'heritage', and which most often political and administrative authorities have been at first glance considering as an unbearable financial burden if not assumed by private or state investments.

Large industrial heritage is not easily handled, being not just a collection of more or less valuable single monuments, either technical or architectural. Moreover, in the case of high-density industrial districts, the 'heritage' constitutes a new kind of geographical landscape, possibly in the dimensions of an extensively urbanized region (such as the Ruhr area, or Emscher Park, in Europe, or some parts of New Jersey and Pennsylvania).

The heritage of industrial society, in such conditions, can only be rescued under two conditions. First, an intensive effort to help the survival of a collective memory among the post-industrial generations regarding such ensembles, by making them globally intelligible after their loss of function. And, second, a mobilization of imagination, invention and creativity in view of re-integrating them into daily life, employment and other cultural or public service needs of the inhabitants.

Such uneasy achievements have been reached, for instance, in several major industrial cities of Nordrheinland-Westfalen, Germany, namely under the impulse of the IBA (Internazionale Bau Ausstellung) during the 1990s, and are also on the way to being successfully achieved in Sesto San Giovanni in Milan, Italy, in parallel with an expected nomination for the World Heritage List in the category of evolved cultural-industrial landscapes.

Conclusion

It goes without saying that the heritage of industrial societies should be considered and used, in the present times more than ever, as a heritage for the future. However, the processes of safeguarding and re-interpretation should not prevent us from looking at the subject with a critical eye. The heritage has also conveyed to us major deficiencies, such as the lack of solutions to the problem of a world running short of irreplaceable energy sources and raw materials; or of the endless quest for an efficient theory of an harmonious relationship between capital and labour. We should be ready to discuss the question: will a new industrial age be able to fill the gap?

Further reading

BERGERON, Louis and PONTOIS, Maria Teresa: *Architecture and Engineering. American Ingenuity 1750–1950*. New York: Harry N Abrams, 2000

HAWKINS FERRY, W.: *The Legacy of Albert Kahn,* Detroit: Wayne State University Press, 1987

LOCKE, Tim and LOCKE, Anne: *Bridges of the World: an illustrated history.* Introduction by Eric DeLony. Basingstoke: AA Publishing, 2008

OLMO, Carlo: *Il Lingotto. L'architettura, l'immagine, il lavoro.* Torino: U Allemandi, 1994

Patrimoine de l'industrie / Industrial Patrimony. 2007, 18, 2

PINON, Pierre: *Un canal, des canaux.* Paris: Picard, 2000

Part II

Understanding the evidence

5

Industrial archaeology

Patrick Martin

Introduction

The disciplined study, preservation and interpretation of the industrial heritage began as a passionate pastime which in recent decades has become a profession. The earliest use of the term 'industrial archaeology' has widely been credited to Michael Rix in Britain in the 1950s, and while this may well be the first use of the phrase in English, an earlier Portuguese writer, F M Sousa Viterbo, appears actually to have coined the term in 1896. The better-known British version of the field arose in the context of amateur enthusiasm as a means of preserving the cherished remnants of an important history; much of the initial work was undertaken by avid amateur archaeologists in adult continuing education courses. The pursuit of knowledge and understanding of industrialization has gradually evolved beyond those early roots into an approach to scholarship and practice that laps over several academic disciplines and government agencies worldwide.

The term industrial archaeology is still widely used in the UK and the US, but the topic is now more commonly called Industrial Heritage Studies, *industriekultur*, *patrimonio industrial* or *patrimoine de l'industrie* in international contexts, reflecting the expansion of coverage to include much more than traditional archaeology. Perhaps the greatest proportion of attention in the field concentrates on preservation of buildings, landscapes and monuments of the industrial past, along with government policies and private practices that serve these ends.

While arguments still occur about the appropriateness of the various labels, the fact remains that some practitioners of this field *do* still approach the study of historic industry from a strictly archaeological perspective, employing archaeological tools to generate evidence and insights into the industrial heritage that we find so fascinating and influential. This chapter will discuss the practice of industrial archaeology in this more narrow sense of the term, focused on excavation and archaeological analysis as a critical set of methods and perspectives for illuminating industrial sites, structures, landscapes and processes.

Archaeological techniques

Traditional archaeological excavation as a technique in industrial heritage study has been well discussed by several authors in the past (see suggested readings). While there is general agreement that the widespread use of the term archaeology in this context is justified because of the focus on the material remains of past industrial processes, practices and social patterns, the actual use of archaeological techniques in industrial heritage studies is fairly limited. The traditional methods of survey/discovery, excavation, stratigraphic dating and artifactual analysis are most generally applied in circumstances where site locations are poorly known, where they are in advanced states of abandonment and/or decay, or where they are threatened with destruction through actions such as development. Such techniques and perspectives are particularly useful on sites that date early in the history of industrialization, and those that are smaller and more vulnerable than the more established, later sites and complexes that are still or have recently been in use. They are, moreover, well suited to studies of process residues and waste to explore details about materials, production and technology.

Archaeological techniques also lend themselves readily to the study of the social dimensions of industrialization through the examination of workers' housing and material culture in the industrial context. Comparative studies of spatial layout and location allow researchers to contrast the living conditions of workers from place to place and examine change over time, as well as to compare the situations of rural and urban dwellers and the contrasts between workers and managers. Examination of food remains and furnishing reflect on the differences in status and social roles between different categories of people, allowing us to explore our assumptions about social hierarchies and the development of modern societies out of simpler precursors. While documentary sources are often extensive in industrial settings, they are seldom, if ever, comprehensive, leaving open many questions about both technical and social aspects of industrial operations. Archaeological insights may be the only avenue of exploration to answer critical questions, both in the specific circumstances and about more general, abstract and comparative matters about the process of industrialization.

To illustrate some of these principles, the remainder of this chapter will discuss two examples of archaeological investigations focused on North American industrial sites.

The Mill Creek site is situated on Lake Huron at the tip of Michigan's Lower Peninsula, nearly 300 miles north of the nearest substantial contemporary settlement, at Detroit. Established in the 1780s to support the English military occupiers of the region, this farm and mill complex was expected to provide sawn lumber and processed grain for both the military establishment at nearby Fort Michilimackinac and for the settlers that were being encouraged to move to the region. While this settlement ideal was never fully realized, the English, and later American military maintained a steady presence, and the area was a critical transshipment and staging point for the American fur trade, situated as it was at the connection between Lakes Huron and Michigan, close to the outlet of Lake Superior and, thereby, the path to the interior of the continent. Built by an early trader and merchant named Robert Campbell around 1785 and purchased in 1819 by a prominent fur trader and entrepreneur named Michael Dousman, a water-powered sawmill and gristmill were operated at this site until some time between 1840 and 1850. Various observers reported the ruins of the mill and dam during the remainder of the nineteenth and into the twentieth century.

The property was acquired by the Mackinac Island State Park Commission in about 1970, after the archaeological remains of the mill site were rediscovered, with a view to

Traditional excavation and analytical techniques employed at the West Point Foundry, New York. Archaeologist Arron Kotlensky in the buried raceway that flows beneath the blast furnace, visible in the background. (Patrick Martin)

incorporating the site into the interpretive programs of the Park. The Park Commission contracted with The Museum at Michigan State University to help in the historical and archaeological investigation of the site; the author focused on this site during the period 1973–76, ultimately producing a doctoral dissertation on the project, later published by the Park Commission. This work and subsequent archaeology by other researchers has provided guidance for the reconstruction of a sawmill and other buildings as the key elements of a public interpretation program at the site, now know as Historic Mill Creek.

Although square hewn timbers were visible in the stream that bisects the site, and depressions that marked building cellar holes did come to light after vegetation was cleared, Campbell and Dousman's mill and farm had largely succumbed to the ravages of time and nature, receding from sight and memory. After the initial discovery of period artifacts by local history enthusiasts armed with metal detectors and searching for another contemporary site location, it remained for archaeological survey to reveal the extent and nature of the remains. A student team employed a systematic random sampling scheme, a technique widely used in mainline archaeology in the 1970s and designed to reduce bias in the selection of a sample of material to allow subsequent excavation to focus on key elements of the site. This approach revealed the ruins of

The reconstructed vertical blade sawmill interior at Mill Creek, Cheboygan County, Michigan. The project was informed by archaeological study of the site and forms part of the interpretation of Mackinac Island State Park Commission. (Patrick Martin)

several buildings, some of which were not visible from the surface, and generated a collection of artifacts that confirmed the site's occupation range in the late eighteenth and early nineteenth centuries. The testing identified remains of two houses, a blacksmith shop and a storehouse/workshop, along with the base of the crib dam that provided water power.

Subsequent area excavation (an approach of extensive exposure directed by the results of the systematic sampling), produced a wide range of artifacts reflecting the milling and domestic activities, along with some surprises not expected in a frontier mill site. For instance, the blacksmith (and cooper's) shop was attached integrally to one of the residential structures, a spatial pattern not previously recognized. Furthermore, there were significant quantities of artifacts related to the fur trade, items such as beads, silver ornaments, fishing gear and firearms of types that were made specifically for the trade in beaver pelts with native peoples of the region. And there was a surprising number of military uniform buttons in and around the residences. While this was not an official military site, it appears that military personnel, either on active duty or recently discharged, were residing in the place.

Other artifacts and features more directly reflected the residential and industrial activities one would expect: architectural hardware, tools (including some specialized milling tools such as a pick for dressing millstones and a saw set for adjusting the teeth on a large vertical saw blade), firearms for hunting, ceramics, glassware and utensils, personal items such as buttons, musical instruments and smoking pipes, and furnishings such as clocks. The chronological development of the site was partly revealed through the dating of specific groups of artifacts and comparisons between and among the different building contexts. For example, detailed dating of ceramic types suggested that the buildings were not all constructed at the same time, a conclusion supported by a statistical study of the variability of thickness in window glass remnants.

The Mill Creek Site was by no means a highly specialized industrial site, but rather a very early frontier establishment where milling functions were combined with farming, trading and a domicile. However, the recognition of nascent industrial activities and facilities in this remote setting reflects on the expansion of industrialization into the far reaches of the frontier at an early date. A water-powered mill with specialized equipment was a completely new discovery, and the perspective offered through a combination of archaeological excavation and analysis with an understanding of milling supported through the industrial archaeology literature allowed for a richer interpretation of this critical facility.

The second example illustrates several additional dimensions of the role of excavation on industrial sites in a larger, more complex context. The West Point Foundry, in Cold Spring, New York, was one of America's foremost early industrial establishments. Located on the Hudson River about 50 miles north of New York City, this heavy ironworks was opened in 1817 as a key part of the national effort to institute a new system of ordnance manufacturers spatially spread around the country. This distribution aimed to avoid a repeat of the unfortunate destruction of cannon-making capability suffered when the British destroyed the Georgetown foundry near Washington DC in the war of 1812. The West Point Foundry Association was a group of well-connected partners that enjoyed a strong relationship with the government and a steady stream of substantial contracts during the foundry's nearly 100 years of operation. While they also produced a wide range of heavy iron products, such as steam engines, some of America's earliest locomotives, cast-iron architectural parts, and sugar mills, among other things, they made their reputation and a considerable share of their income from the manufacture of cannon and shot. They began making other gun types, but this foundry became the home of the Parrott rifled cannon and projectile, patented by the foundry superintendent Robert Parrott in 1861 and widely used by Union forces in the American Civil War. Following the war, demand for the foundry's traditional cast-iron products waned, the original managers retired, and by 1912 operations had slowed to a stop. A succession of smaller firms used the space, but it was gradually abandoned until only one ruined structure stood on the nearly 100 acre parcel in the late years of the century.

In 1996 the foundry property was acquired by the Scenic Hudson Land Trust as part of its mission to protect open green spaces in the Hudson River Valley. Located on the river and adjacent to both the village of Cold Spring and land protected by another environmental organization, this property is a key element for local preservation; the industrial heritage character of the place was a secondary consideration to the new owners, but was embraced enthusiastically once they came to appreciate its unique importance. In 2001, Scenic Hudson approached the author and the Industrial Archaeology Program at Michigan Technological University (MTU) to develop a research program that would explore the site, with an eye to providing information to support an interpretive program. Over the next several years, MTU students, faculty and volunteers conducted historical and archaeological research focused on key portions of the site. Traditional excavation and analytical techniques offered significant insights into critical factors of operation, change over time, production details, environmental conditions, and a host of matters not fully described or explained in the fairly copious documentary records left by this substantial operation. We shall examine a few of these insights below.

The initial research forays at West Point Foundry involved intensive mapping of visible surface remains. While only one structure actually stood with a partly intact roof, the foundations of many other buildings were evident on or just below the surface in the wooded area that contained the foundry. Mapping those remnants and overlaying them within a Geographic Information System (GIS) that also included a series of historic maps allowed the team to work out a sequence of construction for the site and to target areas where remains were not so readily accessible or visible. Collecting spatial information in a digital format, using a laser-based total station, allowed the team to enter data into the GIS that supports an extensive array of manipulation and analysis capabilities. Overlaying historic maps upon the existing conditions portrays both the visible and the invisible former features of the landscape, providing a rich perspective for understanding change and development over time. Working from this system of maps, we were able to focus attention on topics such as the largely buried water-power system, worker housing, the boring mill and casting house, and the technological shift from charcoal to coke in iron-smelting.

The West Point Foundry was established on Foundry Brook, a small but reliable source of water power. Because all of the foundry's machinery was powered hydraulically, the control and efficient use of the falling water was essential to successful operations. In order to manage this critical resource, the company built a series of dams and raceways to store and channel the water to the wheels that drove the equipment in an orderly fashion. While the dams are obvious, some of the raceways are obscured, both by the degradation of the landscape in the century since abandonment and by the fact that they were fully or partly buried from the outset. For example, a blast furnace was placed just below the largest dam, with a water-powered blowing engine. We are fortunate to have access to a contemporary painting that illustrates the furnace, dam and overshot wheel for the blowing engine, a marvellous piece of evidence to interpret the location and operation of this complex. However, examination of the site itself revealed a small waterway entering upstream and exiting below the blast furnace, and excavation disclosed a channel leading from the stream bed above the furnace under the ruined foundation of the blowing engine and passing beneath the furnace. This arrangement runs counter to most reasoned advice about blast furnace operations; purposefully passing water near the intensely heated masonry mass of a furnace invites problems. However, the physical evidence is irrefutable, and is reinforced by an early twentieth-century photograph that clearly shows the channel leading from the brook toward the furnace, running full of water. Subsequent analysis suggests that this arrangement reflects careful management of resources, allowing waste water off the blowing engine wheel to be combined with water from below the dam and run beneath the furnace into a pond where it was stored for use in the boring mill located further down the valley.

From this storage pond, water was fed through an open headrace to the boring mill, where it exited onto a 36 foot diameter backshot breast wheel that drove the machinery to finish cannons and other products. The water exiting the wheel flowed into a buried tailrace to return to the brook, but the opening at the brook was not

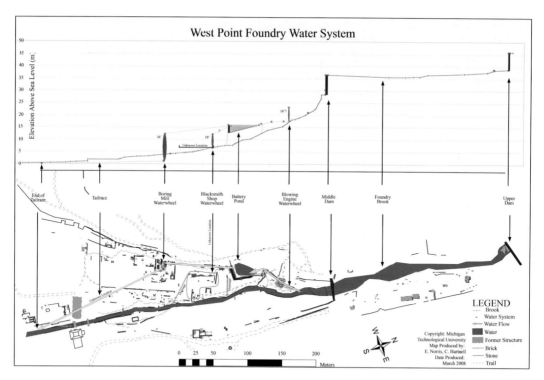

Plan and cross section of the complicated water-power system at West Point Foundry, New York. This synthesis was attained after combining various different techniques. (Michigan Technological University)

immediately evident. The detailed topographic survey of the ground surface in the GIS revealed that the input to the tailrace was actually at an elevation below the streambed at its nearest point to the boring mill, making it impossible to drain water from the mill in the shortest straight-line distance. After excavating the wheel pit, opening the tailrace, and pumping down the ground-water level, the archaeological team deployed a remotely controlled submersible vehicle and attempted to trace the tailrace path. After negotiating some turns and about 50 feet of passage, the submersible was blocked by root growth. Meanwhile we had engaged some remote sensing equipment, including ground penetrating radar (GPR), an electronic technique that projects electrical pulses into the ground and carefully measures the reflected signals to identify and locate buried objects, soil layers and disturbances. The GPR work identified anomalies that proved, through excavation and observation of upwelling water at the stream bank, to reflect the nearly 600 foot long path of the buried tailrace. GPR prospecting, coupled with limited archaeological testing, also allowed teams to identify the extent and locations of a system of buried drains, as well as foundations not visible on the surface. These 'virtual' views of underground features, followed by excavation, provided significant insights into the structural nature of this ruined and largely obscured industrial complex, insights not possible through the documentary record.

In addition to these (and many other) research questions answered by archaeological excavation on industrial sites, this set of techniques has two additional powerful benefits. First, the process of excavation is an excellent tool for public interpretation. As excavators know, visitors love to witness discovery in real time. The work at the West Point Foundry is a classic case in point for this phenomenon. Each field season, the archaeological team held Open House weekends in the early part of the season and again toward the end. Hundreds of local citizens visited daily during these events, fascinated by the discoveries and delighted at the progress. Many people expressed amazement that archaeology, a discipline that in the minds of most relates to the ancient past, could reveal so much about events of a more recent time and about industrial activities, and that interesting evidence lay buried directly beneath their feet. While historical research takes place in some obscure archive or office, the active process of excavation opens a window to the research enterprise that is compelling for the public as they seek to understand the background of the industrial past.

The second benefit offered by excavation, beyond the research dimension, is the simple exposure of the physical evidence for interpretation. Buried foundations, walls, raceways, landforms and artifacts can be incorporated into interpretive schemes for permanent exhibit. While more passive than the dynamic excavation process itself, revealing otherwise invisible evidence is an important result of archaeological research.

Summary and conclusions

Excavation is a critical piece of the toolkit for many, if not all, industrial heritage studies. In circumstances where it is warranted, it is essential for identifying significant remains and exploring particular dimensions of the sites in question. Whether employed for discovery of ruins or artifacts, identification of processes by residue studies, confirmation or denial of documentary or oral history sources, dating and chronological reconstruction of site development or the social dimensions of an industrial community, archaeological excavation can offer an essential key to the understanding of industrial heritage sites. Furthermore, it provides an exciting and engaging glimpse into the research process for visitors who intensely enjoy a visit to an ongoing archaeological investigation.

Further reading

COUNCIL, R Bruce, HONERKAMP, Nicholas, and WILL, M Elizabeth: *Industry and Technology in Antebellum Tennessee, The Archaeology of Bluff Furnace*. Knoxville, University of Tennessee Press, 1992

CRANSTONE, David: 'Excavation: The Role of Archaeology'. *Industrial Archaeology Review*, 1992, Volume XIV(2), 119–25

GORDON, Robert B and MALONE, Patrick M: *The Texture of Industry: an archaeological view of the industrialization of North America*. New York, Oxford University Press, 1994

MARTIN, Patrick E: *The Mill Creek Site and Pattern Recognition in Historical Archaeology*. Archaeological Completion Report Series, No. 10, Mackinac Island Park Commission, Mackinac Island, Michigan, 1985

MARTIN, Patrick E: 'Industrial Archaeology', in *International Handbook of Historical Archaeology*, 285–97, 2009

PALMER, Marilyn and NEAVERSON, Peter: *Industrial Archaeology, Principles and Practice*. London and New York: Routledge, 1998

WALTON, Steven (guest editor): 'Theme Issue on Archeology at the West Point Foundry', *IA: Journal of the Society for Industrial Archeology*, Volume 35, Numbers 1 and 2, 2009

6

Identifying industrial landscapes

Iain Stuart

Introduction

Industrial heritage is rarely confined to a single location or site. More often it is a series of interrelated sites across a wide landscape that contains evidence of how the factors of production were organised, brought to a place where they were transformed into goods and services and from there distributed to their market, leaving waste and landscape change. The term 'industrial landscape' will be familiar to many as a way of referring to an area larger than an individual industrial place (such as a factory site) but less in spatial scale than a region.

It is useful to study the industrial landscape to understand the full historical scope of an industry or a locus of industries and, therefore, fully appreciate their heritage values. This brief discussion attempts to cover the methods for identifying industrial landscapes and touches on many concepts for which there is a great deal of literature but which cannot be discussed fully in a book such as this.

Definitions

At the outset of any discussion of industrial landscapes there is a need to decide exactly what the term means. An industrial landscape is a type of cultural landscape, which may be defined simply as a landscape that has been modified by the effects of human activity. In the case of industrial landscapes the dominant cultural process is one that is broadly termed 'industry'.

Industry is economic activity concerned with the processing of raw materials or the manufacture of goods in factories or services. Economists have identified that industry requires inputs – the so-called factors of production (land, labour, capital and enterprise) – into a production process which transforms these inputs into goods and services. Classical economics did not measure other outputs as they lacked a costing model to quantify them. These outputs are things such as waste material and discharges to land, sea and air which occurred as an integral part of the production process.

Traditionally it was understood that the landscape was 'natural', in some way untouched by human activity, and that 'culture' was imposed on it; however, the reality is that all 'natural' landscapes have some human influence. In the context of an industrial landscape, current industrial processes frequently occur within a landscape already affected by industrial processes. Industrial landscapes often have within their boundaries archaeological evidence spanning a considerable depth of time.

The term 'landscape' has obvious terrestrial limitations, and the term 'seascape' has been used to cover maritime landscapes in the coastal zone and further out to sea. Industrial seascapes cover familiar coastal features such as channels and navigation markers but can also cover such seascapes as fishing grounds (for example, the Great Banks of Newfoundland) and oilfields. In practice the same methods can be applied to both land- and seascapes, with obvious variations.

There have been two dominant ways of viewing a landscape. First, there is landscape as a visual scene – a prospect, scenery, or a view often depicted in artistic images. There is a very considerable body of artistic work responding to industry in the landscape that takes this approach (for example the work of Bernd and Hilla Becher). The second way is the geographic view of a landscape as an area whose morphology can be studied and analysed. This approach is rooted in the intellectual tradition of German geography and was once asserted to be the dominant paradigm of cultural geography. The area approach to landscapes is that taken by most archaeologists, geographers, historians and heritage planners.

In the context of industrial landscapes, however, the two approaches are not mutually exclusive; they represent different ways of 'seeing' the landscape rather than one 'correct' way. The identification, assessment and management of industrial landscapes need to incorporate both approaches.

Categories of industrial landscape

The *Operational Guidelines for the Implementation of the World Heritage Convention*, produced by the World Heritage Committee, helpfully divide cultural landscapes into three main categories: Designed, Evolved and Associative landscapes. These divisions are discussed below with a short example of how they might apply to industrial landscapes

(i) Designed Landscapes

These are defined as, 'Landscapes designed and created intentionally by humans and not restricted to professionally trained architects'. This category includes garden and parkland landscapes constructed for aesthetic reasons which are often (but not always) associated with religious or other monumental buildings and ensembles. Designed industrial landscapes could include industrial estates where the industry and associated residential and commercial areas such as Lowell (Massachusetts, US) or Saltaire (UK), but it is not clear whether designed industrial sites would be considered in this category.

(ii) Evolved Landscapes (or Vernacular Landscapes)

Evolved landscapes are the result of social, economic, administrative or religious activity and have developed their present form by direct or indirect action and/or association with and in response to the natural environment of the area. They can be a single property (such as a farm) or a collection of properties (such as a district of historic farms along a river valley). Two sub-categories have been defined:

A *relic (or fossil) landscape*, in which the social, economic, administrative and/or religious activity has come to an end at some time in the past, either abruptly or over a period of time. Its significant distinguishing features are, however, still visible in material form (or present as buried archaeological remains) but may not be complete or may lack integrity. The Ironbridge Gorge comes readily to mind as a classic relic industrial landscape.

A *continuing landscape* is one that retains an active economic and social role in contemporary society closely associated with a traditional way of life (in the broadest possible sense) and in which the evolutionary process is still in progress, but at the same time it exhibits significant material evidence of its evolution over time. The Ruhrgebiet which, while considerably modified in recent years, is still an active industrial landscape, producing iron and steel, would be an example of this category.

Mullock Dumps at the Sunny Corner silver mine site, in New South Wales, Australia, indicating the position of old mine entries and shafts. The mining landscape's picturesque nature hides a subtler overlay of a later industrial process, that of softwood plantations, whose trees (Pinus radiatia) have colonised the adjacent mining areas. (Iain Stuart)

The former dockyard at Cockatoo Island in Sydney Harbour, Australia, showing the Fitzroy Dock, Turbine Hall cranes and on the left part of the original island. This industrial landscape was created out of a mixture of local and Imperial politics as well as the development of ship technology. (Iain Stuart)

(iii) Associative cultural landscape

The final category is the associative cultural landscape. This is one where the landscape is significant due to the powerful religious, artistic, historical, scientific or cultural associations of the natural element rather than material cultural evidence, which may be insignificant or even absent. An example of such a landscape would be Mount Alexander in Central Victoria (Australia) which was the focus of a major gold rush in the early 1850s. People sailed across the world to go to the 'Mount Alexander diggings'. Mount Alexander itself was simply a prominent and distinctive hill marking the location of the diggings 5 kilometres away. Nevertheless the view of Mount Alexander from the goldfields, and as part of the goldfields route, is of heritage significance.

The practice of landscape identification

The practice of landscape identification varies between the statutory requirements of various jurisdictions, the traditions of heritage identification practice in each country and the purposes of the landscape identification. As a consequence, it is difficult to describe a universal methodology for the process of industrial landscape identification.

A general approach to the question of identifying industrial landscapes is presented below. This is a combination of the United States National Parks Service approach (as outlined in their National Register Bulletin No. 30) and the Historic Landscape Characterisation (HLC) approach developed by English Heritage which is mostly regional in scale.

There are four phases of work in a landscape identification project: Scoping the Project; Desk-based Analysis; Field Survey and Inspection; and Mapping and Reporting.

Scoping the project is absolutely critical as this determines whether the work is effective. It is essential that the ultimate purpose of the work be known as this will influence decisions about how the project is carried out, what resources are needed, how useful the results will be, and how they will be disseminated.

Critically, decisions about the scale of the project will influence the amount of data recorded and how it is used. The data recorded both in the desktop evaluation and the fieldwork needs to be mapped, and the way this is undertaken is dependent on the scale of the project. Mapping at the small scale or regional level is very general, and particularly looking at HLC maps it is difficult to see individual sites or small landscapes. Overall regional trends and landscape character types are easier to identify as this is the level at which heritage in the landscape is managed. Large-scale recording requires more detail which may disappear if the ultimate product is produced at a small scale.

Another critical point is that available data may be provided at varying scales and resolutions, and reliance on some data sets may be limited because of this. Scale needs to be considered at the outset of the project.

The use of Geographical Information Systems (GIS) makes it possible to record information at a large scale and display it at varying scales according to need. However, it is important to realise that GIS is expensive in terms of the cost of the program and data and in getting trained staff to use it. GIS may not be available for some projects, and for other projects traditional techniques of map overlays may be a more cost-effective or practical approach.

It is critical to define project boundaries at this stage. Boundaries can be fixed, permeable or impermeable. A study of a local government area might be limited by the boundaries of that area, and the boundary itself may be impermeable so that nothing beyond the boundary may be considered. On the other hand, in practice the boundary of a project area may not be easily read or might in fact be gradational from one landscape to another. Furthermore, the vistas from a landscape may extend to key features outside the project boundary. Defining the nature of project boundaries at the outset of the project avoids having to make on-the-run decisions when these issues are identified.

It is also important to develop a thesaurus for the project as this will ensure that everyone understands the meaning of terms such as *building, hill, slope, structure, feature, podzol* ... etc. There is such a diversity of views on definition and nomenclature that chaos is inevitable unless strict definitions are applied at the outset of the project. In

Australia many of the definitions used in characterising environmental attributes for environmental studies are found in the *Australian Soil and Landscape Survey Handbook*. It is assumed that most countries would have similar works available for use.

The term *desk-based analysis* covers a multitude of tasks involving the collection and organisation of relevant data sets. There are obvious sources for information – previous studies, maps, aerial and satellite photography, and so on – which are particular to an individual locality and cannot be usefully discussed here. At this point, questions about the relationship between the data sets, in particular between the natural environment data and historical and archaeological information about industry, need to be considered.

Historical information about the landscape should be researched and placed into broader historical contexts. The American methodology emphasises the importance of developing historical context. An historic context is defined as an important theme, pattern or trend in the historical development of a locality, state, or the nation, at a particular time in history or prehistory. Within each theme, and according to landscape characteristics, historical information can be organised into patterns on the landscape. In a similar way HLC relies on the development of Landscape Character Types based on historical research at this stage of the project.

The historical information should be mapped at an appropriate scale and integrated with other information into a series of map overlays that provide an initial characterisation of the landscape. This model of the landscape can then be evaluated by the field survey program.

Field Survey and Inspection almost seems redundant in this era when a landscape can be viewed with Google Earth and Street View. Why go into the field at all? Nothing online can replace the sense and understanding that comes from actually being in the landscape and moving through it. Once there, it is simply easier to understand key attributes by experiencing them. Furthermore, as some studies of landscape design have identified, moving through the landscape often shows how features such as plantings or buildings can create vistas or landmarks, and these have been linked to expressions of power and of control. These things are not easily understood by reading maps in an office or by looking at a computer screen.

Typically, information should be recorded on a field record sheet designed specifically for the project. This encourages surveyors to make systematic observations and to record them in a consistent way. Written records should be supported by photographic images, and, since most cameras are multi-functional, video images as well. Locational information should be recorded on field maps. Global Positioning Systems (GPS) are readily available (although varying in precision) and can be used to record locations and landscape features.

It is important to collect field survey metadata such as to the areas surveyed and the depth and quality of coverage (for example, windscreen survey versus field-walking). Some GPS units can track routes, which provides a useful record of where the surveyors were. Photographs can also be geo-referenced using GPS routes or by reference to maps.

The task of *mapping and reporting* involves the correlation of information gathered through historic research and field survey to define the industrial landscapes and their characteristics and extent. If significance assessment is part of the project, it is at this stage that considerations of the integrity of the landscape should also be undertaken – that is, the degree to which a landscape reflects the spatial organisation, physical components and historic associations that it attained during the period or periods of significance. The key question is to what extent the surface landscape can be 'read' to demonstrate the characteristics for which it is significant.

The significance of industrial landscapes is evaluated no differently than other types of heritage sites using standard heritage criteria. These vary of course in their precise form between statutory jurisdictions, but they are best summarised by Article 1.2 of the *Burra Charter*, 'Cultural significance means aesthetic, historic, scientific, social or spiritual value for past, present or future generations'. English Heritage regards characterisation as being best done as a 'neutral' and descriptive process, simply identifying the differences in character between different areas, and avoiding giving values to different character types. If significance is required to be assessed then it is best undertaken in the context of a specific development proposal.

Conclusion

Industry has had a powerful although often subtle impact on our environment over time. The identification and analysis of industrial landscapes is an important tool for understanding how industry worked, and created and shaped our environment, and in identifying the heritage values that flow from that activity. The methodology outlined here is only a general indication of what will be more detailed as the practice of identifying industrial landscapes is developed.

Acknowledgements

For this chapter I drew on help from Messrs Herring and Thomas of English Heritage to help understand HLC and on material prepared and discussed by the ICOMOS (Aust.) Cultural Landscape scientific committee of which I am a member.

Further reading

ALFREY, J and CLARK, K: *The Landscape of Industry: patterns of change in the Ironbridge Gorge.* London: Routledge, 1993

BECHER, Hilla and BECHER, Bernd: *Industrial landscapes.* English language edition, Cambridge: MIT Press, 2002

McCLELLAND, L F, KELLER, J T, KELLER, G P, and MELNICK R Z: *How to identify, evaluate and register Rural Historic Landscapes.* National Register Bulletin No. 30, Washington, D.C.: National Parks Service, 1999

MCDONALD, R C, ISABELL, R F, SPEIGHT, G, WALKER, J and HOPKINS, M S: *Australian Soil and Land Survey: Field Handbook.* Canberra: CSIRO, 2011

RIPPON, Stephen: *Historic Landscape Analysis: deciphering the countryside.* York: Council for British Archaeology, 2004

SAUER, C O: The Morphology of Landscape. *University of California Publications in Geography,* 1925, 2(2): 19–53

7

Recording and documentation

Miles Oglethorpe and Miriam McDonald

Introduction

The Nizhny Tagil Charter is very clear about the fundamental role of recording the industrial heritage as a vital means of assessing its value and context, educating generations of people about its importance, and prioritising work on its conservation. In particular, the charter stresses the need for the establishment of typologies to identify the extent and nature of the industrial heritage and the subsequent building of searchable inventories that are publicly accessible to all, aided by ever more powerful computer technologies. This, of course, is reflected in the other chapters within this book, most of which link back to the need for reliable records. Recording, therefore, is a fundamental priority for all those concerned with managing, protecting and utilising the industrial heritage, so it is important that it is done to the highest possible standard.

The special challenges of industrial heritage

Industrial heritage has several characteristics which can make it especially daunting to those used to more traditional recording challenges. Perhaps most significant is scale – it can vary from the small to the truly vast. It can therefore range from very large industrial landscapes to individual machines or small pieces of machinery or equipment. Alongside this is the fact that it can be immensely complex, sometimes incorporating in the one site very specialised and often bewildering ranges of technologies.

Equally, while recorders are frequently presented in the field with what appears to be a snapshot in time, the industries whose remains are being studied were often immensely dynamic entities; for this reason, trying to capture information that truly represents fabric and process can be extremely difficult, as can the gathering of information that genuinely captures the change itself. Many industries are fundamentally transient in nature, and the material remains that survive are not necessarily representative of what occurred during the most significant periods of industrial activity. These factors need to be taken into account when planning and executing recording activity.

There can also be a range of obstacles or hazards that are particular to industrial sites, some of which can impair access and impede recording efforts. Much depends on the ownership of the properties. Where the industries are themselves still operating, issues such as commercial sensitivity, security, and health and safety, can result in access being restricted or obstructed. At the same time, some owners can be defensive about the potential for their properties to be given statutory protection, fearing that recording might in some way detract from their commercial value.

Perhaps most significant are the dangers that many industrial properties present in terms of on-site hazards and health and safety, which can have wide-ranging ramifications including problems with insurance cover. Hazards can range from a legacy of toxicity caused by pollution, such as heavy metals, hydrocarbons, explosives residue or asbestos, through to dangerous terrain and collapsing buildings and structures, and even hostile people, and intimidating animals and vegetation.

Such factors can conspire to make the recording of the industrial heritage an unattractive option. Add to this the low regard in which industry can be held within many cultures, the lack of self-esteem among current and former workers, and a lack of interest in what is often perceived to be the mundane, and it is easy to see why the recording of industrial heritage can be given a low priority.

In practice, no industrial heritage is unrecordable, and many of the attributes of industry that are seen as unattractive or unworthy are in fact key features that are in themselves worthy of record. Today there is a large armoury of techniques and technologies that can help record industrial heritage, so the purpose of this chapter is to discuss briefly the evolution of industrial heritage recording in recent decades, and then to focus on new priorities and opportunities.

Early survey initiatives

It is useful at this point to consider the example of how industrial heritage recording evolved in the UK over recent decades. It first began to take shape in the 1960s and focused on identifying and documenting industrial sites using standardised record cards. Thousands of cards were distributed to groups of activists and volunteers, and, although relatively crude, the information gathered greatly assisted subsequent survey work and helped to spawn a range of thematic and regional publications promoting industrial heritage.

In subsequent years, data gathering was consolidated, and advisory panels made recommendations for the more detailed recording and statutory protection of the most important sites that were identified. The resulting accumulation of record cards and associated data was later integrated into National Monuments Records, and has subsequently been digitised, now forming the backbone of the UK's national databases.

There is no doubt that today similar initiatives in countries across the world could amass, and in some cases, will have already rapidly gathered, valuable data using manual or virtual card recording systems. This approach is not dependent on the acquisition and maintenance of new technologies, and is therefore universally sustainable, making it an essential starting point for many countries that are beginning projects to document their industrial heritage. A major challenge, however, is the establishment of common data standards, including geo-spatial referencing and the use of standard terminology and classification systems. In the UK these issues were tackled during the 1990s by the development of an agreed thesaurus of terms and an associated classification system by the Royal Commission on the Historical Monuments of England (RCHME) and English Heritage.

Field survey

In the meantime, the actual field recording of archaeology and historic buildings focused on terrestrial photography and measured survey using traditional survey equipment such as plane tables, measuring tapes, chains, and poles, alidades and theodolites, which were applied both to archaeology and buildings and gradually extended to industrial subjects. A notable example of high-quality output from detailed industrial surveys in this period occurred in Scotland, the results of which can be seen in Hay and Stell's 1986 *Monuments of Industry*.

This was relatively modest compared with the growing work of the Historic American Engineering Record (HAER), which is based at the Library of Congress in Washington. From 1971 to 2003, HAER was directed by Eric Delony, and his staff and students produced extraordinarily detailed and beautiful records of a wide range of industrial and engineering structures across the United State, setting a high standard for others to follow.

At the same time, survey methods were beginning to benefit from the onset of new technologies and the advent of laser-driven electronic distance measuring devices (EDMs), which were to have an especially significant impact on landscape surveys. These technologies were applied very successfully to a variety of industrial subjects.

For example, the RCHME amassed an enviable expertise in recording techniques and technologies and applied them to industrial heritage very successfully in the 1980s and 1990s, harnessing the capability of ever more sophisticated computer-aided drawing (CAD) software, initially converting data gathered using manual survey and then increasingly automating the survey process. Other innovations included the use of aerial photography, which was especially valuable when surveying industrial landscapes.

RCHME was subsequently merged with English Heritage in 1999, and the two organisations' combined survey expertise is now captured in excellent summary guidance on understanding landscapes and historic buildings, provided by the Historic Environment Local Management (HELM) service.

Improvisation in the face of crisis

The rapidity and scale of de-industrialisation in some areas during the 1970s and 1980s was especially challenging, and with entire classes of industrial monument disappearing, more formal survey programmes were proving to be ill-equipped and unwilling to tackle such widespread change. Against this background, in 1977 the Scottish Industrial Archaeology Survey (SIAS) was formed at the University of Strathclyde in Glasgow by John R Hume following a courageous diversion of archaeology field survey funds away from excavation. The survey unit's work differed radically from other survey programmes in that its remit was threat-based, so it deliberately prioritised extant and sometimes working industries and focused on themed survey initiatives.

Led by a mechanical draughtsman, Graham Douglas, a cost-effective and rapid survey campaign ensued. The resulting survey records took the form of measured (but not normally to-scale) annotated site sketches which captured the fabric, function and processes of industrial sites, supported by informal photography and historical maps. The survey also collected documentary material on site, and all these records were

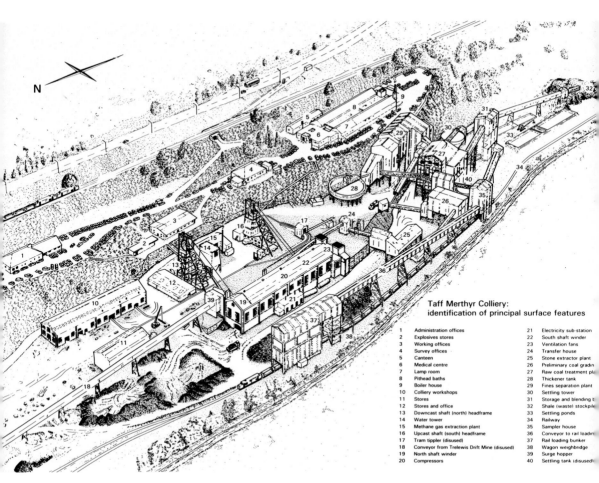

Taff Merthyr Colliery:
identification of principal surface features

1	Administration offices	21	Electricity sub-station
2	Explosives stores	22	South shaft winder
3	Working offices	23	Ventilation fans
4	Survey offices	24	Transfer house
5	Canteen	25	Stone extractor plant
6	Medical centre	26	Preliminary coal gradin
7	Lamp room	27	Raw coal treatment pla
8	Pithead baths	28	Thickener tank
9	Boiler house	29	Fines separation plant
10	Colliery workshops	30	Settling tower
11	Stores	31	Storage and blending t
12	Stores and office	32	Shale (waste) stockpile
13	Downcast shaft (north) headframe	33	Settling ponds
14	Water tower	34	Railway
15	Methane gas extraction plant	35	Sampler house
16	Upcast shaft (south) headframe	36	Conveyor to rail loadin
17	Tram tippler (disused)	37	Rail loading bunker
18	Conveyor from Trelewis Drift Mine (disused)	38	Wagon weighbridge
19	North shaft winder	39	Surge hopper
20	Compressors	40	Settling tank (disused)

Malaws' 1997 recording of Taff Merthyr Colliery in Wales, UK, before it closed. This and other drawings could not have been achieved by conventional recording techniques. The work drew on a wealth of existing records as well as aerial photography and the expertise of coal miners who remained at the site. (Crown Copyright RCAHMW)

gathered together in 'survey packages'. They were notable for their ease of use and for the mechanical and technical information that they contained, as well as for the sometimes esoteric nature of the material gathered at the site. As a means of rapid survey the SIAS proved to be very successful and could be emulated elsewhere where new survey technologies are not available.

New recording initiatives

A major requirement when recording more extant industrial heritage is an understanding of the *processes* that occurred or are occurring at the site, together with their associated technologies. Without this knowledge, important features of the plant, layout and fabric of industrial sites and landscapes will not be understood, and may even be ignored completely. This was one of the reasons for the founding of SIAS, with the processes themselves forming a key element of the recording programmes.

Process recording was subsequently taken to much greater levels of sophistication by the Royal Commission on the Ancient and Historical Monuments of Wales (RCAHMW), where the recording work of Brian Malaws set the standard. A particularly good example was the recording of Taff Merthyr Colliery before its closure. The level of detail captured in this and other drawings and documentation could not have been achieved by conventional recording techniques, and would not normally have been possible as it was rare in the past for working sites to be recorded. The work, which utilised aerial photography, also benefited greatly from being able to draw on a wealth of existing records, as well as the expertise of coal miners who remained at the site.

Process recording has continued to be carried out in various forms across the world, and has sometimes formed the basis of thematic surveys. Initiatives in the Antarctic and Arctic resulted in the recording of whaling stations, a process that has been continued by the multi-national LASHIPA (Large Scale Industrial Exploitation of Polar Areas) project, which has also included mining landscapes in the Arctic archipelago of Svalbard.

Since the 1990s, industrial survey and associated documentary research have demonstrated the value of thematic studies and access to associated industrial archives and records. In the UK, this has manifested itself in a number of ways, not least in the recording of the textile industries in Yorkshire and Lancashire. Thematic survey work

A digital image comprising a point cloud generated by the 3D scanning of the New Lanark World Heritage site, an eighteenth century cotton mill and model setlement on the River Clyde in Scotland, UK. (Centre for Digital Documentation and Visualisation LLP)

often takes on a regional quality because of spatial concentrations of specific industries. Recording programmes that create regional, national or international collections and inventories can be very useful, sometimes challenging existing understanding of industries and processes. Impressive examples of recent work include published reports on the mining landscapes of the Colline in Tuscany, Italy, and regional cross-border surveys and inventories in Hungary and Slovakia.

New recording technologies

Since the 1980s, field recording armouries have been steadily reinforced with an ever more potent array of digital recording technologies. Of these, satellite-guided Geographical Positioning Systems (GPS), combined with digital mapping and increasingly portable, powerful and robust computers, have transformed field recording, building on the advances brought about by the EDM survey technologies mentioned earlier.

A particularly significant new development was 'Cyrax', which was one of a small number of portable high-definition 'time-of-flight' 3D laser scanning systems patented by Ben Kacyra and partners in the late 1990s. This new technology was developed for an industrial market where it was able to record in detail buildings, plant and machinery, and, with the aid of rectified high-definition photography, to provide a reliable record from which maintenance and other work programmes could be planned.

Laser scanners have evolved rapidly in subsequent years, and have become cheaper, opening them up to wider use. Inevitably, they are now used extensively in the heritage sector by architects and archaeologists. These scanners are especially well suited to the recording of often large and complicated industrial sites.

The technology is, however, expensive, and requires skilled, experienced people to operate it effectively. Equally, the survey itself is often the easy part of the project. Considerable time and expertise are required to convert the raw data – clouds of millions of 3D co-ordinates – into something useful, usually in combination with the rectified photography. Other serious considerations include the sheer volume of the data generated, which needs to be managed, protected and migrated as computer hardware, software and web-based services evolve.

The output from the 3D laser scanners has many potential uses, especially as digital technologies are opening up new opportunities for dissemination. The charitable foundation Cyark, for example, which was founded by Ben Kacyra, is developing apps which can be used on portable devices and which can help guide both actual and virtual visitors around industrial heritage sites. In addition to promoting access, this technology can, through the creation of accurate records, also promote subsequent condition monitoring and computer modelling that can test the potential impact of proposed development on heritage sites.

Laser technology is, meanwhile, not solely restricted to terrestrial use, and has been applied very successfully to remote sensing. Light Detecting and Ranging (LIDAR) has had a range of applications for many years, including archaeology, and has been used to great effect to record both rural and urban landscapes. Indeed, it can be deployed in combination with terrestrial 3D scanning, and can be very effective for the recording of industry and infrastructure.

One final note of caution is also necessary at this point. The exceptionally high-quality records generated by the new technologies have on a number of recent occasions encouraged the view that if such records can be created, there is no longer any need for the sites themselves to be conserved. In such cases, there is therefore a danger that the power and sophistication of the recording technology will inadvertently accelerate the demise of the heritage it is supposed to be protecting.

Recording with existing industrial documentation

The nature of rapid de-industrialisation does not only endanger the historic industrial sites themselves. Records and memories associated with industry also tend to perish, and it is with this in mind that in many countries there have been major initiatives in recent years to safeguard and rescue records held by a number of industries. In many instances there can be no better record of an industry than its own business and technical documentation, yet this is often discarded in periods of transition and closure. Indeed, there are many examples where fine leather-bound ledgers containing financial records are salvaged, leaving the technical drawings, photographs and other documentation to be destroyed.

Perhaps the most ambitious recent example of recording live industries through the acquisition and safeguarding of existing records has been the offshore oil and gas industries in Norway, where the first oil and gas field, Ekofisk, has been defined as being part of Norway's industrial heritage with national value. The Norwegian Directorate for Cultural Heritage characterised Ekofisk's installations as 'some of the largest and most complex cultural monuments of our time'. Using the statutory provisions of Norway's Cultural Heritage legislation, the Directorate persuaded Conoco Phillips Norge and other licensees to embark upon a major documentation project.

This ran from 2002 to 2004 and was based in the Norwegian Petroleum Museum in Stavanger. The Directorate for Cultural Heritage was a key partner in initiating and following up the project, emphasising the importance of State support. Work on collecting, selecting, registering and storing source material was carried out in collaboration with the National Library of Norway and the Stavanger department of the National Archival Services of Norway. The results can be found online at http://www.kulturminne-ekofisk.no/), and have recently been emulated by the Frigg project in partnership with heritage bodies in Scotland (see (http://www.kulturminne-frigg.no/). Frigg has also resulted in the establishment of a UK offshore oil and gas industry recording project called 'Capturing the Energy'.

Lessons from the offshore experience

The recent rapid and catastrophic closure and disappearance of the coal-mining industry in many industrialised countries demonstrates how easy it is to ignore contemporary, omni-present industry and allow its records to be lost during periods of decline. In the UK, although some records survive, these are only a fraction of what once existed, and the disappearance of so much of the good material helps to explain why the national memory of the British coal industry is so flawed and negative.

In many ways, the offshore oil industry presents a similar narrative of heroism, sacrifice, and technological innovation as occurred in the coal industry, but its scale, complexity and dynamism are of a different order entirely. Against this background, the achievement of the Norwegians is extraordinary. Clearly, however, very few countries in the world have a strong enough state apparatus and the available resources to conduct an industrial heritage recording project on this scale.

Conclusion

Working with live industries has many advantages, not least sometimes rescuing and usually making the best of existing records and tapping into existing expertise, knowledge and experience of the industry and its production processes. This can inform field recording activity and oral history work, and can provide the basis of a powerful education resource with applications inside industry itself, but can also be used much more widely in informal and formal education.

There will always be a place for field recording of industrial heritage and for the detailed examination of rare or threatened industrial sites and landscapes. These can be recorded where resources are limited by more traditional survey techniques, but today new technologies allow for rapid and extremely detailed digital surveys which can be put to use in digital applications and disseminated without the need for separate digitising processes, all of which can be achieved at a quality unimaginable twenty years ago.

Perhaps the biggest lesson of all is that in the first instance priority needs to be given to those historic industries which continue to operate but are most endangered. In the past, much information has been lost while major industries have been eradicated with little if any recording activity having taken place. Very significant periods of history have therefore disappeared almost without trace because recording resources have continued to be channelled into 'mainstream', conventional projects. There is no excuse for allowing this situation to continue.

Further reading

ENGLISH HERITAGE, *Understanding Historic Buildings. A Guide to Good Recording Practice.* Swindon: English Heritage, 2006

FALCONER, K: 'The industrial heritage in Britain – the first fifty years', *La revue pour l'histoire du CNRS.* 14, 26-33, 2006

HAY, Geoffrey and STELL, Geoffrey: *Monuments of Industry.* Edinburgh: HMSO, 1986

MALAWS, Brian A, 'Process Recording at Industrial Sites'. *Industrial Archaeology Review*, XIX, 1997, 75–98

PREITE, Massimo, Preite, M: *Masterplan: a Valorizzazione Del Paesaggio Minerario / The Development of the Mining Landscape.* Florence: Polistampa, 2009

STAMM, Alicia and PEATROSS, C Ford (ed.): *Historic America: Buildings, Structures, and Sites Recorded by the Historic American Buildings Survey and the Historic American Engineering Record.* Washington: Library of Congress, 1983

8

Process recording

Gustav Rossnes

Introduction

Our professional engagement and activity associated with cultural history and the preservation of historic industrial monuments should be based on documentary knowledge of the objects. Large sections of our cultural heritage are rapidly disappearing due to the hurried reorganisation in industry. It is only possible to preserve a minute

Prince Olav Harbour shore whaling station, South Georgia, the flensing plan surrounded by cookeries for blubber, meat and bones. The station was operated by the Southern Whaling & Sealing Company before production ceased, and the whaling station was abandoned in 1932. Later it was bought by Chr. Salvesen & Co. of Leith, Scotland, and used as a spare parts supply for the Leith Harbour whaling station farther down the coast. (Gustav Rossnes)

part of today's industrial plants complete with their production equipment and existing functions. So the task of recording becomes even more important as a basis for research, for the dissemination of knowledge and for management so that knowledge of important production facilities is secured through archival preservation.

To summarise the situation:

- De-industrialisation has provided an increasing category of cultural heritage; that of disused industrial facilities

- Both the nature and scale of many of the more complex industrial structures of the twentieth century are a profound challenge to all cultural heritage bodies

- Recording, documentation, and information management are among the central activities of the decision-making process for heritage conservation management – and a fully integrated part of research, investigation and treatment (see Letellier 2011:11)

- Documentation represents an alternative solution when physical preservation is not practical or economically feasible – 'preservation by record' secures the historic source values of industrial structures in an archival form

Recording and documenting industrial sites or structures can be defined as:

> ... the process of obtaining factual information by direct observation in the field. Its purpose is to create an archive, usually both written and illustrative, for permanent storage, a process usually described as 'preservation by record', and in many cases to provide an interpretation of the site or structure. The term 'recording' covers a wide range of techniques from the provision of a written description to a fully measured site plan and researched report (Palmer & Neaverson 1998:82).

Objectives for the documentation of industry

- Document functional relationships, spatial layout, the organisation of production lines, and interaction with the surrounding landscape

- Identify details which are essential for the function of the process

- Documentation of the above in such a way as to enable future access and analysis

The material should illustrate various facts about the chosen subject for survey, not only from a technical constructive point of view but also to inform about visual aspects as well as social, economic and historical conditions. The various types of information thus gained during the fieldwork should build up and complement each other, and interpretations and later analysis of the data should illustrate the many variables that the industrial sites reveal.

Techniques of process recording

Measured drawings are a powerful medium for displaying significant facts and relationships about a site that simply cannot be entirely captured by photography or writing. The drawings will determine and show the relationship between the activity, building construction and site use. A site plan should be included so as to place the industrial complex in its topographical and environmental context. The plan should show existing site conditions – and feature site boundaries, transportation systems, drainage, production lines and significant site structures and services.

If a site is of interest because of its function, documentation should focus on how production was carried out – how and why the work was organised and executed in a particular way in order to explain the way the workers, machines, tools, and materials worked together to perform a task – and what the consequences of these choices were.

The most important aspect of an industrial plant is the production process – the qualities that make the plant effective for the production of goods for a given market. Process recording, then, should be a study of all aspects relating to the physical operation of a site.

- The 'input' side – how the site relates to its surroundings; its proximity to raw materials and transport systems

- Choices, design and adaptation of technologies and organisations to local environmental, political and geographical contexts

- How material is processed within the works – what type of machinery and techniques are employed; whether 'standard' applications have been adapted and developed for local conditions (human nature and traditional working methods, economics of operation, nature of material and market requirements)

- The 'output' side – how the product is stored, loaded and transported to market

Malaws (1997:77) has stressed the importance of recording industrial production processes with the following points:

- Recording of the industrial process will complement a structural or building survey, provide a more complete and integrated site record and allow a mutually enhanced understanding of both the operation and architecture of the individual site. The resulting records will allow the more confident creation of typologies, drawing on several aspects which may have influenced development of the particular area of interest

- Study of industrial processes will give an insight into the reason for the location of particular industries in a region and in relation to their immediate environs

The documentation of a production line can also be useful in the evaluation of a historical industrial monument: 'One of the most valuable uses of understanding and properly recording a process in relation to its surrounding structures is to give an insight into the relative importance of those structures and draw attention to those worthy of further recording or even preservation.' (Malaws 1997:77)

This means that the measured drawings will give a better understanding than that which a more general description of the work process and site conditions could offer. Such a level of detail is necessary in order to give an understanding of the interplay between activities, area use and layout of the buildings, installations and production processes.

Personal interviews are an integral part of the fieldwork. Interviews on site and parallel with other documentation have enormous potential as sources of important information. Such information is best documented in written form. The information thus received can often have a corroborating or corrective effect on the adopted procedure for the rest of the documentation.

Collaboration between measured survey, room inventory and interview during the fieldwork is therefore of greatest importance. In order for the measured drawing to show the essential elements in the process, it is necessary for the recorder to get a gist of the production plant and workplaces relevant to the inventory. Interviews contribute to this general understanding, just as the drawings will, during their production, give the recorder and interviewer a better feeling for the plant's area planning, room arrangement and organisation of production.

The interviews also play a decisive role in the documentation of the social historical aspect of the factory and the lives of the workers. Interviews with both workers and management are necessary to describe any particular company's culture.

Explanatory illustrations should be produced in order to show the relationships between machines, work processes and production lines, which otherwise can be difficult to understand. In this way it is possible to cross-refer and integrate elements by collecting details otherwise dispersed throughout the written, photographic and measured material, and as such help the user to discover important relationships otherwise difficult to see solely through the other media. Such explanatory illustrations are also useful in the building analysis.

Interpretative drawings go beyond orthographic views to clarify, explain and emphasise distinctive relationships between physical features of the site and its functions. Such drawings may range from exploded axonometric projections, cut-away views, step-by-step schematics illustrating how a crucial machine or process functions, or flowcharts of industrial processes. A flowchart is a type of diagram that represents a process, showing the steps as boxes of various kinds, and their order by connecting these with arrows. Process operations are represented in these boxes, and arrows connecting them represent flow of control. Flowcharts are used in analysing, designing, documenting or managing a process or program in various fields. In other words, this type of diagram may serve as an investigative and interpretative drawing tool that combines various methods of recording to understand a site, building, or object. The diagram thus represents the relationships between elements in order to understand how they interact (Eppich 2011: 186).

Drawings can vary from the schematic to more complicated versions. Schematic movement studies are effective in showing stages in the treatment or forming of raw materials between components in a production line. Isometric or perspective drawings, which show the relationship between components, can often explain physical ties, relative size, functional parts or other conditions when surrounding elements are removed in the graphic presentation. Clarity is of utmost importance, but this does not necessarily mean simplicity. Several levels of detail or types of information can be presented together without blurring understanding – as long as each category of information clearly illustrates differing aspects of an object or theme.

The production line

A production line is a set of sequential operations established in a factory whereby materials are put through a refining process to produce an end-product that is suitable for onward consumption; or whereby components are assembled to make a finished article.

All cultural heritages represent historical sources; they tell about a business activity and society, social structures, technology and use of materials, market connections and attitudes to the surroundings. Following the production line through a manufacturing plant is a practical way to give a consistent structure to the documentation work and the report giving account of the collected material describing the process flow through the plant. Depending upon the scope or objectives of the investigation there are a lot of questions that can be formulated and documented at the different stages along the production line.

The production equipment employed tells about the technological level of the factory and the producers and origins of machinery and equipment. Whaling, for instance, was a very capital-intensive industry, applying cutting-edge technology from leading producers from all over the industrialised world. A survey of the equipment of a whaling station can tell much about who were the leading manufacturers of the time. Much of the technology developed for the processing of whales later spread to neighbouring industries, for example for the production of herring oil and fish meal, demonstrating the development, application and diffusion of technology.

A production line diagram is also a practical tool for mapping and describing the social organisation of the production, elucidating questions such as who were manning the different stations or taking care of different working operations: skilled or unskilled labour, the recruitment to the different tasks, high or low in the hierarchy, monotonous but easy work or arduous and intensive, demanding dexterity and special skills. Video technology is an electronic tool used to capture and process a large number of images and sound in a sequence. It is therefore the ideal tool to record motion and processes (Eppich 2011: 186). Accordingly, filming manual working operations is an excellent way to document and visualise the movements and handiness accomplished in its context and entirety.

The social context of production

In a fully researched report, there should also be a contextual site history. Any industrial structure is not an isolated monument but part of a network of linkages relating to the methods and means of production. These associations include not only the economic ones of sources of raw material, methods of processing and transport networks, but also the social context of production. It is a vital element in understanding the relationship between components of complex sites and their social symbolism. If the purpose of a site's documentation is to provide information contributing to an understanding of the whole process of industrialisation, it should have a broad scope:

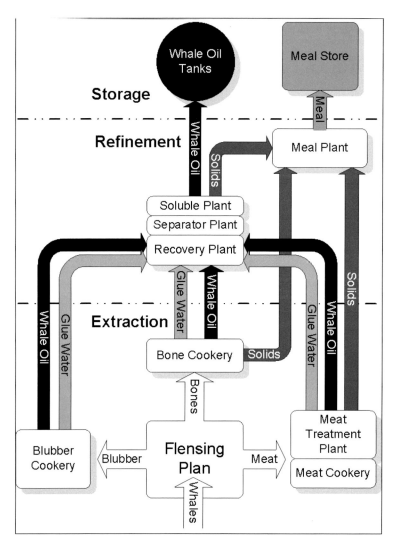

Diagrammatic expression of a production line at a whaling station – production of whale oil and meal (guano). The first is the extraction stage where oil was separated from the blubber, the meat and the bones. The output of this stage was oil and residuals (grax). In the second stage, the oil was refined in various separators, while the residuals were dealt with in the guano plant. The purified oil and the whale meal were then stored in tanks for the oil and bags for the meal – the third stage.

Little has been said, until recently, about the human side of industrial archaeology, for example, housing, churches, schools and other parts of the built environment associated with industry. The rapidly disappearing craft skills which were so necessary in the early phases of the industrial revolution need to be recorded wherever possible. Such skills are now being replaced by automated machines and by robots. In addition, little attempt was made to understand the conditions to which working people were subjected at home and in the work place in the early phases of the industrial revolution (Kemp 1996:5).

Too often social contexts are treated and analysed as a separate entity from the actual production. However, social variables such as salaries, leisure activities, design of accommodation and hierarchical divisions should be analysed as an integral part of the production process since they influenced the output and success of an industrial product. Recording of social aspects, in relation to the physical qualities of the working environment, thus reveal insights into a largely overlooked aspect of production.

Conclusion

Not much has been said about the techniques of documentation and recording. What is for certain is that hitherto expensive and advanced technology will be more easily available for smaller heritage institutions in the field of laser measuring and CAD (Computer-Assisted Drawing).

But technology cannot exempt the need to reflect on the objectives of documentation. These will often be recording the organisation of machinery and equipment, the production processes/lines of production, the functions of buildings and spaces, and social history. Recording industrial process will complement a structural or building survey, provide a more complete and integrated site record and allow a mutually enhanced understanding of both the operation and architecture of the individual site.

Recording an industrial site implies multiple choices and decisions, and a documentation team must identify and assess each and every structure and make value judgements as to what structures are of greatest interest and significance. Documentation is by nature selective and interpretive; a method that seeks to understand and explain the significant aspects of the site. It is therefore the responsibility of the documentation team to collect structured observations and historical sources that constitute an adequate and consistent archival material that can tell a story of that particular site.

We cannot be sure to what uses, demands and questions future generations will put this material. But we can, with available resources, try to provide as rich and comprehensive a historical source material as possible.

Acknowledgements

I owe a large thank you to my friend and colleague Ulf Gustafsson for his contribution to this chapter, through discussions, mutual experiences on field works and his proposals for improving the text.

Further reading

EPPICH, R (ed.): *Recording, Documentation and Information Management for the Conservation of Heritage Places: illustrated examples.* (First published by The Getty Conservation Institute, Los Angeles 2007. Republished with revisions). Vol. 2. Shaftesbury: Donhead Publishing, 2011

KEMP, E L (ed.): *Industrial Archaeology: techniques.* Malabar, Florida: Krieger Publishing, 1996

LETELLIER, R: *Recording, Documentation and Information Management for the Conservation of Heritage Places: guiding principles.* (First published by The Getty Conservation Institute, Los Angeles 2007. Republished with revisions. Vol. 1. Shaftesbury: Donhead Publishing, 2011

MALAWS, B A: Process Recording at Industrial Sites. *Industrial Archaeology Review.* 1997, *Vol. XIX.* 75–98

PALMER, M, and NEAVERSON, P: *Industrial Archaeology: principles and practice.* London: Routledge, 1998

9

Industrial archives and company records

Belem Oviedo Gámez

Introduction

The protection and conservation of industrial records is relatively recent in the world of archives. Why and what to keep of industrial documents? Why are they important to historians? These are some of the questions that need to be answered to justify their protection. On the other hand, and based on the fact that in most cases professionals from various disciplines work in industrial archives, albeit rarely as professional archivists, this chapter will give some indications of best practice in classification and cataloguing.

Origins of archive conservation

The first steps in preserving industrial archives were taken in 1905 when the archives of Krupp in Essen, Germany, were arranged on a scientific basis in order to protect them. A year later the first Centre for Business Archives was created in Köln with support from the Chamber of Commerce, and the First Congress of Economic Archives was held in 1913. In the meantime, the archives of Siemens in Munich and Bayer in Leverkusen were organised. Since then, many large corporations have conserved their archives, and some smaller companies or those with fewer financial resources have gathered their records in shared archives such as that in Dortmund, which hosts the documents of some 300 companies in eight kilometres of documents.

In the 1920s, Harvard University in the United States received archives from many companies, giving teachers and researchers the opportunity to work on them. The Business Archives Council was established in the United Kingdom in 1935, including archives, libraries, museums, archivists, historians and business organisations. German companies deliver their archives to the state when they lack the funds to keep them. In the UK, universities fulfil this role, one of the most important being in Glasgow, which holds documents from 1,200 companies.

In 1949, the National Archives of France began to recover industrial archives, and twenty years later the Mining Historical Centre was created in the northern French coal district. *Les Archives des Entreprises: conseils practiques d'organization* was published in

1980 and a few years later, at the premises of what was once the Mitte Bossut cotton mill, the National Archives of the World of Work were established, composed of industrial and commercial enterprises, banks or insurance companies, professional organisations, trade unions and societies, many of them private. Currently the National Archive of France has a law which obliges companies to conserve and catalogue their archives, but this does not apply to private archives; advice is also offered to companies concerned for the preservation of their documents.

Interest in economic history is, as we have seen, the trigger for many of the rescue projects of business and industrial archives. In Italy this dates back to 1971 with the archives of Fiat, Alfa Romeo, Ebel and Ansaldo, while in Belgium the work in favour of industrial heritage 'has been the promoter of the conservation movement, prioritizing the historical, testimonial and heritage value of the documents of companies' (González, 2010). Mexico is no exception, where the Archivo General de la Nación (National Archives) has the authority to request government bodies to transfer their archives but cannot compel private firms to preserve and catalogue their

An original plan for the installation of a hydraulic wheel and two Jenisch mills in 1892 at the Hacienda de Beneficio de San Miguel Regla, Hidalgo, Mexico. The documents are conserved at the Archivo Histórico de la Compañía de Minas de Real del Monte y Pachuca (AHCRMyP), Fondo Siglo XIX Sección: Correspondencia Serie: Varios a Compañía Subserie: Varios (Archivo Histórico y Museo de Minería, A C)

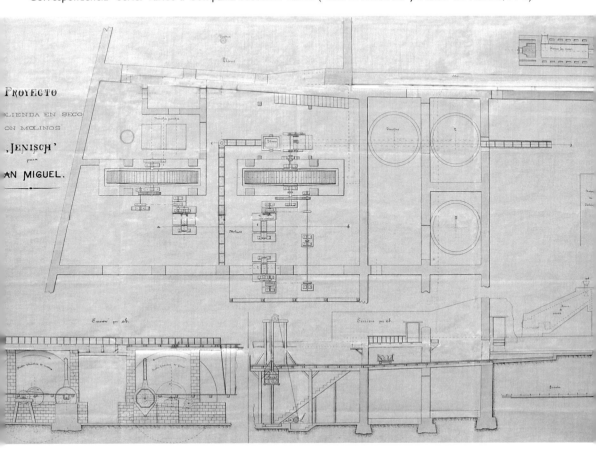

documents. Among its archives are those of the Comisión de Luz y Fuerza del Centro (State Electric Company), which were first gathered together in 2011. Within the private sector, one of the early works of preserving records of companies in Mexico began in 1981 with the recovery and classification of a significant portion of the documents produced during the nineteenth century by the Societat Real del Monte and Pachuca (CRMyP) in Hidalgo. Nowadays, these historical archives are 2,700 m long, covering a chronological period from 1616 to 2002. In recent years the concern in preserving industrial archives has grown thanks to the efforts in favour of the industrial heritage. In 2003 the Mexican Association of Economic History organised a forum on business archives, and the international seminars of TICCIH Mexico always include a workshop on this topic.

The importance of industrial archives

The records generated by industrial activity are essential to understand not only its own history and technological changes, but also the history of economic, technological, social, trade union, political and even cultural development of the region. They represent an invaluable testimony to the contribution to the origin and development of the towns and regions that emerged alongside these industries.

In many cases, records come with books, periodicals and photography, providing information which is without doubt a fundamental tool for drawing up conservation plans, preservation schemes and plans for the re-use of industrial sites, to mention just a few practical examples.

It is also important to take into account the protection of trade union archives, which have the greatest risk of being lost, and although they are not considered true industrial archives they do have a close relationship with the companies, not least because in many cases the unions were created by the companies themselves.

The contribution of archives to local history is essential, thanks in many cases to their continuity and because they do not depend on political factors for their creation, permanence or organisation. They are as large or small as the company that originated them; their history is not only of the company itself, but of a productive activity and its relationship to the external world such as the manufacturing towns which developed from the foundation of the company.

In times of political or economic disruption many industries continue to work and produce information. Much can be known through these records of political relationships between entrepreneurs and governments, the formation of unions and their struggles, the development of banking and commerce and the international relationship between the exchange of technology, labour and supplies.

In the case of the industrial heritage, the written information contained in archives, machinery and tool catalogues, periodicals and photographs of that time is of great help in carrying out comprehensive projects for rescue, restoration and re-use.

Best practice for organising archives

Cleaning. It is frequently the case that industrial archives, especially the ones belonging to the oldest enterprises or recently closed ones, are literally stacked up in boxes – at best – or form piles of paper in a warehouse. The first thing to do is to collect everything and move them to a proper site where, as a first step, cleaning can be performed. Ideally, they will also undergo a thorough a process of fumigation, but unfortunately that is something that rarely occurs.

Classification. Before attempting to classify information it is essential to study and understand the production process and the administrative structure of the company. It is not possible to understand the documents without knowing the organisational chain, how and why it was generated.

However, it is possible to propose a small scheme for classification and cataloguing, based on the idea that all companies have a similar administrative structure and the experience accumulated over twenty-five years working on industrial archives. First of all, we must respect basic archival principles:

> The principle of provenance and the principle of original order. While the former is inflexible and is related to an issue of utmost importance to the archival profession, the second involves mainly aspects of convenience and ease of use. The principle of provenance concerns the integrity of the files, the preservation of evidential values that are inherent in their organic status … The principle of original order relates to the use or convenience. (Scellenberg, 1982)

Once classification charts are established based on the administrative organization, it is recommended to carry out an initial separation of documents which may correspond to a particular historical period of the company or a particular authority. This chart is complemented by sections, series and sub-series. The first correspond to the departments, branches or sections of the company. A chronological sequence must be maintained, starting from the earliest date to the latest, respecting the dates of each of the subsets, numbering each subset from 1. The volume, which can contain multiple records, is assigned a sequential number, according to its place within the collection.

Depending on the characteristics of the volume and integration of the archive, it can also be classified by independent collections or as part of an archival fund if there is a relationship among several of them, and ordered thematically and chronologically. As an example, the Colonial Fund of the Historical Archives of the Society of Mines of Real del Monte and Pachuca (Mexico) is enriched by the addition of copies of documents from other archives, resulting in the following collections: General Archives of the Indies (Archivo General de Indias), General Archives of the Nation (Archivo General de la Nación, Mexico) and Romero de Terreros. The original classification of previously organised archives should be respected.

A general inventory should be made at the same time as the work of classification. This will give an overview of the wealth of information which they contain and will serve as an instrument of control. Inventories are also the first tool to support research, both from the company and from outside researchers, so it is recommended that the archives are open for public consultation, under rules set down by their owners. The information contained in the inventories is simple: file number, beginning and end dates, folio number, theme and observations where it is important to note the physical condition of the document and the existence of external elements that enrich it such as photographs, stamps, brochures and so forth.

The General Fund Guide. Once these two tasks – classifying and inventorying – are completed it is possible to develop a general guide to the archive, in which each record group may include a brief synopsis of its material and intellectual content:

- Origin: address or department that originated the information.

- Chronological period: end dates, putting in brackets the dates of the documentation and in parenthesis the years of single documents. For example 1975–1988 [1975–1984] (1985–1988), indicates that the group described includes information from 1975 to 1988, concentrated between 1975 and 1984, with few documents for the period from 1985 to 1988.

- Volume: total number and volume described in linear meters: 92 volumes, 3.12 linear meters.

- Arrangement: chronological, alphabetical or numerical.

- Consultation tools: all the material that may be helpful to the researcher, such as inventories.

- Informative description: overview and the most complete panorama of unit of description.

- Additional sources: identify what other funds or collections related to the information can be located, if possible include other archives, libraries and collections (Oviedo, 1993).

Cataloguing. This is one of the tasks that demands most time and concentration. It requires prior intellectual work on the history of the industry related to the archive, the history of the company including understanding of their production system, and a capacity of synthesis that allows the most important themes of the files to be extracted. It is a difficult and individual task which cannot be speeded up using electronic means except for capturing the information that will shape the catalogue. If we really wish to support research it is advisable to prepare this tool in the best possible way so as to facilitate access to the sources for consultation. Catalogues are enriched by including personal names and place-names indexes. Research is accelerated if catalogues are released on compact disc, which can deploy only catalogue cards containing the name of the person or place of interest of the researcher. This is probably possible in the great national archives, but is rarely seen in industrial archives.

Catalogue cards ought to include the following fields: section, series, sub-series and file volume number, chronology, dates, places, observations such as state of preservation, graphics, prints, number of pages and a content summary record.

All issued consultation instruments should be viewed as general bibliography, for both specialists and people in search of research topics, hence the need always to annex a glossary of terms used, since more often than not the reader is not familiar with the industry in question.

Diffusion and public service. If the service is available, it is convenient to microfilm records as a way to preserve the information so as to disseminate the contents of the

The landscape around the Mina de Acosta, Real del Monte Hidalgo in Mexico. Silver and gold mining started here in 1727 and ended in 1955. The Spanish, English, Mexican and American involvement can be traced in the mine archaeology and followed through the documentary archives. Since 2001 it has been a museum with access underground guided by former miners. (Marco Antonio Hernandez Badillo)

files. Another means of diffusion is to publish guides with the documentation, written and graphic.

In today's globalised world and with the advance of communications it is important to have a website linked to other sites that share an interest in archives, history, industrial heritage and so on.

Industrial archives should be the cornerstone and the historical and academic foundation for re-use projects for industrial sites. Coordinated work between the archive and industrial museums is one of the best examples of their 'socialisation'. Museums are the main promoters of archives among students, researchers, tourists and the local population in which the industry was located. In many cases a weekend visit to one of these museums ends in the archives, generating feedback between the archives and museums.

Conclusion

This chapter has dealt with companies interested in preserving their cultural heritage. There are researchers who are motivated by working in economic history, industrial history and industrial heritage who are willing to save their archives, to organize and to awaken the interest of owners of companies to protect them. However, in reality most countries have no legislation to protect them; moreover, there is little awareness of the need for safekeeping, of investing time, effort and money in their conservation. Even within specialised agencies there is little discussion about industrial archives. In numerous conferences, seminars or meetings of experts on industrial heritage, few projects present the rescue and protection of archives, even if these have already been classified. At the international level, projects on large buildings or machines and the research on industrial heritage are privileged. The search for the origins and development of industry can also be read in the written story by employers, employees and workers.

Finally, a reflection on the Nizhny Tagil Charter. Industrial heritage is based primarily on the study of land: a site, a specific place, a situation related to a place where the records and inventories originated. Hence the urgent need firstly to protect the archives generated by the companies, and secondly to open them to researchers. The values of industrial heritage are materialised in, among other things, written and graphic documentation. As the Charter says, it is necessary to foresee in the legislation the closure of industrial sites to prevent the destruction or removal of significant elements, where the archives are the most vulnerable. Everyone interested in industrial heritage ought to reflect on how far the often self-appointed custodians and specialists are responsible for the destruction of what we decide not to save and apply the wisdom of 'silence gives consent'. There is an ethical responsibility for the real protection of our historical memory.

English translation: Miguel Iwadare

Further reading

GONZÁLEZ PEDRAZA, José Andrés: Los archivos de empresa: un estudio comparativo. España, Arch-e, *Revista Andaluza de Archivos*, January 2010, Nº 2, 31–57

KUHNMUNCH, Annie: Les Archives du Centre Historique Minier. Constitution des Fonds et Exploitation, Actes du VIIIe. Colloque National sur le Patrimoine Industriel, Lille, 7–8–9, *L'Archéologie Industrielle en France,* May 1987, No. 17–18

OVIEDO GÁMEZ, Belem (ed.): *Guía General del Archivo Histórico de la Compañía de Minas de Real del Monte y Pachuca. México,* PLACE: Archivo General de la Nación, Compañía Real del Monte y Pachuca, AHCRDMyP, 1993

OVIEDO GÁMEZ, Belem and HERNÁNDEZ Badillo, Marco A: Un archivo de empresa, base para el rescate y conservación del patrimonio industrial: El Archivo Histórico de la Compañía de Minas de Real del Monte y Pachuca (1556–1967), *Memorias del Primer Encuentro Nacional de Arqueología Industrial,* DATE, VOLUME, 143–9

SCHELLENBERG, T R: *Principios archivísticos de ordenación.* PLACE: Archivo General de la Nación, Serie Información de Archivos, 1982

10

Photography and image resources

Jan af Geijerstam

Introduction

Images, especially photographs, are sources to read the past and a way to interpret and convey history. This chapter gives a short overview of the significance of photography in industrial history and as a source for the understanding and interpretation of industrial heritage sites. It also introduces some basic notes on the collection, cataloguing, interpretation and use of images.

Photography in the industrial society

The history of photography – that is, the making of durable images by recording light or other electromagnetic radiation – is an integral part of the history of industrial society. It was developed as a usable process with daguerreotypes in the first half of the nineteenth century, during the classical era of the first industrial revolution. The era of widespread mass photography commenced with George Eastman's first camera in 1888, during the second industrial revolution of mass consumption. In a third phase, and on a commercial scale since the early 1990s, we have seen digital photography gradually replacing the use of light sensitive photographic film and chemical processing in photography, in the era of the third industrial revolution.

Photography has thus passed through a number of different technologies, which have influenced not only how it has been used, but also set the conditions for the safeguarding of photographs for the future. The daguerreotype, with a long exposure and a complicated chemical processing, created a single, unique and very sensitive image on a piece of glass. With digital techniques of today images can be caught in a fraction of a second and be spread over the world almost instantly.

Images and industry

The camera has been a central tool for industrial companies in their daily work. Depending on the size of the firm and the branch of industry and its products, the scope of photography has varied. It has been used in research and development, in the study

Two images of a worker's room by the blast furnaces at the steelworks of Fagersta, Sweden. The colour image, from 2005, resembles the typical abandoned site photographs produced by urban explorers. The possibility of contrasting it with an image while the works were running, here from 1978, brings a number of new insights into the reading of the site. The men by the table are Olle Lindstedt and Torsten Forss. If images are saved at the sites where they were taken their potential as a source to the past and in the reconstruction of an industrial heritage site is greatly increased. (Peter Nyblom)

of production processes, and in marketing and public relations. Images have been used to create, convey and firmly establish the ideology and identity of a corporation among its employees and outwards to capture markets. Images are part of a social context; they are acts of communication – and of power.

Photographs of larger industrial corporations were normally carefully collected and recorded in archives. These often still exist, and two examples suffice to indicate their wealth. The Krupp Historical Archive in Duisburg, Germany, contains some 1.9 million photographs dating from 1860 and onwards. The Archives of General Electric in Schenectady, New York, contain some 1.5 million images (1891–1960). Even a small steel-making community such as Fagersta in central Sweden has a community archive with some 250,000 photographs (1860–c.1980) in which the company archives is an important part. Added to the stills these archives also contain films, that is moving images, of immense importance.

In general, industries as such, as well as industrial communities and their social lives,

Number 1 steelworks at Fagersta was commissioned in 1949. When the top photograph was taken ten years later, the characteristics of the steel were still determined largely by which process was used. There were five steel processes in the same bay, and pride was taken in being able to produce 'the right steel for every purpose'. In the foreground is an open-hearth furnace, with a charging machine, and behind them an electric arc furnace and a Bessemer furnace. Between the latter two there are also high-frequency furnaces. The smelter with three blast furnaces is hidden behind the Bessemer plant. The image of 1959 is essential for the interpretation of the present-day abandoned mill, in the lower image in 2005. (Fagersta Ironworks Museum/Peter Nyblom)

have been important themes for photographers from inside and outside the companies. The camera has been a tool in the hands of employees and external observers, for personal memory or publication, in order to support or to examine critically. Several world-renowned *photographers/artists*, on commission from industrial corporations or mass media or in a more personal exploration of industrial society, have documented industrial life. And in our own times, in the so-called post-industrial era, the structures, landscapes and social life of industry continue to be important themes.

Photography of industry as art might be considered as a special genre, with photographers such as Tom Paiva (US), Naoya Hatakeyama (Japan), Edward Burtynsky (Canada), Andreas Gursky and Bernd and Hilla Becher (Germany), among the most renowned, with their photographs represented at world-leading art galleries. Another example of contemporary industrial photography, of a totally different kind, is the continuous documentation of abandoned sites of industrial society made by different strands of the movement denoted *urban exploration*. Their work can be described as an existential interest in and representation of life and death, of time passing. *Ruins of Detroit*, by Yves Marchand and Romain Meffre (2010), is an artistic and high-quality expression of the same strand of photography of industrial society in transition. A common feature of these groups of images is that they depict merely the traces of human activity with an emphasis of form, light, pattern and colour. It is an aesthetic of decline, but mostly devoid of history or of active human presence.

Another and more important category of photography is the documentation of industry as a human activity, as a site of work, production and social interaction. This brings to the forefront the very essence of industry – and industrial heritage. It is not buildings and sites, but men, women and children in the complexities of human life. The British photographer Ian Beesley has integrated images and writing in an active, participatory fieldwork. He strives to encourage the workers he portrays to participate and contribute to his projects. He stresses the importance of their active involvement in decision-making and control in the documentary process and establishes their ownership of the documentation and of the interpretation. Another example is the Brazilian/Portuguese photographer Sebastião Salgado, who has systematically documented life and work on all continents in his immensely forceful volume *Workers. An archaeology of the industrial age* (1993). Salgado also brings forward the basic fact that industry is not a thing of the past but is at the core of modern society, in ever-new forms and changing circumstances.

Why use photographs as industrial heritage?

The use of photographs in the area of industrial heritage is a hitherto all too neglected field and historians in general have been sceptical of the use of visual media. If photographs are used it is most often made with a minimum of analysis and contextualisation. The primacy of the written word remains uncontested, seldom letting images into an active dialogue with the text or the physical heritage site. If used, images are all too often reduced to decoration. This is paralleled by an all too common neglect of the archival safeguarding of photographic evidence from the past.

Systematic studies of photography and industry are also scarce. Possibly the most extensive analysis of a single photographic archive that is connected to both a site and a company is the research connected to the Krupp archives, which has resulted in two big and most informative volumes (Tenfelde 2005 and Stremmel *et al.* 2011).

At the same time, media increasingly affects our lives, and the visual has become central to modern communication. It has even been described as a key to the cultural construction of social life in western society. The difference between the practice of historians and the societal use of images increases, and it is necessary to bring up and emphasise the importance of images in research and the interpretation of industrial heritage.

Images can readily be used as a basis for the interpretation of industrial heritage sites – alone or preferably in combination with other different sources, such as the site itself in its physical context, the living memories of employees, text archives, and so on. Through an analysis of photographs we can explore the physical layout of plants as a whole, as well as of industrial workshops and single workplaces.

Photographs are also essential in the exploration and analysis of the social order and organisation of work, and they enable us to put these into their wider societal context.

Images can reinstate life into abandoned and often tidied industrial heritage sites. They bring people and life back into being, and reconstruct the site, as it actually was, at least at one point in time in its shifting past. Torn-down buildings, scrapped machinery, railroad tracks of old reappear.

The complexity of the images raises questions and insights of a new character. It should also be remembered that images can be a most usable way of initiating discussions, bringing memories to life (photo elicitation).

Finding and collecting photographs

The most immediate sources of images of an industrial site are the company itself, its archives, its employees, the local administrative authorities, professional and semi-professional photographers, and the local newspaper(s). In cases of already existing archives the survival of the photographs is hopefully secured, but often work on industrial heritage can lead to discoveries of extensive and important collections, which might also be hidden away and maybe forgotten, in public, private or personal archives. It might require considerable research, knowledge and perseverance for such resources to be found, and the systematic collection of images should be considered as an integrated part of industrial heritage preservation.

Important collections of images can also be found far beyond the local context. Especially in colonial or post-colonial contexts, it is important to consider how the company has been owned and structured over the years. Most big corporations have had a global scope for a very long period, and as archives reflect the structures of power, immense numbers of photographic records from 'foreign' lands are saved far away from the sites where the photographs were taken. The essence and basic reasons for using the camera was to report and document in order to show others what things were like. In these contexts the past is a foreign country, in a very double meaning. The most important images are normally saved at the site of power, at the headquarters of transnational corporations. My own research regarding early efforts to introduce industrial iron-making processes in India in the mid-nineteenth century disclosed images relating to the period 1861–63 – which were to be absolutely decisive for the outcome of the investigation – in an archive in Sweden.

Saving, protecting, interpreting and using images

The main role of archives is to guarantee the conservation and future accessibility of documents from the past for possible future use. In a well-managed photographic archive each specimen should be documented, sorted, marked, housed and stored in a safe way in order to safeguard not only the images as physical objects but also complement them with metadata on their content and context.

A central task is thus to invest in accessioning, not only photographs but also data connected to them. It is literally of vital importance to spend time gathering information since a photograph without annotations loses nearly all of its potential importance. The history of industry can be contemporary, but time passes, and information is always more accessible today than it will be tomorrow.

In cataloguing images the way one sets up keywords will direct and confine future studies. The cataloguing of images demands extra care as it reduces the photograph to the elements recorded in that specific cataloguing programme. Every database is conceived of to satisfy a finite (no matter how high) number of questions.

An essential rule is to not over-categorise and to save any original order and arrangement scheme of the collection. Seven features merit special attention, most of them reaching back to the original site of the production of the photographs: creator name, context and role; title; date; extent and physical description; subject; notes; and identification number. These points of information should always be present in any register to a collection.

Preservation and digitisation

Photographic records are often very complex, with diverse formats and materials. Some of these are especially unstable and require special care, but all benefit from well-defined

During the early 1860s three Swedish engineers were commissioned by the British to build an ironworks in India, based on charcoal. The image shows the construction of the iron and steelworks in Dechauri, north of Delhi, photographed by one of the Swedish engineers in early 1863. In the centre, the lowest part of one of the blast furnaces is visible, parts of which still can be identified at the site. (Carl Gustaf Wittenström/ National Museum of Science and Technology, Stockholm)

preservation practices, stable environmental conditions and careful handling. Most important is to replace enclosures and storage furniture, which can damage the photograph, and to establish a duplication programme for unstable materials. Digitisation might thus be necessary.

The introduction of digital technologies has made new, powerful tools available for conservation and access requirements, and almost all photograph archives are today involved in electronic cataloguing and photographic print and negative digitisation projects; at the same time, new methods of online consultation have been developed. This is a decisive shift, making the images accessible from far away and also democratising the archives.

At the same time digitisation can never be a substitute for saving the original images, and the 2009 Florence Declaration explicitly calls for the preservation of analogue photographs. Any archival measure implies the selection of documents considered worthy of being conserved, and digitisation implies a further stage of selection. Just like industrial heritage remains, photographs are objects endowed with materiality that exists in time and space and they have to be preserved as such. An analogue photograph and its digital reproduction are not the same thing. If internet access is ideally independent of place and time, it is also limited to a single component of the photographic object: the image as such.

Digitisation is also extremely onerous in terms of cost, time and human resources. No matter how much money is invested, it is not realistic to convert all photographs into digital format along with all of the metadata connected to them. It is also necessary to bear in mind as yet unresolved questions relating to future obsolescence and the instability of digital formats.

Interpretation

In many industrial communities the mill or factory was, or still is, the heart and focus around which life was lived. It became an icon of stability and of the future. It dominated the physical, built layout of the community. It set the timings of daily life. Its sounds, smells and dirt were felt in most of the town.

Photographic archives are part of the history of the community and of the transformation of industrial society. The images are often saved together with text-based archives. In image research this gives room for an analysis not only of the images as such, but for studies of what photographs do socially, in the construction of landscape, identity and place. They can also be used in the study of the history of photography, the shifts and changes of technology and the position of the photographic image in society in its variety of uses.

Gillian Rose (2012) distinguishes between three different *sites* in the analysis of an image. The sites are the production of the image, the image itself and finally where it is viewed and used. In each of these cases we also should consider three different *modalities*: the technology used, the material qualities of the images and social context. This schematic layout supplies the basic tools for a full understanding of an image or a group of images. What kind of photograph is it, and when, by whom, for whom and why was it made using what technique? How is the image composed and what meaning does it carry? How was it used and interpreted?

Conclusion

Images are split-second remembrances of a part of the past, but in the present, as in the past, they are also objects telling about relations in the making and articulating of histories. Images are acts of communication. It is thus of immense importance that they are safeguarded in the sites where they have the strongest potential to act as relational objects. It should be an aim to keep them in the context where they once were incepted, created and used. For full and informed use of images, they need to be closely linked to their 'original documentary universe'.

Archives are also active agents in the creation and maintaining of memory and identity. They influence the ways in which society seeks evidence of what its core values are and have been. Archives are sites where social power is negotiated, contested, confirmed.

Maintaining a direct connection between images and other archives and the local society and space gives the fullest possible prerequisites to a nuanced analysis. It carries the possibility of shifting the balance of power in the interpretation of industrial heritage, regarding which stories are favoured and which are marginalised.

Further reading

Florence Declaration. Recommendation for the Preservation of Analogue Photo Archives, Kunsthistorisches Institut in Florenz, 2009 (<http://www.khi.fi.it/en/photothek/florencedeclaration/index.html>)

RITZENTHALER, Mary Lynn and VOGT-O'CONNOR, Diane: *Photographs: archival care and management.* Chicago: Society of American Archivists, 2006

ROSE, Gillian: *Visual Methodologies: an introduction to researching with visual materials*, 3rd edn. London: Sage, 2012

SALGADO, Sebastião and NEPOMUCENO, Eric: *Workers: an archaeology of the industrial age.* New York: Aperture, 1993

STREMMEL, Ralf *et al.* (eds): *Krupp. Fotografien aus zwei Jahrhunderten.* Berlin/München: Deutscher Kunstverlag, 2011

TENFELDE, Klaus (ed.): *Pictures of Krupp: photography and history in the industrial age.* London: Philip Wilson Publishers, 2005

Part III

Realising the potential

11

Choosing what to preserve

Paul Smith

Introduction

This chapter takes a look at the criteria for the study and the protection of the industrial heritage as they have been developed in France. Under the influence of initiatives in industrial archaeology in Great Britain during the 1950s and 1960s, a new awareness of the importance of the physical vestiges of industrialization began to emerge in France during the 1970s. After the post-war years of growth and prosperity known as the *trente glorieuses*, this decade witnessed numerous closures of sites, particularly in the traditional sectors of textile production, iron- and steel-making and coal-mining. As elsewhere, the appearance of what the French call *friches industrielles* – industrial wastelands or brownfield sites – began to provoke concern as to the place of this industrial heritage within the national heritage as a whole, and a consciousness that once-familiar factory buildings with their north-lit roofs and smoking chimneys were gradually, or perhaps rapidly, becoming a thing of the past.

Among the figures who played a part in drawing attention to the urgency of recording and preserving the physical evidence of France's disappearing industrial landscapes, mention may be made here of the historian Maurice Daumas, author in 1980 of a seminal book on industrial archaeology in France, of the historian Louis Bergeron, specialist of the banking and manufacturing institutions of the revolutionary period (and subsequently, of course, president of TICCIH between 1990 and 2000), of Denis Woronoff, historian of the iron and steel industries, and of Serge Chassagne, historian of the French cotton industry. Despite this powerful academic input, the movement in France was by no means confined to university spheres and was also strongly influenced by novel approaches to the way museums can interpret the industrial environment, pioneered at the celebrated eco-museum that was founded at Le Creusot in 1973. The movement also mobilised a certain number of architects who appreciated the potential of disused textile mills for accommodating new, non-industrial uses and demonstrated how the adaptive re-use of such buildings could assure their preservation. These different strands came together in 1978 with the foundation of France's national industrial archaeology association, the Comité d'information et de liaison pour l'archéologie, l'étude et la mise en valeur du patrimoine industriel, (CILAC), which publishes the review *L'Archéologie industrielle en France*, organizes national conferences and represents TICCIH in France.

Although the industrial heritage in France is made up largely of the sites and landscapes bequeathed by the country's industrial development during the nineteenth and twentieth centuries, there was an awareness from the outset that the special attention focused in Great Britain on the physical heritage of the Industrial Revolution was not directly applicable to the chronology of France's industrial history. France today can boast the preservation of above-ground remains of an industrial site dating from the second century, the Barbegal Gallo-Roman milling complex at Fontvieille near Arles, where a succession of overshot waterwheels was estimated to have been capable of powering machinery to grind up to five tonnes of flour a day. The French industrial heritage also comprises a number of seventeenth- and eighteenth-century manufactories founded with royal privileges and specialising in the production of high-quality broadcloth, of paper, of glass or of fiscal commodities such as salt and tobacco. Founded by Colbert in the 1660s, the royal arsenal at Rochefort retains many of its original buildings, including the spectacular 1670 rope works and one of the world's first masonry dry docks, the *vieille forme* of 1666.

One of the best-known industrial heritage sites in France: the Menier chocolate factory at Noisiel, to the east of Paris. The 1871 mill, astride a branch of the river Marne, was protected from 1986 and subsequently restored when the whole site was transformed by the architects Robert & Reichen to accommodate the French headquarters of Nestlé. It is now on the French Tentative List of World Heritage nominations. (Paul Smith)

Alongside these prestigious establishments which were invested with royal authority, French industrial heritage is also characterised by its wealth of surviving water-powered sites. If the Industrial Revolution in Great Britain was largely a steam-driven thing, industry in France was primarily water-powered up to the last decades of the nineteenth century. What is often termed the Second Industrial Revolution of the late nineteenth and early twentieth century, based on electricity and the internal combustion engine, gives the French industrial heritage another special feature. In the early years of the twentieth century France led the world in the motor car and aviation industries, and several sites in the Paris region and at Lyons bear witness to this advance.

L'inventaire general du patrimoine culturel

In 1983, under pressure from the industrial heritage 'lobby' that had coalesced around le CILAC, and which had been given considerable impetus by the organization at Lyons and Grenoble of TICCIH's fourth international congress in 1981, and in the context too of a renewal of heritage policies under the aegis of President Mitterrand's Minister of Culture, Jack Lang, the study of industrial heritage was officially embraced by his ministry. A small industrial heritage 'cell' was set up within the ministry's national inventory service originally created by André Malraux in 1962 with a mission of identifying, studying and sharing knowledge about France's national heritage. In the 1960s, of course, this *Inventaire general des monuments et des richesses artistiques de la France* as it was then called (today it is known as the *Inventaire general du patrimoine culturel*, the General Inventory of the Cultural Heritage) paid little attention to sites of industrial production, concentrating on the study and documentation of more traditional forms of heritage such as churches, manor houses, farm buildings and so forth. The new industrial heritage cell began its work by supporting thematic surveys, inspired by questions of historical research coming from the university, for example on the place of hydraulic energy in French industrial development, looking at the location of sites in different hydrographic basins, examining the continuity and changes in their use over time and paying particular attention to the technical development of water wheels and turbines, a field in which French engineers and inventors were particularly innovative. Another thematic survey plotted and recorded the built vestiges of the French iron and steel industries, developing new interpretations of the geographical diffusion of charcoal-fired blast furnaces from the sixteenth century. These early research inventories were carried out either by field workers already employed by the regional services of the *Inventaire* or by associations or research bodies supported with grants. They were designed in part to demonstrate the pertinence of the industrial archaeological approach, drawing new historical evidence from the physical remains of sites, their buildings, their machines and transport infrastructures, and comparing that evidence with other printed or archival sources. Other research projects undertaken by the industrial heritage cell were inspired more by considerations of urgency. An inventory was launched, for example, on the coal-mining heritage in the Nord-Pas-de-Calais and Lorraine coal basins, and another on the car factories of Paris and its western suburbs, the birthplace of this quintessential twentieth-century industry.

The industrial heritage location survey

In 1986, in a change of strategy and in response to recommendations drawn up by the Council of Europe at a 1985 colloquium at Lyons entitled 'The Industrial Heritage, What Policies?', the cell launched its *repérage du patrimoine industriel*, a nation-wide location survey of industrial heritage, department by department. This location survey was to be completed within a few years in order to provide a general overview of French industrial heritage at the end of the twentieth century. Its objectives were both scientific and administrative in nature. In scientific terms, the identification and documentation of all the sites of industrial production in existence at the time of the survey were intended to produce a better global understanding of France's industrial history and geography, and to single out sites of particular interest worthy of further analysis. In administrative terms, the findings of the survey, by identifying such exceptional sites, were destined to underpin policies of heritage preservation at national and regional levels. It should perhaps be mentioned here that the General Inventory is a research body with no direct responsibility for the statutory protection of the heritage, a mission which is under the control of another administration within the Ministry, the historic monuments department, which dates back to the 1830s.

Drawing on the *Inventaire*'s existing expertise in heritage documentation, and computerising its results from the outset, the industrial heritage location survey was launched in 1986 in four of France's twenty-two metropolitan regions. The methodology for the operation was elaborated at the same time and comprised the realization of several thesauri in order to classify the sites identified in the field and to designate their different constituent parts. The *dénominations* (monument type) thesaurus was organised hierarchically and subdivided into industrial sectors (energy production, mining, metallurgy, mechanical engineering, ceramics, etc.) while the constituent parts (components) thesaurus identified elements such as warehouses, different types of workshop, office buildings, housing, water towers, chimneys and so on. The aim of these thesauri was not to propose unequivocal descriptive terms for all aspects of industrial reality, but to facilitate the management of machine-readable records and different researches in these records. For each site identified in the field a documentary file was established, including reproductions of historic representations such as extracts from old maps, architectural drawings, old photographs or postcards, but comprised essentially of the photographic coverage realised by the service's professional photographers. To begin with these photographs were in black and white, but today they are in colour and are integrated, in digital form, into the database. A standardised file orders the data collected on each site into several information fields under the general headings of designation, localization, history, description, interest, property and so on. For those interested in these aspects of the French industrial heritage inventory, which at the time were considered as admirably Cartesian and highly innovative, the General Inventory's web site (www.inventaire.culture.gouv.fr/) gives access to all the methodological resources as well as to the different databases on buildings, on the moveable heritage and on images.

Criteria for selection

At the same time as these tools were being forged, considerable thought was also given to what exactly we intended to inventorise, in other words what criteria could be applied to identify the industrial heritage. The definition given by the *Inventaire* for its location survey was a deliberately restrictive one. What we planned to identify and analyze were the sites of industrial production, rather than the heritage of industrial civilization as a whole. Railway heritage and engineering structures such as canals, roads or bridges were not included in the remit, unless they were an integral part of the production site under consideration. This is not to say that such elements are not studied and documented by the services of the General Inventory, but they are not dealt with by the industrial heritage location survey. For sites of industrial production, the aim of the operation was to provide an agreed minimum of information on all of the sites in existence at the time of the enquiry. No distinction was made here between sites still in activity and those which were abandoned or had been converted to new uses. As a heritage survey rather than a programme of historical research, the criterion of the physical survival of the site was of course a crucial one but, in keeping with the *Inventaire*'s practice with regards to other types of heritage, it was accepted that certain exceptional sites could be the object of documentary files even if they had disappeared, as long as the documentary and iconographical material allowed for a relatively detailed restitution of what the site had once been. Obviously, a fairly large proportion of the sites recorded in the 1980s and 1990s have since disappeared, and the inventory files now constitute a precious record of such sites now lost.

In chronological terms, no *terminus ante quem* was fixed and, as we have seen, the survival of production sites dating from before the Industrial Revolution was one of the specific characteristics of France's industrial history that we were anxious to record. At the beginning of the operation, it was decided that the survey would aim for the complete identification and coverage of all industrial sites dating from before the 1950s. For sites created after that date, it was left to the initiative of the field researchers to decide whether or not they would open a file, according to the perceived interest of the site concerned and its importance in architectural, economic or landscape terms. Much discussion was of course devoted to the notion of industrial production and how to distinguish it from artisanal or craft production. Here, once again, rules of thumb were suggested as criteria for industrial activity, such as the existence of mechanised production, the importance of the workforce (more than ten workers) and the distribution of finished products beyond the confines of a local community. As the survey advanced, it also became necessary to institute 'collective' files for nebulous groupings of small workshops which, taken individually, might not be considered as of great significance but which, collectively, represent an important local industry. This was the case, for example, for the small workshops constituting the cutlery industry around Thiers, or the *fruitières* of the Jura, small depots for the preliminary transformation of milk into cheese. At another scale, it was also necessary to create special files for industrial 'ensembles', large sites composed of different installations not necessarily close to each other but forming a single and coherent industrial complex. This type of file was necessary, for example, for the car factories of the Paris suburbs or for some large-scale complexes of the chemical industry.

A recent study undertaken for the General Inventory by Marina Gasnier and published under the title *Patrimoine industriel et technique, perspectives et retour sur trente ans de politiques pubiques au service des territoires* has provided an historical analysis of the operation and its achievements. The Mérimée database on the built heritage today includes some 14,000 notices produced by the industrial heritage location survey,

The Clément-Bayard factory at Levallois-Perret, a suburb to the west of Paris, was one of the first purpose-built automobile factories in the world. It opened in 1898 and was demolished in 1988. This restitution, based on archival material and on the Inventaire's photographic record, was developed by the research project entitled 'Usines 3D, Histoire industrielle et reconstitution virtuelle'. (Loïc Espinasse, Laboratoire ArchéoVision, Université de Bordeaux 3-CNRS)

and the operation has covered 21 per cent of the national territory. The survey has been completed in two of the country's metropolitan regions (Poitou-Charentes and Champagne-Ardenne). A further 26 per cent of the territory is presently under study, but 50 per cent of mainland France remains to be dealt with. Thirty years after its initiation, then, the operation is half successful or half disappointing, according to one's point of view. There is no doubt that the initial objectives of finishing the operation by the end of the twentieth century were naively optimistic, and the human resources made available for the operation – roughly one researcher and one photographer per region – woefully inadequate. But these statistical results of the operation do not do full justice to its scientific accomplishments. As well as a computerised database, the *Inventaire*'s mission of sharing its knowledge is also pursued by means of publications, and nearly a hundred books devoted to industrial heritage have been published over the past thirty years.

Survey results

The administrative aspect of the location survey in underpinning policies of protection has also borne its fruits in a coherent movement, or 'chain', leading from identification to understanding and to reasoned protection. In some cases, the completion of the survey was immediately followed by a campaign of statutory protection, under the terms of the French law on historic monuments, dating from 1913, which provides for two levels of protection known as *classement* and *inscription*. For the Orne department in Normandy, for example, preliminary archival research identified some 2,500 industrial establishments active in the nineteenth and twentieth centuries, of which some 300 survived to be documented. Ten of these were then given statutory protection in order to preserve a representative selection of monuments bearing witness to different aspects of the department's industrial past in flour-milling, textiles, ceramics, paper-making and metallurgy. Knowledge provided by the location survey allowed for the protection of the best preserved and most remarkable sites in each sector, particularly those that retained their industrial equipment.

During the 1990s, then, the progress of the industrial heritage survey provided better appreciation of France's industrial history and encouraged demands for the statutory protection of certain sites. Fully aware that, as it was often repeated at the time, 'we cannot keep everything', and that it was not possible to create industrial museums everywhere, efforts were made to define some theoretical criteria for deciding objectively which sites were worthy of protection. In a 1994 article published by the review *Monumental*, Claudine Cartier, the head of the industrial heritage cell, outlined four such criteria which could serve as guidelines in this process of reasoned selection:

- the historical criterion, or criterion of being exceptional, concerning industrial sites related to a particular historical or technical event with an impact on subsequent industrial and social development;

- the quantitative criterion allowing for the selection of a representative exemplar within a given industrial sector, at regional or national levels;

- the criterion of noteworthiness, identifying remarkable buildings in terms of their architectural design, their engineering aspects or the celebrity of the industrialist associated with the site;

- the technological criterion, where the plant bears witness to a particular industrial process or to a specific technological innovation.

In reality, between the exceptional and the representative there is a whole range of sites that are exceptionally representative and in point of fact, one of the principal criteria for the protection of an industrial site in France is what may be termed social demand, the mobilization of voluntary associations and friends of the heritage for the preservation of a site under threat. The scientific justifications in terms of representativeness or uniqueness will often come as a consequence of this social demand. An analysis of the industrial monuments protected in France carried out by the CILAC and published in its review in June 2010 identified a total of 830 sites that can be considered as industrial, out of a total stock of some 43,000 historic monuments in France, protected since the 1840s. Of these 830 monuments, more than 300 are in fact small wind- or water-mills, keenly defended by a variety of associations since the 1930s. Another well-protected sector, reflecting research priorities, is the charcoal-based iron and steel industry, with more than sixty sites protected altogether. The surviving royal manufactories of the seventeenth and eighteenth centuries also enjoy statutory protection today. Not surprisingly however, the twentieth-century industrial heritage is less well protected, and only a handful of monuments bear witness, for example, to the motor car and aviation industries.

In terms of the preservation of the industrial heritage, however, the statutory protection of individual sites is not the only tool available, and other forms of preservation under terms of local planning regulations, for example, are equally important. After thirty years of research and inventory initiatives, the French industrial heritage now enjoys full recognition as an integral part of the national heritage. Although the unthinking demolition of industrial sites is not entirely unknown, the main priority today, in terms of good practice, is the preservation of historic and heritage values in re-use projects involving conserved industrial buildings.

Further reading

BELHOSTE, Jean-François and SMITH, Paul (dir.): *Patrimoine industriel, cinquante sites en France*. Paris: Editions du Patrimoine, 1997

DAUMAS, Maurice: *L'Archéologie industrielle en France*. Paris: R Laffont, 1980

GASNIER, Marina: *Patrimoine industriel et technique, perspectives et retour sur 30 ans de politiques publiques au service des territoires*. Lyon: Lieux Dits, 2011

TRINDER, Barrie (ed.): *The Blackwell Encyclopedia of Industrial Archaeology*. Oxford, Cambridge (Mass.): Blackwell, 1992

WORONOFF, Denis: *Histoire de l'industrie en France du XVIe siècle à nos jours*. Paris: Editions du Seuil, 1994

L'Archéologie industrielle en France, review of the CILAC association

12

Legal protection

Keith Falconer

Introduction

The legal protection of historic industrial sites is a means to an end. The benign management and conservation of the sites should be the primary aims, and this might involve differing levels of protection ranging from local lists and conservation areas through statutory designated individual sites at varying grades up to World Heritage Sites and landscapes. Each country will have its own designation codes, some of which will have been developed and refined over more than a century, so these will vary widely from country to country. This chapter will not attempt to survey the many different national codes but will, by focusing on those familiar to the author, attempt to draw out common threads leading to best practice.

The earliest examples of historic industrial sites being legally protected date from

a century ago, when national perspectives and agendas were perhaps quite different from those of today. Thus the seventeenth-century Frohnauer Hammer, a complete water-powered hammer mill, was protected as early as 1907 in order to celebrate Germanic vernacular traditions and thereby inadvertently became Saxony's first technical monument. Much more recently, in Japan thematic groupings or 'constellations' of sites have been identified to represent the many facets of the country's industrialisation, while in northern France they are seeking in the Bassin Minier World Heritage Site bid to preserve a living cultural landscape.

Legal protection is usually the end result of an assessment of significance and therefore it is the veracity of the processes of identification and assessment that are crucial to the effectiveness of the protection, and these can change greatly over time. Thus a site that may have been common a few decades ago may have now achieved great significance as a rare survivor. It follows that, ideally, all assessments should be regularly reviewed and updated if necessary – perhaps a vain hope.

This chapter will concentrate unashamedly on the British experience, but hopefully with some justification. Just as Britain pioneered global industrialisation three centuries ago, it pioneered the recording and protection of industrial heritage fifty years ago. Britain took a great many incremental steps on the path to industrialisation – some down blind alleys – and similarly has, at times, made hard work of identification, documentation and protection; its experience is therefore perhaps salutary. A common strand throughout that journey has been an alliance between volunteer expert knowledge

The Colònia Sedó (1846) outside Barcelona, Spain. The colònia of Catalonia are over a hundred self-contained industrial settlements along the river valleys with housing, churches, shops and schools clustered around a water-powered textile mill. Most failed in the 1970s. Some buildings have been adapted to new industrial uses and a museum, but maintaining the historic value of ensembles and the spaces between them is challenging. (Pepe Cornet – Creative Commons)

and the official use of that knowledge. This too has evolved constantly over a period of fifty years; now much expertise resides with official bodies, and much use is made of paid consultants, but some of the best work is still achieved through the use of expert volunteers as witnessed by a recent report of historic breweries produced for English Heritage by the members of the Brewery History Society.

The development of legal controls

Let us review that long, and at times tortuous, journey. In the nineteenth century a pre-occupation with both antiquarianism and the history of technology led to the formulation of the Ancient Monuments Acts from 1883 onwards and to the creation of the Science Museum in London. That the Ancient Monuments Acts should be invoked in the second quarter of the twentieth century to protect industrial heritage would have surprised the originators of the Acts, while the Science Museum has become a network of museums comprising not only treasure-houses of pioneer steam engines and machinery but encapsulating the very latest social developments and inventions.

The systematic study, identification and preservation of historic industrial sites really began in the UK from 1920 onwards with the creation of the Newcomen Society, dedicated to the study of the history of technology. Thus by the 1930s a group of Cornish beam engines had been preserved along with numerous wind and watermills, while the Iron Bridge had been scheduled in 1934 as an Ancient Monument. By the end of the 1950s a dozen further industrial sites had been scheduled. However, it was the aftermath of the destruction of historic sites in World War II that led to widespread protection of historic buildings under the Town & Country Planning Acts. Henceforth it became easier to designate buildings, and important sites such as Arkwright's Cromford Mills were soon listed as Historic Buildings but very much on an *ad hoc* basis. The lack of any coherent government policy towards industrial sites led the Council for British Archaeology (CBA) to convene a conference in 1959 at which a resolution was passed urging the formulation of a national policy of protection and recording. Subsequently a list of 127 sites was presented by the CBA for consideration for designation by the two government departments concerned. However, an official acknowledgement that the staff in those departments did not have the necessary expertise or national context to assess the sites delayed implementation, and in 1961 the CBA initiated some regional surveys using a specifically designed record card, which was printed in bulk to ensure uniformity.

Continued public pressure – which was increased greatly by the needless demolition of the classical archway in front of Euston railway station in London – led in 1963 to the part-time appointment by the Ministry of Works of Rex Wailes, a noted expert on wind and watermills, to co-ordinate a national survey to identify sites for protection. As an aid to the survey, from 1965 onwards the CBA record cards completed by volunteers were to form the National Record of Industrial Monuments (NRIM) administered by Angus Buchanan at the University of Bath. The survey was put on a full-time basis in 1971 with the appointment of the author, who became the conduit for identified sites between the expert volunteers and an advisory panel composed of representatives of national agencies and museums. The panel could make recommendations for designation or for recording or for museum preservation. The Industrial Monuments Survey conducted two types of survey – county surveys which identified all types of industrial sites meriting designation within a defined area, and thematic surveys of sites such as steam pumping engines, seaside piers, brickworks, canal structures and signal boxes. Between 1963 and 1981 the Industrial Monuments Survey looked at over 4,000 sites and submitted 2,325 sites to the Advisory Panel.

In 1980 a quirk of fate – the demolition of the Art Deco frontage of the 1929 Firestone Building in London immediately prior to its proposed listing – so outraged the Secretary of State for the Environment that he ordered a major acceleration in the rate of assessment of historic buildings. The massive increase in staff resources now being applied to these surveys around the country rendered the efforts of the lone IMS survey officer rather puny, and in 1981 the IMS was transferred to the Royal Commission on the Historical and Archaeological Monuments of England (RCHAME) upon the condition that the Survey Officer should continue to advise the DoE on the assessment of industrial sites. The NRIM, which by then contained some 8,000 entries, was closed and absorbed into the National Monuments Record.

English Heritage was created in 1984 and, in the aftermath of the accelerated survey, immediately undertook thematic designation programmes which were primarily to encompass industrial sites. The Monuments Protection Programme (MPP) was initiated in 1986 and was undertaken by external consultants. It developed a systematic approach for classifying, evaluating and selecting sites for designation and for other forms of management. It was, however, very expensive as it involved two stages of sector consultation, and the industrial component of MPP ground to a halt in 2004. Nevertheless, reports had been produced on 33 industries, and nearly 5,000 sites and buildings had been evaluated in the field, with recommendations for over 1,000 new Scheduled Ancient Monument designations and around 350 candidates for listing consideration. These national overviews retain high research and operational value and, as they constitute an authoritative source of information on industrial heritage, are being made accessible on the English Heritage web pages.

A second programme – Thematic Listing Review – was born out of an appreciation that the traditional geographical approach to listing had not provided adequate cover for many specialised types of building. Two approaches were adopted, to attempt as comprehensive cover as possible for each building type or, alternatively, to evaluate a number of examples of each building type that would then serve as a benchmark for further listing. The former approach, when focused on small areas such as the Birmingham Jewellery Quarter, worked well, and a comprehensive conservation strategy emerged from the large number of listings. However, of the larger regional textile mill surveys, for example, only the Greater Manchester survey has as yet been carried through to logical conclusion.

Following the end of MPP in 2004, a less resource-hungry successor programme, the Strategy for the Historic Industrial Environment Reports, was begun. National in scope, these projects were designed to provide an introduction to historic industries and to assess the current state of the resource providing sufficient contextual information on levels of survival, protection and significance to guide future designation. Lack of resources has impeded their progress but the two published reports – on maltings undertaken by a lone consultant and on breweries undertaken by the Brewery History Society – have ably demonstrated the potential of these national contextual reports. Thus it was found that in 2004 out of some 600 extant sites identified as maltings there were only six traditional floor maltings still operating. By 2007 there were only two, and this certainly concentrated the mind as to where priorities should lie. Similarly, out of

The conservation of McConnel & Kennedy's Mills and A & G Murray's Mills (1797–1820) bordering the Rochdale Canal at Ancoats in Manchester has been the catalyst for the regeneration of the area. (English Heritage)

several thousand breweries that supplied local needs at the end of the nineteenth century only 40 pre-1940 breweries were still working. The county by county summaries of the resource have provided the context to inform greatly subsequent designation. The reports on the Atomic Age and Engineering Works, though as yet uncompleted, are already informing English Heritage's involvement in those fields.

All the many thousand sites mentioned in these various reports are entered in the national database which is then shared with regional databases maintained for planning purposes. This ensures that historic industrial sites are noted in any proposed development, an essential first line of defence.

Thematic surveys

Meanwhile, alongside these evaluation surveys, throughout the 1980s and 1990s academic surveys of key types of historic industrial sites were undertaken by internal staff. These have included textile mills in West Yorkshire, Greater Manchester, East

Cheshire, North East Derbyshire and the Derwent Valley, workers' housing in West Yorkshire, potteries in Staffordshire, waterworks, military gunpowder and explosive works, ironworks in Furness and workshops in the Birmingham Jewellery Quarter and in Sheffield. These have also greatly informed designation by establishing typological frameworks and consequently highlighting significant structural and technical features.

These various surveys and studies have now enabled the heritage sector in Britain to aspire to a comprehensive overview of the industrial heritage resource, and this has facilitated the selection of thematic industrial landscapes to be nominated as World Heritage Sites. Internationally, sites celebrating industrial heritage have proliferated in the last decade. In 1999 there were just 20 sites, and only one British; now, following the successful implementation of the 1999 UK Tentative List, the UK share has risen to eight out of 42. These eight landscapes – the Ironbridge Gorge, Blaenavon, Derwent Valley Mills, New Lanark and Saltaire textile mills and settlements, Liverpool Maritime City, Cornish Mining Industry and the Pontcysyllte Aqueduct (along with 10 kilometres of canal approaches) – represent Britain's outstanding contribution to global industrialisation. English Heritage's Industrial Archaeology Panel was instrumental in elaborating the concept of such thematic landscapes. Further sites may be developed for pioneer railways, naval dockyards and monuments of Welsh slate-working, and key structures such as the Forth Bridge (due in 2014 to become the first site from the UK World Heritage Tentative List to be nominated in the new round).

There are now more than 30,000 designated industrial sites in England alone at various levels of statutory protection (4 per cent at the highest grades); countless more are situated in industrial conservation areas which have a lesser degree of protection, but cannot be demolished without permission, and many more still in the local Historic Environment Records which are a material consideration in the planning process.

What examples of best practice can be learnt from the British experience?

1. The value of volunteer expertise: for every subject there are likely to be single-minded enthusiasts, and their knowledge and passion should be harnessed to good effect. English Heritage works closely with the Association for Industrial Archaeology (AIA) and the Council for British Archaeology (CBA) to maintain a vision for the stewardship of the industrial heritage.

2. The use of an advisory panel composed of experts and representatives of official agencies gives a degree of transparency to the consideration of sites for protection.

3. Assessments of significance must be kept up to date as they can change greatly over time.

4. Good contextual frameworks allow prioritisation of scarce resources.

5. All sites of interest should be entered in official planning databases or their equivalent, both by private individuals as well as official agencies. This allows a constructive dialogue between property developer and conservationist with both sides having bargaining chips.

6. The compilation of comprehensive overviews of the historic resource permits selection of outstanding sites whether for protection at the highest levels or for nomination for World heritage status.

7. Public opinion is very important and must be nurtured. It was crucial to the development of the initiative in 1962 with the demolition of the Euston Arch in London while a public attitude survey in 2011 found that 85 per cent of the respondents agreed that it is important to identify industrial heritage sites of significance so that they can be protected.

Conclusion

Once appropriate protection is in place the challenge has just begun – the sustainable management of the resource becomes paramount. Some sites can be simply monumentalised or allowed to become ruins; others may be turned into working museums; but most will need to be re-used in some way or other, and this may involve some compromise of integrity. The particular significance of the heritage asset, the types of use and the degree of intervention then become the issues. At the protection level of conservation areas, guideline manuals of permitted repairs and alterations can achieve much. For instance, in company settlements these can preserve uniformity of appearance while allowing modernisation of facilities.

'National Heritage Sites' would, for many countries, be a way of recognising industrial assets that cannot quite compare with the classic World Heritage Sites of global 'outstanding universal value' but nevertheless for domestic reasons need some international recognition.

Legal protection can be used very constructively and can be the catalyst for regeneration, as demonstrated by the historic textile mills bordering the Rochdale Canal at Ancoats in Manchester. The statutory designation of the mills at a high grade ensured their future was discussed at an equally high level in the planning process. The involvement of local enthusiasts, city planners, developers, a buildings trust and English Heritage, all positively, engaged has resulted in the rehabilitation of the two prime complexes of late eighteenth-century mills, McConnel & Kennedy's Mills and A & G Murray's Mills. It has also provided the spur for the regeneration of the surrounding area. Similar examples can be found all around the world, including the textile mills at Roubaix in France, Schio in Italy, New Lanark in Scotland and in the *colònia* around Barcelona in Spain or coal mines and steelworks in the Ruhr or in Japan. Indeed, the sympathetic re-use of historic industrial sites has spawned a specialised sector in the real estate industry, and this has only come about by sensible use of the powers of statutory protection.

Further reading

COSSONS, N (ed.) *Perspectives on Industrial Archaeology.* Science Museum: London, 2000

English Heritage *Conservation Bulletin 67: Saving the Age of Industry.* English Heritage, 2011 and *Research News 17/18* English Heritage, 2012

PALMER, M, NEVELL M and SISSONS, M: *Industrial Archaeology: a handbook.* Council for British Archaeology: 2012

ROSE, M with FALCONER, K and HOLDER, J: *Ancoats – Cradle of Industrialisation.* London: English Heritage, 2011

STRATTON, M, (ed.): *Industrial Buildings: conservation and regeneration.* London: E&FN Spon, 2000

13

Urban regeneration and planning

Massimo Preite

Introduction

Beginning in the 1990s, industrial cities faced a new cycle of transformations which, unlike the renewals of previous years, saw abandoned production and manufacturing sites not as obstacles to be removed, but as opportunities for development. This phase in the recent history of the industrial city began to be called urban regeneration and involved a new planning mode inspired by the principles of strategic vision, public and private partnership, sustainability and urban heritage enhancement. This chapter reports on a sample of well-known examples: in England, the late eighteenth-century textile mills of Ancoats and the Castlefield canal basin and warehouses, both in Manchester, and the Albert Dock warehouse complex in Liverpool; the textile manufacturing towns of Elbeuf in France and Norrköping in Sweden; the Finlayson Mill area beside the Tammerkoski rapids in Tampere, Finland; and lastly the IBA (International Building Exhibition) Emscher Landscape Park in the Ruhr, Germany, one of the most celebrated experiences of large-scale industrial heritage regeneration. Through these examples the key issues of urban regeneration plans are highlighted: sources of financing, models of governance, the relationship between the plan and the project, and the goal of conservation in relation to the other goals of regeneration.

Sources of financing

There is a wide range of funding for urban regeneration programmes in Europe that started in the 1990s. A crucial role was played by European Union Structural Funds, without which the rescue of a large part of the industrial heritage would not have been possible. Many projects benefited from the European Regional Development Fund (ERDF) under the terms of the Convergence and Regional Competitiveness and Employment Objectives. As a rule, ERDF funding was granted only to bodies able to meet 40 per cent of the total investment from their own resources (state, regional or municipal public funds, or private financing).

In the ten years in which the IBA operated for the Ruhr regeneration, €2.5 billion was invested, of which €1.5 billion came from public sources (federal government, EU

The coke plant at the Zollverein XII mine in Essen, Germany, was one of the four flagship projects of the IBA Emscher Park. There is ice skating on the frozen tank in winter. (Benjamin Fragner)

funds) and €1 billion in private resources. Of the €250 million spent via a rotating fund set up by the North Rhine Westphalia government a large part came from EU structural funds (Regional Competitiveness and Employment Objectives).

The ERDF Convergence Objective funds proved to be equally crucial for financing both the programmes for the regeneration of Liverpool, including the redevelopment interventions for the Albert Dock, and the projects for the renewal of the former textile mills in Ancoats in Manchester, jointly financed by English Heritage, the Heritage Lottery Fund and charitable trusts.

However, there are many projects which drew on sources other than EU channels. The urban regeneration of Elbeuf began from the renovation of the Blin et Blin factory, closed in 1975. In this case, the operation was wholly funded from the public sector. To prevent the factory (of great architectural quality) from falling into decay, the municipal council bought the whole complex and appointed the architects Bernard Reichen and Philippe Robert to draw up a project for the transformation of the factory into 170 social housing units, within the framework of the *Fond d'Aménagement Urbain,* Urban Development Funds whose beneficiaries are municipalities launching social housing programmes.

Meanwhile, at the opposite extreme, is the renovation of the Finlayson Area in Tampere, in southern Finland, which was financed wholly by the private sector. To execute the project, investments were needed in excess of €100 million, and it was funded via bank loans which were repaid by means of the rents of the renovated buildings.

Models of governance

Examples of urban regeneration show extremely varied approaches and are therefore hard to ascribe to a single model. A common denominator in Europe is interactive planning, namely a form of planning in which the public authority no longer has a monopoly on decisions but carries out tasks of policy guidance and coordination within a cooperative and pluralist decision-making process. Only in one of the cases considered, Elbeuf, was the public administration the principal player, especially after 1975 when a new cycle of interventions began aimed at conserving rather than erasing the industrial evidence, as unfortunately happened in the previous cycle from 1960. At the opposite extreme we can place the conversion of the Tampere textile complex, which was sponsored, implemented and run by Tampereen Kiinteistö Invest Oy (TaKI), a private company set up in 1987 with the task of redeveloping industrial premises. In order to monitor the restoration, a coordination committee liaised between the municipal council and TaKI, and the private projects had to fall into line with the city's zoning and the guidelines of

The Frenckell chimney and boiler room, Finlayson factory and the hydroelectric power plant at the Tammerkoski Falls in the very centre of Tampere, Finland (Benjamin Fragner)

the National Board of Antiquity. However, it is undeniable that TaKI is the sole body responsible for all the projects, not just those involving property but also infrastructure (main roads and secondary roads, water networks and drains, lighting etc.) set to pass to municipal ownership. So Elbeuf and Tampere represent two extreme cases, one a wholly public intervention, and the other a completely private one.

In a midway position there are other case histories giving rise, as protagonists, to 'atypical' bodies which, to a certain extent, have had to take the place of the traditional local authorities which proved to be unsuited to dealing with the reconversion of major industrial areas that fall into disuse. In Britain, for example, in the 1980s, Urban Regeneration Corporations were set up: private companies that sought to achieve a radical physical transformation of their areas through masterplans and co-coordinating financial assistance to developers, from both the public and private sector. The role played by these corporations as replacements for the public administration was especially clear in the case of the 1846 Albert Dock in Liverpool. Following closure in 1972, first Liverpool City Council and then the wider Merseyside County Council tried in vain to draw up solutions for the re-use of the complex. The stalemate was resolved at the initiative of the Merseyside Development Corporation in 1981, which negotiated with private investors the establishment of the Albert Dock Company, the real sponsor of its regeneration. Similar agencies were responsible for the salvaging of the Castlefield and Ancoats areas in Manchester: the former as part of a larger regeneration programme got under way by the Central Manchester Development Corporation (1988) for the city's central area, and financed by a combination of private investments and government grants. In the regeneration of Ancoats an Urban Village Company became involved.

However, the replacement of the ordinary public administrations with *ad hoc* agencies is not a feature exclusive to Britain. The same phenomenon was seen in Germany in the redevelopment of the Ruhr, except that in this case the replacement body was not private, but public. IBA Emscher Park, which was behind a ten-year regeneration project extended to an entire region, was an agency set up by the regional North Rhine-Westphalia government with coordination tasks which traditionally are the responsibility of local authorities. IBA came into being, and has since operated, in full independence from the traditional system of local institutions, relieving them of authority after years and years of operational paralysis caused by their inability to co-operate over common development projects. In this respect, the experience of IBA Emscher Park is fairly unique: IBA was an agency with a very limited budget, enough to organise international architecture competitions. IBA did not engage in any planning activity, nor did it have resources for carrying out interventions. Its role was solely that of selecting the projects presented, on the basis of a series of very high-profile criteria: architectural quality, energy savings, landscape planning, local participation, and so on. As stated, IBA did not have funds to allocate, but it is equally true that when it turned down a project, that project was excluded from all forms of public funding. Only when the project got past the IBA quality-control screening process could it embark on its institutional and procedural process, and get channelled into ordinary administrative management.

Plan and project

Traditional planning follows a top-down model which establishes a hierarchical procedure in the decision-making chain: the overarching plan predetermines the content of the project, and the ways in which it is implemented. In urban regeneration schemes things go differently, and the relationship between the plan and the project is less straightforward and less linear. The order is often reversed, with projects coming before plans. The actual plan only comes afterwards, being drawn up when the transformation process has already been started, representing a sort of crowning moment of projects conceived *ex ante*.

This should not be too surprising: abandoned industrial areas do not, in an initial phase, offer special attractions to property investment: their state of neglect, the high costs associated with site clearance work, and the negative image often associated with such areas are all factors which initially discourage the administration, the local community and economic operators from imagining a possible re-use of former manufacturing structures. The role of *flagship projects* has been crucial in overcoming this reluctance. These have served to give a persuasive demonstration that the recovery of industrial buildings is not only feasible but also can be profitable: reused industrial sites have proved to be able to create an added value which new, replacement buildings would not have generated.

One can take the French case of Elbeuf. In a preliminary phase from 1960 to 1975 'progressive' planning policies were carried out with a view to 'urban renewal'; in their radicalism, they led to the demolition of pre-existing structures and to their replacement with new housing schemes. The trend was only reversed with the salvaging of the Blin et Blin factory, leading to a reassessment of the industrial heritage, and a halt to its destruction. There was a similar course of events at Norrköping. Threats to its industrial landscape were avoided by the success of the flagship projects drafted between 1989 and 1997 which allowed the salvaging of former industrial buildings for new, high-status urban functions. A plan for the industrial landscape was only drawn up in 2003 when the flagship projects, which paved the way, were already completed.

Another case also comes from the Ruhr. The IBA, as stated above, was the overall overseer of the transformation. The regeneration of the Emscher Park is not the fruit of a predetermined plan. As noted by Kunzmann, 'No blueprint or comprehensive physical masterplan has been designed for the region. Individual projects followed a vague long-term vision' (Kunzmann, 2004). The project began life from a strategic document – the project memorandum of 1986 – which restricted itself to setting out the guidelines of the programme: ecological transformation and revitalisation of a derelict landscape, the renaturalisation of the Emscher River; brownfield redevelopment; conservation of the industrial heritage, etc. The real process of transformation sprang above all from the salvaging of four flagship sites, the coal mine complexes of Zeche Zollverein in Essen and Zeche Nordstern in Gelsenkirchen, the Landschaftspark former steelworks in Duisburg, and the Jahrhunderthalle in Bochum, the former gas and power station of a steel mill, which brought about a thorough change to the image of the region and led to new opportunities from which further interventions benefited. In this case, too, the full-scale plan intervened only after the transformation was already under way, or rather after the IBA had concluded its work. It was Project Ruhr, the new company which took over from IBA to continue the conversion of the Ruhr, which drafted the 2010 Masterplan.

Norrköping and Emscher Park are thus fully demonstrative examples of the twin consequences of the flagship projects: a *multiplier* effect which triggers a chain of other projects involving the re-use of the abandoned industrial heritage; and a *leverage* effect insofar as, compared with a new replacement building, a re-used industrial building, as a piece of heritage, generates new added value.

While it is true that flagship projects are carried out in the absence of a general plan (indeed, it is precisely thanks to them that the conditions are encouraged for its formulation 'after the event'), it is equally true that their success has been facilitated by a parallel salvaging intervention, involving the free areas to be converted for new use as a public space. Herein lies the real start of the urban regeneration. In the schedule identified by Legnér for the regeneration of Norrköping, the phase which really gets the process under way is the appropriation of the free spaces by the local community by means of three initiatives (1983–1988):

- enhancing the attractive views of the water-course; the local community mobilized against plans to reduce the flow of water;

- improving communications alongside the river with new footbridges and quays;

- opening up the industrial areas and mills that were still closed off to pedestrian circulation.

The urban redevelopment of Castlefield also owes its high quality to the restoration of the canals, and to the creation of a refined network of pathways, bridges and rest areas which make the newly created public space attractive. The guiding idea behind the salvaging of Finlayson was to transform an area which had been inaccessible (while manufacturing was on-going) into a new opportunity of expansion for the urban centre of Tampere by way of plans for a network of paths. This was designed to break the former isolation and give greater access to new businesses.

And finally the Ruhr. It must not be forgotten that here the guiding idea was to turn an industrial area into an extensive river park, Emscher Landscape Park, whose goals, clearly stated right from the start, related above all to the network of paths: preserving the remaining leftover landscape, linking up the isolated areas in the agglomeration, re-zoning separate areas as parkland and creating green corridors connecting several industrial sites. Put simply, we can say that urban regeneration, as seen in some of its best manifestations, begins more from the re-planning of the 'spaces' than from the re-planning of its 'solid volumes'.

Conservation versus transformation

From the case studies outlined above, one can clearly see the active role of industrial heritage in urban regeneration programmes: what is known as *regeneration through heritage*. However, we still have to examine how this heritage has been preserved, how far its original characteristics have been respected, and how far it had to be modified to adapt the structures to new end uses: repurposing or adaptive re-use.

In the 'half-twentieth century' of industrial archaeology (its official debut came in

Merchants' warehouses surround the canal basin on the 1764 Bridgewater Canal in the central area of Castlefield, Manchester, UK. The oldest canal warehouse opened in 1779. The regeneration programme was a 1988 initiative of the Central Manchester Development Corporation. (Benjamin Fragner)

1962, with the demolition of the Arch into London's Euston Station), the most famous examples of conservation are those that have transformed the industrial heritage into a museum of itself, such as the Ironbridge Gorge Museum, the Völklingen Hutte ironworks, the Verla Board Mill in Finland or the woollen mill occupied by the Museu de la Ciència i de la Tècnica de Catalunya in Spain. But while there are significant examples of museum developments in the cited experiences of urban regeneration, it is certainly not the dominant solution. On the contrary, new functions have been assigned to most of the salvaged heritage sites and these have sometimes imposed a decisive transformation.

This has led to a reformulation of the goals of conservation. Indeed, conservation no longer constitutes an absolute objective, inasmuch as it has to be increasingly integrated in the multi-task system of the intervention programme. The modern regeneration project aims at achieving an economic boost, creating new jobs, revitalising depressed urban areas, building a new community or generating a 'vibrant' atmosphere so as to prompt innovation and creativity. Conservation is no longer an end unto itself, but is conditioned toward achieving other objectives which demand a search for mediation between economic interests while protecting historical values.

In the case of Tampere, as well as being tempered by variations in the use of the buildings, conservation saw a radical reformulation of its theoretical principles. The salvaging of the Finlayson area was exemplary above all in terms of the extreme variety of functions for which the former industrial structures were adapted. The repertoire of new end uses is striking, to say the least: more than 100 commercial premises, a health care business, a private hospital, three museums, a cinema complex, the Polytechnic School of Arts and Media and eighteen cafes and restaurants. Such multi-faceted functions were achieved by renouncing all principles of 'fundamentalist conservation'. On the contrary, instead of restoring the former forms, there was a preference for intervening in line with the centuries-old process of *layering*, by which, in a gradual way, with each intervention, Finlayson had grown. The absolute novelty of the heritage preservation programme relates to the fact that the conservation objective was shifted from the mere built heritage (Finlayson as it now appears) to the rules which generated it. By preserving those rules, and continuing to apply them, it became possible to manage in the best possible way the transformation of the abandoned industrial buildings and their adaptation to new end uses, without betraying their historical and structural identity: '... The preserving and restoring approach used has been based on identifying old and authentic working methods, textures and details and reintroducing them as parts of a vibrant whole. The layering of time periods has been reinforced by finding the original, oldest and most valuable parts under the more recent layers, and marrying them with the new ...' (Architectural Bureau Poussinen Oy, no date).

Risks for successful conservation

A successful outcome of 'conservation by means of adaptation' is not always guaranteed. There are several different obstacles along the way. Sometimes these relate to the poor mixture of functions that has been created, while other times they derive from the limits of adaptability of the buildings themselves. Elbeuf, for example, seems to suffer from a regeneration programme centred predominantly upon social housing. In the opinion of the writer (a subjective opinion derived from a recent personal visit), the restoration of the Blin et Blin textile factory, while admirable for the successful adaptation to its new residential function, without compromising its historical and architectural identity, does not make it safe from the potential risk of a 'second' cycle of decay following de-industrialisation, as a consequence of the fragile economic conditions of the new residents. It is to be hoped that the new functions of excellence which other valuable former industrial facilities enjoy (the Institut Universitaire de Technologie in the former Sodidro soap factory, the Fabrique des Savoirs in an old textile plant) can amplify these effects of 'urban revitalisation' which, so far, do not seem to have manifested themselves with resolute intensity. The warehouses of Manchester show, by contrast, that the margins for adapting heritage sites are not infinite. As stated by the English Heritage guide, 'The earlier canal warehouses tend to have low floor-to-ceiling heights and smaller window openings. Both can pose a challenge in terms of adaptation for new uses ...' There is a risk of promoting interventions 'that retain only a minimum of historic fabric. There are examples of façadism and of retention of the shell of the building around a new internal structure.' However, one cannot fail to acknowledge the fact that the adaptive re-use of the Castlefield warehouses is a textbook case. In salvaging the Merchants Warehouse and the Middle Warehouse (transformed into offices and luxury hotels) ingenious solutions have been devised for making space for technical services (fire prevention, ventilation, heating and sanitation) in glass blocks added at either end of the building.

There is, in addition, a third category of risk to the built heritage, which depends on the excessive success of regeneration through heritage: the most representative case is Norrköping, where the creation of the Pronova Science Park and the opening of the new university campus have accelerated the pace of rising real estate values and gentrification in the area. As noted by Legnér, 'the presence of the university has pushed out economically weaker operators, such as sweet shops and small independent stores; there is now much less affordable, bohemian and creative space than there was as recently as ten years ago.' Unlike Elbeuf, where the heritage is at risk owing to new forms of social marginality, the industrial heritage salvaged at Norrköping suffers from a fading of its character and of its suitability for functioning as an urban site of social aggregation owing to an excessive rise in property values.

This short overview of regeneration through heritage would, however, be incomplete without a brief mention of the experience of the Ruhr, where adaptation of the heritage has also seen transient forms of re-use. The abandoned areas and industrial buildings, being subject to less stringent building regulations and security norms than those normally in force, offer greater conditions of flexibility and lower operating costs than those of a traditional building. This combination of factors makes them particularly attractive to start-ups and new businesses in the cultural sector and in the creative industry, which require spaces for short-term use, with low levels of investment.

Further reading

Architectural Bureau Pussinen Oy: *Future of the City: Finlayson, Tampere.* No date

BERENS, C: *Redeveloping Industrial Sites: a guide for architects, planners, and developers.* Hoboken: J Wiley & Sons, 2010

JÄRVI, M: 'The History and the Reuse of the Industrial Buildings on the Banks of Tammerkoski in Centre of Tampere', in HINNERICHSEN, M (ed.): *Reusing the Industrial Past by the Tammerkoski Rapids.* Tampere: City of Tampere, Museum Services, Pirkanmaa Provincial Museum, 2011

KUNZMANN, K R: 'Creative Brownfield Redevelopment: the experience of the IBA Emscher Park initiative in the Ruhr in Germany', in GREENSTEIN, ROSALIND and YESIM SUNGU-ERYILMAZ, (eds): *Recycling the City: the use and reuse of urban land.* Cambridge (Mass.): Lincoln Institute of Land Policy, 2004, 201–17

LEGNÉR, M: 'Regeneration, Quarterization and Historic Preservation', in LEGNÉR and PONZINI (ed.): *Cultural Quarters and Urban Transformation.* Klintehamn: Gotlandica förlag, 2009

TAYLOR, S, COOPER, M and BARNWELL, P S: *Manchester: the warehouse legacy,* London: English Heritage, 2005

14

Adaptive re-use

Benjamin Fragner

Introduction

Little has done so much to heighten the amount of attention and interest shown in industrial heritage as recent conversion projects targeting abandoned warehouses, textile mills, factory halls, breweries, iron and steelworks and power plants. These projects chime well with current trends in art, enjoy public popularity, and are becoming increasingly common. Projects for adaptive re-use are a hot topic in architecture and urban studies today and almost overshadow issues of heritage conservation. Adaptive re-use is often mentioned as a tool with which to preserve threatened values and presented as a sustainable development strategy.

However, the conversion of a structure to serve a different purpose almost always requires interventions and changes to adapt it to the new function. How far such interventions go will determine if the conversion and functional transformation is not, paradoxically, to efface the assets that led to the decision to conserve the industrial site in the first place. And this is true even if the site is not yet a protected monument.

It would be misleading to speak of contemporary projects for the adaptive re-use of industrial heritage as one group. A wide variety of methods is employed in these projects, from preserving the integrity of industrial heritage through conservation (in a manner suited to its heritage value), to searching for the right degree of new, creative (primarily architectural and artistic) interventions, to abuse (*adaptive miss-use*) through the destruction and devaluation of surviving features. It all depends on the given situation and available options how much we are able – and willing – to carry over from the past and to absorb in the present; and above all, on what the reasons were for bringing the industrial heritage site back to life.

First steps and arguments

While there have always been buildings that have survived beyond their original function and then been renovated for a new one, or that have even served multiple different uses over time, having been adapted by builders again and again for a different purpose, and what we now call adaptive re-use was historically something that was driven by common sense and economy. We can see examples of this in cities such as Lucca, Italy, where the remains of a Roman amphitheatre can be traced in the structural outlines of the city;

The conversion of the gasholder and the blast furnaces of the Vítkovice steelworks in Ostrava, once the most industrialised city in the Czech Republic, shows the interpolation of modern architecture into a historical structure. Conversion by AP Atelier Josef Pleskot, investor Vítkovice, Vítkovice Heavy Machinery a.s. (Tomáš Souček)

or in the late eighteenth-century Habsburg monarchy, where various monasteries and churches were shut down and turned into storage spaces and manufactories; changes in use were also common as technological advances were made in production, but usually with minimal and only the most economical structural alterations.

These lessons from the past, however, are rather different from the situation today, and there are many reasons for this. Since the 1980s, with accelerating de-industrialisation, an incomparably larger number of abandoned buildings and sites have accumulated within a short period of time that are facing an uncertain fate and await new use or demolition. And they all vary in size, spaciousness, complexity, structural diversity and the environmental burden they represent.

Another difference today, however, relates to the social roles and ambitions of the professions that make decisions about and execute conversion projects: investors, including newly anonymous developers, with no personal relationship to the resulting use; builders, equipped with aggressive techniques; architects trained more in designing structures from scratch; and heritage workers, who are still trying to find their way to industrial heritage.

Moreover, a new and previously unknown argument has emerged that relates to the historical and cultural values of the material remains of a vanishing industrial age. This argument gained in intensity in the 1950s and then especially in the 1960s and 1970s as the movement to protect industrial heritage gained in strength, something described in more detail by other contributors.

But there is something else that warrants mention in order to understand the motives for projects of adaptive re-use. The atmosphere that led to the first efforts to protect industrial monuments and to the interest in industrial archaeology derived from a keener appreciation of environmental issues and awareness of the need to rejuvenate the environment and cities, the kind of perceptivity that Jane Jacobs wrote about in 1961 in her now classic book *The Death and Life of Great American Cities*. This perspective has moved to the fore and may continue to predominate. Adaptive re-use – alongside arguments for the conservation of industrial monuments – has become a part of the process of architectural creation and an essential feature of the more natural development of human settlements. It corresponds with a layered reading of the architecture of a city. Another part of the new urbanism is citizens' participation in the decisions about the places that are undergoing change.

Memory of place

As the physical appearance of the city changed over time there was a sudden appreciation of the distinct and raw qualities of the industrial setting, with workshops and factory halls transformed into lofts and studios and eventually into clubs and art centres. This began among the abandoned factories, workshops and warehouses that neighboured the skyscrapers of Manhattan and SoHo in New York and reflected the alternative lifestyle of the local arts community. In the 1970s and 1980s this development was repeated in most large industrial cities. One of the first and most important urban projects for the adaptive re-use of an industrial heritage site emerged in the mid-1960s in the former Ghirardelli Chocolate Company on Ghirardelli Square in San Francisco by architects Wurster, Bernardi & Emmons.

In the 1970s a unique plan was introduced into the declining industrial city of Lowell, Massachusetts, which was aimed at revitalising the city by combining the industrial past of the place with various new economic and tourist activities. And in the 1980s, another project with similar goals was launched, its aim being to transform the neglected industrial area of Castlefield in Manchester by moving the Museum of Science and Industry into the abandoned Liverpool Road railway terminus, which was built in 1830. Public investment in this project was followed by more, usually private, initiatives and by conversions of the surrounding warehouses and textile mills, some with support from the city, the national budget and eventually EU funds. This general tendency is one of the best and most commonly quoted examples of the adaptive new use of industrial heritage in the wider urban context as part of the vast transformation of an area while preserving the network of railway viaducts, bridges, sophisticated inland canals and the central part of the former docklands. Recent projects have continued in other parts of Manchester, most notably in Ancoats, with its unique collection of historic textile mills and engineering shops.

One of the most important projects for the development of an entire city undertaken since the year 2000 is the transformation of the large cluster of the Finlayson, Tampella, Frenckell textile mills in Tampere, Finland, into an urban recreation centre.

When sites undergo a radical structural transformation, memory of place becomes just an isolated or even fragmented reminder of a defunct human activity. A single building on large industrial sites, left-over technological equipment, such as the enormous disused F60 spoil conveyor bridge in the open-cast mine in Lichterfeld near Finsterwalde in Germany, water and mining towers and chimney-stacks, towering in isolation over demolished sugar refineries, brickworks and boiler houses, or the remnants of the railway and tracks of the High Line in New York, which was given a new recreational function: all these continue to exist as symbolic edifices, as beacons, though the information they convey has been torn from its historical context.

Strategies and programmes

Every re-use project is unique unto itself. But here we can at least mention some of the more typical strategies employed. If it is possible to identify what makes a particular structure special, it is easier to evaluate the potential risks and benefits.

One strategy that has proved itself well is the now classic story of Salt's Mill and the workers' colony in Saltaire in Bradford, UK. In the late 1980s the decaying textile factory, at risk of demolition, was bought by Jonathan Silver, a businessman and art collector. He resisted the lure of showy and expensive projects that would have involved the radical reconstruction of the site and instead took the surprising first step of opening an art gallery devoted to the work of David Hockney. This set the stage for subsequent development; it attracted publicity, and it changed the way the public and business partners looked at the future of a derelict industrial monument. Step by step, using income from rents and developing businesses, the building was repaired and adapted to serve a new function, and it brought the surrounding housing estate back to life. And all this was done without any radical structural interventions, so that the historical value and attraction of the site were maintained and have grown over the years. In the meantime, or more accurately as a result, in 2001 the 'model estate' and the textile mill made it on to the UNESCO World Heritage List, which extended the financial assistance available to it from public sources. A wide spectrum of activities and tenants helped it to surmount the risks of investment, activities ranging from art to information technology, inexpensive letting of office space to start-up firms, or creative arts studios. The model created by this project continues to be recommended today: it is effective and acts as a defence from the consequences of a developers' crisis.

The principles of economically sustainable investment and management of industrial heritage monuments, with the support of the private sector and public funding, are now applied to a number of projects. The Regeneration Through Heritage initiative under the Prince's Regeneration Trust is one example in Perth, Scotland, where Stanley Mills is now a museum successfully combined with residential housing.

However, the public takes more notice of those examples that fit the current media atmosphere. Investors focus almost exclusively on iconic structures and tend to bet on big names when commissioning projects. The best-known examples are the Bankside Power Station, converted into the Tate Modern in London by architects Herzog & de Meuron, and the reconstruction of four gasholders in Simmering, a former industrial

Salt's Mill (1853) and the adjoining village of Saltaire near Bradford, UK, is a World Heritage Site. The conversion of the mill to an art gallery, shopping and restaurant complex and business space was carried through by an independent entrepreneur, Jonathan Silver. (Benjamin Fragner)

neighbourhood on the outskirts of Vienna, by Manfred Wehdorn, Jean Nouvel, Coop Himmelb(l)au and Wilhelm Holzbauer. The costs of these conversion projects tends to be higher, but thanks to the publicity they garner they are able to secure more funding from sponsors and public sources. While heritage professionals tend to be wary of such popularised projects, they have the effect of significantly increasing public interest in industrial heritage and attracting more investors for other abandoned buildings in the immediate area. But this approach cannot be applied everywhere, and it usually requires bigger interventions into the structure and appearance of the building in order to increase the site's attractiveness.

One success has been the ability to link up thematically- or regionally-connected model projects, the aim being to achieve more wide-ranging regeneration of an area, including giving its positive social impacts a wider reach. This principle was the starting point for organisers of Emscher Park International Building Exhibition (IBA) in the Ruhr district in Germany. On an area of 800 square kilometres they concentrated more than 120 model examples of the adaptive re-use of the grounds of run-down steelworks, abandoned mines, filled-in docks, the conversion of abandoned buildings for various public and commercial functions. It also includes the post-industrial Landschaftspark in Duisburg on the site of the nineteenth-century Meiderich steelworks, where the original technological equipment is exposed and authentically preserved, where the blast furnaces now serve as a viewing platform for looking out onto the changing landscape, the remains of concrete ore bunkers are used as climbing walls, the gasholder contains a diving tank and gym, and the machine hall in the power plant hosts rock concerts and official receptions.

What is crucial is the discovery of a new 'programme', or function for the site. This is more easily found for universal industrial objects that are amenable to multiple types of functions and have usually suffered less contamination. A long and illuminating list could be compiled of the many textile mills and warehouses that have been converted into flats, offices and hotels, examples that could serve as sources of inspiration for other places still in decay. Examples can be found from Manchester to Venice, in the luxury hotel in Molino Stucky, a factory, on Giudecca Island, or in the Manufaktura Centre (developer: Apsys) in the huge Poznanski factory in Łódź, Poland. Small halls and workshops also offer possibilities and are especially well suited for use as studios, clubs, or even shopping centres, such as the *Designer* Outlet Shopping Mall (developer: BAAMcArthur/Glen) on the former grounds of the Great Western Railway Engineering Works in Swindon, UK.

With single-purpose production and technical structures things are more difficult, and the technology on these sites tends to be directly built into the construction and shapes the layout and appearance of the site. These objects are often very large and heavily contaminated; examples include power plants, mining buildings and metal-working sites. They are usually unique structures that are visually striking and impossible to overlook and tend to dominate the area in which they are located. They can be useful in initiatory projects concentrating on key areas, where they serve as the focal point and catalyst for the regeneration of the entire area. Such are the aims of the grand project to convert and give new use to the former Vítkovice steelworks, Czech Republic, which is an important monument to industrial heritage of European significance (conversion: AP Atelier Josef Pleskot). The gasholder has been converted into a multifunctional auditorium, around which a university campus should be built within several years. This represents a source of hope for Ostrava, which until quite recently was the biggest industrial city in the Czech Republic and has since experienced a dramatic decrease in heavy industry.

Form and meaning

More than ever before, adaptive re-use constitutes an unfinished dialogue on continuity and the risk of fleeting decisions. The development of a conversion project may also be prompted by an appreciation and recognition of the remarkable features of industrial architecture and a fascination with its aesthetics. It certainly provides a deeper and more lasting experience than what is offered by rootless contemporary creations.

Its appeal lies in its many layers of meaning, where utilitarian and decorative, minutely crafted, details come together. It typically unites technological requirements and the economics of production (still apparent in the typology of the vacated structures, for instance, in the silhouette of a brewery, the rhythm of the window openings of a textile mill), with representative and stylistically expressive architecture that drew attention to the economic, technical and artistic ambitions of contemporary entrepreneurs, engineers, builders and artists.

This architectural quality, the representative and even ostentatious design of many industrial buildings, can be successfully put to use to bring out the ambitions of today. Proof that this pays off is the often-publicised example of the Nestlé Headquarters in Noisiel, outside Paris, which is located in one of the most important industrial monuments in France, the former Menier Chocolate Factory (conversion project by Reichen & Robert Architects).

Another example is the smokestack of Lister's Manningham Mills in Bradford, England, richly decorated in an Italian neo-Renaissance style, which at the time the structure was completed in the 1870s was meant to announce to the world that this was an important and successful business. Today, in circumstances where the use and perception of architecture is completely different, this representative function of architecture is similarly used by investors to further commercial interests. This is one of the reasons why the more exciting and ambitious project of converting a run-down site into fashionable flats was adopted for Lister's Mills and helped to save it (developer: Urban Splash; architects: David Morley Architects and Lathams). The 'advertising' effect of attention-grabbing architecture also works 'to promote' industrial heritage.

Alongside historical architecture, another prominent theme is the current level of reflection of contemporary art trends. New projects of conversion allow structural details and fragments of the original technology to come to the fore. They retain authentic surfaces and materials. They enrich the perception of the structure with the story of its origin and evolution.

In the prestigious Massachusetts Museum of Contemporary Art (MASS MoCA), North Adams, Massachusetts in the US, in the nineteenth-century Arnold Print Works cloth-printing factory, the wall structures, chipped and stained with paint, have been preserved as autonomous artistic artefacts – in the immediate vicinity of contemporary art (conversion: Bruner/Cott & Associates). The traces and reminders of defunct activity, the passage of time and human existence, have also an aesthetic and cultural value.

This is not just the experience of a contemporary art museum. Entering any of the luxury flats in Lister's Mills in Bradford, overt traces of the defunct original functions are preserved in the structure of the plaster on the ceilings and walls, as though in the place of framed classical paintings.

The layers of meanings, styles, experiences and information are an asset. An industrial structure imbued with something new gains in credibility, which is lacking from places and structures with no past. This was the guiding principle of the transformation of the boiler house of the Zollverein mine in Essen into the German Design Centre (conversion by Norman Foster – Foster & Partners Architects), another of the projects developed as part of the international exhibition at IBA Emscher Park. The boiler house's technological equipment seems fixed in the moment when it went out of service and has been transformed into a backdrop for the modern design objects. For effect, this gesture hints at questioning the point of exhibiting consumer items.

Conclusion

Adaptive re-use above all means a different experience to a world of disposable things. This method is not about superficial exploitation, nor is it a bottomless reservoir of material, energy and meanings, which some examples might suggest. The principle of sustainability, adherence to which is not always successful, lies in the arguments, structural interventions and architectural designs that leave enough room for future decisions and for uncovering new meanings in situations that we cannot yet foresee. It lies in preserving room for continuity.

Further reading

LATHAM, D: *Creative Re-use of Buildings* (vols 1 and 2*).* Shaftesbury: Donhead Publishing, 2000

MUÑOZ-VIÑAS, S: *Contemporary Theory of Conservation.* Oxford: Elsevier, 2005

POWELL, K: *Architecture Reborn: the conversion and reconstruction of old buildings.* London: Laurence King Publishing, 1999

STRATTON, M, (ed.): *Industrial Buildings: conservation and regeneration.* London: E&FN Spon, 2000

TIESDEL, S, OC, T and HEATH, T: *Revitalizing Historic Urban Quarters.* Oxford: Architectural Press, 2001

UFFELEN, C van: *Re-Use Architecture.* Salenstein: Braun Publishing, 2011

15

Financial and fiscal incentives

Bode Morin

Introduction

Industrial heritage provides social value in multiple ways. Through its study, we gain a greater understanding of the forces and personal experiences that shaped our industrial and post-industrial cultures. Through its re-use, we keep demolition materials from landfills and encourage sustainable practices and economic development. Through its conservation, we provide an indelible link for current and future generations to identify with, and appreciate the character of, earlier generations and places.

Some preservation projects are realised for the public benefit they bring, or are accomplished by non-profit-making bodies, or have public grants and other types of philanthropic funding available. However, many other projects are private, for-profit developments that do not have the same financing options available. Despite the often varied nature of preservation funding, the value of keeping and maintaining historic structures is well recognised and understood and includes issues of regional identity, economic development, neighbourhood stabilisation and sustainability. The sustainable approach should be for tax mechanisms and credit policies to favour conservation and re-use over new construction. Because heritage preservation is an important social and economic component of modern cultures, governments create incentives not only to promote non-profit and public heritage projects but also to encourage private efforts to stimulate the revitalisation of redundant sites or blighted areas and to promote sustainable practices through adaptive re-use. By deploying public investment in industrial heritage as a 'lever' to raise investment from the private sector, there can be an overall gain for the heritage as well as tax revenues for the public budget.

The greatest effects can usually be achieved through a combination of different funding mechanisms, such as grant aid, low-interest loans and tax incentives. Many of the outstanding cases of best practice in funding through the careful deployment of public funds are discussed in the preceding three chapters. For best practice in the application of fiscal incentives for heritage conservation, the United States can serve as a good example.

The US recognises the social and economic value of preservation, while at the same time not providing as great a level of public financial support and protection as do many European states. In the US, several levels of incentives at both the national and the state levels are geared toward re-using buildings and redeveloping redundant lands. Although the Society for Industrial Archaeology (SIA) awards grants to non-profit industrial heritage projects, and the Society for the Preservation of Old Mills (SPOOM) offers technical advice to owners of historic mills, and a few states even have mill-building restoration programs, in general there are few incentives specifically tailored for the adaptive re-use of industrial structures. However, a number of financial incentives exist for general heritage preservation projects and other incentives exist for the reclamation of brownfields. Both of these can be applied to industrial heritage sites.

Federal and state tax incentives

While the federal preservation tax incentive program discussed below has been fairly stable since its implementation in 1977, in general US tax laws at the federal and state levels tend to be quite fluid and prone to rapid changes, periodic renewals and abrupt cancellations.

At the federal level, the National Park Service (NPS), State Historic Preservation Offices (SHPO), and the Internal Revenue Service (IRS) administer the Federal Historic Preservation Tax Incentive Program. Tax incentives take the form of a credit against tax owed and are limited to a tax reduction of 20 per cent of the amount spent in a *certified rehabilitation* or 10 per cent spent to rehabilitate non-historic buildings constructed and placed in service prior to 1936.

The larger, 20 per cent rehabilitation tax credit must be applied to a 'certified' building, which means a structure already listed on the US National Register of

The Edenton cotton mill (1899) in North Carolina was rehabilitated using the state's tax credits, in many cases passed along to the buyers of the apartments in the mill. It is estimated that the re-use for homes and adjacent mill village added over $20 million to the local tax base. (Preservation North Carolina)

Historic Places, or within a US National Register District, or eligible for listing on the National Register. The credit is available for depreciable properties, such as those used in a business where value losses or acquisition costs can be deducted from income over a period of time. These buildings must ultimately be rehabilitated for commercial, industrial, agriculture or rental residential purposes, but the credit is not permitted for an owner's private residence or for non-building structures such as bridges, railroad cars or dams. In general, the credits are claimed the year a building is put back into service but could be phased in over time provided substantial work has been done over a two-year period. Further, the building must be owned by the claimant for five years following the credit or the claimant will suffer graduated repayment penalties based on when the building was sold or transferred. A 'certified' rehabilitation also requires that character-defining elements of the property be protected during the project and that the rehabilitation plans be reviewed, approved and officially certified by the National Park Service on the recommendation of the appropriate State Historic Preservation Office. Official certification is required by the IRS prior to allowing the tax credit.

The 10 per cent rehabilitation tax credit is also limited to depreciable buildings placed in initial service prior to 1936 and rehabilitated for non-residential, commercial purposes. While the 20 per cent credit requires the protection of character-defining elements, the 10 per cent credit has a more formal specification for the retention of walls and structural elements. To be eligible, at least 50 per cent of the exterior walls that existed at the start of the rehabilitation must be present at its completion; at least 75 per cent of the building's existing external walls must remain in place either as external or internal walls; and at least 75 per cent of the building's structural framework must remain in place at its completion. No certification is required for the 10 per cent credit, but approval is still necessary for tax purposes, and buildings already listed on the National Register and thus eligible for the 20 per cent credit are not eligible for the lower credit.

States too, recognise the value of promoting historic preservation. In fact at least 30 individual US states offer preservation tax benefits similar to the federal program, and 25 offer some form of local property tax relief for approved projects in approved areas. In fiscal year 2010, 47 per cent of the federally certified projects also included state incentives and other forms of tax relief. Further, many states also offer additional credits for owner-occupied structures and specific low-income housing with individual credits ranging from 10 per cent to 30 per cent.

Another type of preservation tax credit available at the federal and some state and municipal levels is through easement donations. Under these considerations, a credit can be claimed if a property owner places deed restrictions on future developments or changes to an historic property to ensure that significant elements are protected even over multiple later ownerships. These easements are then donated to a local preservation or conservation organisation and the owner can claim an income reduction as a charitable contribution, essentially trading some of their property rights for tax considerations. These are often long-term agreements and are commonly used to encourage the preservation of façades and street vistas.

Brownfield tax credits

The broader tax incentive program that is more specifically applicable to industrial sites is the brownfield tax credit. Like the preservation credits, brownfield programs exist at the state and federal levels and are designed to encourage the redevelopment and re-use of economically distressed areas. By definition, brownfields are abandoned or idle properties that ceased productivity due to concerns over environmental contamination. Under the federal program, certain clean-up and remediation costs can be claimed at 100 per cent in the year they were incurred. Unlike the rehabilitation tax credit, which directly lowers the tax burden, brownfield tax incentives can be claimed as deductible expenses that reduce overall income thus indirectly lowering taxes and tax brackets. The credits, however, can only be taken against efforts to reduce directly the contaminant hazards of the site and not for preservation or other redevelopment activities, although they can be combined with other federal and state preservation tax incentives.

To be eligible for the brownfield credit, a site must be owned by the taxpayer incurring the clean-up expenses, be used in a trade or for the production of income and have extant hazardous substance or petroleum contamination. Furthermore, the owner/taxpayer must provide certification from the state's environmental agency that the site qualifies as a brownfield. With the petroleum inclusion, former gas stations and underground storage tank sites became eligible, but sites listed on the US National Priorities List for environmental remediation are ineligible, because their inclusion on this list triggers a federal clean-up under the EPA's Superfund legislation.

Historically the federal brownfield incentive has never been enacted on a long-term basis. Since its inception in 1997, Congress has allowed the program to lapse five times only to renew it at later dates. The most recent federal brownfield tax incentive program expired on December 31, 2011. In years past, it was renewed with other tax changes later in the year and applied retroactively to the date of the last expiration. Like the rehabilitation tax credits, several states offer a variety of incentives to promote redevelopment of brownfield lands. Seven states offer some a form of targeted financial assistance such as loan guarantees for clean-up projects: four states offer incentives such as tax credits for approved clean-up expenses or cancellation of delinquent taxes; two offer planning, assessment and clean-up programs to aid assessment planning; and one has an infrastructure development program aiding new transportation and community redevelopment projects using brownfield lands.

Other federal programs

Other federal programs that exist to promote underdeveloped neighbourhoods, economically declining regions or lower-income housing have potential implications for industrial heritage. The US Department of Housing and Urban Development (HUD), for instance, administers the Community Development Block Grant program geared toward generating affordable housing and public improvements to encourage economic revitalisation. While planning funds are available to communities or economic development groups directly under the block grant program, preservation funds for rehabilitation, preservation or restoration projects are available directly to public or private historic preservation projects for properties either listed or eligible for listing on the National Register. The key restriction is that the property must not have a government function when completed. Further, at least 70 per cent of the funds acquired from HUD must be used to benefit low- and moderate-income persons, and must at a minimum also be applied to reduce blight, or address community development health and welfare needs.

Examples of state programs

States also recognise the economic benefits of historic preservation especially when directed toward reversing economic trends in blighted or post-industrial areas that have direct implications for industrial heritage. In addition to state historic preservation tax credits and brownfield tax deductions, the Commonwealth (state) of Massachusetts has a tax law encouraging the redevelopment of abandoned buildings. The Commonwealth allows a state income tax deduction equal to 10 per cent of the costs of renovating a qualifying abandoned building in a designated Economic Opportunity Area. Once designated or certified by the Economic Assistance Coordinating Council, the deduction may be taken in addition to any other federal or commonwealth tax or financial incentive available to developers.

Although currently suspended (summer 2012) due to budgetary constraints, The State of Rhode Island allowed for tax credits against the cost of preserving certified industrial mill buildings of the state's former textile industry, in certain approved communities. The program permitted credits up to 10 per cent of the cost of an approved renovation, plus additional incentives for employment tax credits if the development was located in an enterprise zone. The program was primarily designed to revitalise pre-1950s mills that had sat largely vacant for more than two years.

Like the Rhode Island incentive program, North Carolina maintains an historic mill preservation program targeting the state's numerous former tobacco, textile and utility structures. Through the efforts of Preservation North Carolina, the state passed the Mills Tax Credit in 2004 specifically to support the revitalisation of vacant mill structures for income and non-income producing projects. The state program allows owners to claim up to 40 per cent of eligible rehabilitation costs as state tax credits for work on a certified rehabilitation of a National Register listed, National Register district located, or State Register listed property. The level of the available credit is dependent on its location in the state and the economic conditions of the surrounding area. In addition to its historic character, the building must have been 80 per cent vacant for at least two years and certified 'eligible' by the State Historic Preservation Officer. Owners claiming the Mills Tax Credit, however, are not eligible for other state preservation tax credits. As of 2010, the North Carolina program had generated $304 million (US) in rehabilitation expenditures.

In 2004, South Carolina passed the similar Textile Communities Revitalization Act to provide tax credits against the rehabilitation costs of abandoned textile manufacturing sites in that state but, unlike its neighbour to the north, only requires a one-year vacancy. Similar programs exist in other states to promote the preservation of barns, lighthouses, courthouses and other iconic structures, but, in general, incentives for private US industrial heritage are rare, requiring planners and developers to pursue incentives within general historic preservation planning.

Grants and loans

Industrial heritage preservation benefits from much more direct economic support in Europe, where it tends to be largely publicly funded and based around grants. These extend from the international level of the European Union, as discussed in Chapter 13, through support from national administrations, including funding from public lotteries, to grants distributed at the local or municipal level. In recent years, financial awards have increasingly preferred areas suffering from structural industrial decline and are usually intended as catalysts for regeneration, rather than responding to the special technical or historical interest of particular sites. These frequently form part of the suite of initiatives which go under the umbrella of Regeneration Through Heritage, many of them pioneered on historic industrial properties.

Low-interest loan facilities, such as through revolving fund mechanisms, are also an effective funding mechanism that is widely used in Europe, especially to finance adaptive re-use projects where there is a good possibility of giving former industrial buildings a financially viable new use. Revolving funds are financial endowments set up to make loans for a conservation project. When the money is paid back, usually after the sale of the restored building, it is loaned out again for a new project, at interest rates well below those offered by the banks.

Conclusion

Tax credits and other incentives have been used successfully in the Untied States to promote and encourage the preservation of heritage that does not qualify for direct public funding. US federal historic preservation tax credits alone have supported and generated significant preservation investment by promoting new economic development in economically declining areas.

From 1977 to 2010, 37,364 rehabilitation projects have been certified eligible for the 20 per cent tax credits which, with the projects eligible for the 10 per cent credit, have leveraged or generated nearly $59 billion in private investment. Many of these projects, however, have not relied exclusively on federal tax incentives. State preservation

The Boilerhouse restaurant at the Rosie the Riveter National Historical Park, Richmond, California, is one component of a private, mixed-use facility, formerly the Ford Assembly Plant. This National Register listed former auto and military production plant was a certified rehabilitation in the mid-2000s and eligible for federal tax credits. (Photo 2012 ©www.hustacephotography.com)

tax incentives, brownfield tax incentives at the state and federal level, and specific state programs such as the mill tax credits have created an entrepreneurial atmosphere around re-using heritage buildings in the US leading to the recapturing and redevelopment of culturally important landscapes and structures.

Best Practice: Ford Assembly Plant, Richmond, California

Although federal incentive programs in the US do not specifically promote the redevelopment of industrial sites for commercial use outside of brownfield clean-ups, the indelible character of industrial structures coupled with the available incentives have promoted the adaptive re-use of many former industrial sites. While loft developments have been the most visible form of rehabilitation across the country, several significant sites have been repurposed, leaving important structures, regional character and identity intact for future generations, and new spaces available for community re-use.

One of the best of these projects was the 2004 rehabilitation of the former Ford Motor Company assembly plant in Richmond, California, by Orton Development. Once the site of the largest assembly plant on the West Coast, the 1930 Albert Kahn-designed building was transformed into a significant military vehicle production facility during World War II and later resumed auto assembly for several years before manufacturing ended in 1953. The 520,000 square foot building lived on sporadically. It was later used as a movie set and book depository before being added to the US National Register in 1988. By the 2000s, however, the building had sat vacant for years and suffered structural damage from earthquakes. However, the iconic factory was never completely forgotten, and plans for its restoration and re-use then began in earnest. The multi-year rehabilitation was carried out in phases, initially by the City of Richmond which raised nearly $19 million from federal agencies and invested more than $16 million of city funds before the building was purchased by Orton Development. In total the project required $55 million in rehabilitation work. With Orton's involvement, the project was certified by the National Park Service and was therefore eligible for 20 per cent federal preservation tax credits and some state incentives, although the exact dollar amount eligible for credits was not disclosed. Today the site is home to several manufacturers of environmentally sustainable products, a large convention and entertainment venue, and is part of the Rosie the Riveter National Historical Park which celebrates the role of women and other non-military personnel supporting manufacturing on the World War II home front.

Further reading

ENVIRONMENTAL PRESERVATION AGENCY. *A Guide to Federal Tax Incentives for Brownfields Redevelopment.* Washington DC: USEPA, 2011

HOWARD, J Myrick: 'Financial Incentives for Saving Industrial Heritage in North Carolina'. *Forum Journal.* National Trust for Historic Preservation, 2011, 25(3), 47-52

NATIONAL PARK SERVICE: *Federal Tax Incentives for Rehabilitation Historic Buildings, Annual Report Fiscal Year 2010.* Washington DC: USNPS, 2011

NATIONAL PARK SERVICE: *Historic Preservation Tax Incentives.* Washington DC: USNPS, 2009

PICKARD, Robert: *Funding the Architectural Heritage: a guide to policies and examples.* Strasbourg: Council of Europe Publishing, 2009

16

Heritage at risk surveys

Jaime Migone

Introduction

Heritage sites can be at risk from two sources: first, an external threat of some form; and, second, the risks and problems inherent in any intervention that might be necessary to mitigate or eliminate those risks (itself a very difficult, indeed near impossible, task). In these circumstances the acceptance of some risk becomes necessary, as failure to intervene might well be counter-productive: in essence, one would be waiting for the threat or risk to materialise. What *might* happen then stands a good chance of becoming a reality.

Yet intervening does always involve risks. There is nothing more hazardous than flawed interventions that are carried out for a good cause. Yet, often due to the urgency involved in acting to reduce risk, or to poor understanding of the issue, coupled with a lack of experience in developing solutions, this latent risk emerges. By doing things badly the solution can be turned into a bigger, unsolvable problem in the medium or long term.

This threat is also associated with abundance. There is nothing worse for heritage than an excess of resources and over-intervention, the motives of which are often more political than technical. Attempting to reduce risks within limited timeframes with non-technical criteria and the political logic of 'cutting the ribbon' – so as to appear to lower the danger to heritage sites – itself becomes an on-going threat.

The word risk comes from the Italian words *risico* or *rischio*, which have their roots in the classical Arabic *rizq* meaning 'what providence brings'. Risk to a heritage site refers to all those vulnerabilities, inherent in the site or its context, that threaten to detract partially or totally from its value, either by altering part or the whole of that heritage site. The management of risk concerns the entire future of the site.

Preventative conservation

Analysis of a heritage site is absolutely necessary to understand the processes of degradation and the risks they face for its future conservation. Analysing a heritage site is an on-going and multidisciplinary necessity. It must be on-going because corrosion and decay are constant and persistent; we can try to slow them down or limit them, but ultimately deterioration can never be completely stopped. And it is multidisciplinary, because this process affects the monument in various ways and such effects differ according to the particular perspective we have of the heritage site. As such, understanding the value of a monument is the first aspect to consider when prioritising future actions for its conservation.

Analysis must also be continuous because reality is itself dynamic and complex. Values in society are changeable and must be reviewed regularly. Physicochemical alterations in structures can be evident and easily detected – changes which are observable via known and identified pathologies and established diagnoses and treatments – but there are also changes that are very slow and not easily detected, and which become apparent only after long periods of time. This means it is necessary for continuous comparative analysis to shed light on changes that are not visible to the naked eye – signs that, once detected early, can without a doubt help with the preservation in time of historic sites.

It is clear that prevention is always better than cure. It will always be less invasive and traumatic to take action before and not after pathologies have seriously damaged a monument's materials. And preventative conservation furthermore has another substantive virtue in solving the issue at hand: it is always much cheaper and more accessible. It can be developed with applied intelligence and planning. Vast resources are not required, compared with intervening once the damage has been done and its progress is physically apparent.

Every heritage site faces risks and threats from a variety of sources, including its climatic context, seismic risk, unnecessary interventions and tourist overuse, and so on, and preventative conservation should be used in order to prevent deterioration and increased threats in the future. It is necessary to understand all of these factors so as to be able to develop management plans that are adequate for each heritage site.

The first premise must always be that each site is unique and unrepeatable and by extension, so are the problems it faces, so the solutions to such problems will naturally also be unique and unrepeatable. The solutions in evaluating a heritage site are unique in terms of their heritage characteristics and values, as well as all the problems and threats they encounter.

Evaluation entails examining the monument so as to understand its particular problems and needs, which can be done by analysing documentary records and the general history of the site in depth. Such research essential to understand the reasons behind its construction and appearance. This study must be complemented by a detailed analysis through field examination of the fabric and its current state.

Such an understanding of the monument through direct sources allows us to ascertain its current condition, determining the pathologies, damage, needs and threats affecting it.

With a thorough understanding of the origin, development and future needs of the site, we can undertake a comparative analysis with its current state of conservation, which will allow us to determine, at a given moment, the values and reasons for which society appreciates and recognises it. Such recognition is apparent in the preconceived ideas of its conservation in the future. While in many cases a monument may have lost its functionality and role within human activity, especially its economic function, society may value it for its symbolic, historic, testimonial or evidential status.

A comparative analysis, then, between indirect and direct sources will help us determine and understand the monument's current value. Given the dynamic nature of real-world situations, this can and surely will change in the future, but focusing on them will help define our actions in terms of conservation and movement into the future.

Developing and applying a management plan on which to base a restoration project should be founded as scientifically as possible on such knowledge. This is an argument that supports interventions whether they be merely for conservation purposes, rehabilitative with new ways of using the material, recycling so as to give society a new use for the site, restoring the monument to its figurative original image, or incorporating it into a new contemporary design that assumes and promotes a modern vision.

It is essential, therefore that the evaluation thesis receives the consensus of society and be made publicly available, as part of the social integration strategy that heritage requires. An informed society is the best guarantor of maintaining heritage.

Case study: mining sites in the Atacama Desert, Chile

In Chile there are two important industrial World Heritage Sites, representative of the exploitation of saltpetre during the nineteenth and part of the twentieth century, the Sewell copper mining plant 150 kilometres south of the capital Santiago, and *Oficinas Salitreras de Humberstone y Santa Laura* (Humberstone and Santa Laura Saltpeter Works) 1,600 kilometres to the north in the Atacama Desert.

The Santa Laura Saltpeter Works, Chile, was inscribed on the World Heritage list in 2004 and simultaneously put on the List of World Heritage in Danger. It was an example of mining exploitation in extreme geographical conditions which presents very serious conservation challenges. The deterioration of the wooden structure and corrugated iron covering is due to the aggressive atmospheric conditions that hamper a comprehensive and long-term resolution. (World Heritage nomination file)

Humberstone was declared a World Heritage Site in 2004 and the Sewell camp site in 2005. Both have more than a hundred-year history of development and activity, involving minerals essential for the social and economic development of Chile.

In the surviving structures of these sites there is a permanent degradation of materials, which has not been analysed in depth. The vast majority of the buildings were built using Oregon pine (*Pseudotsuga menziesii*) and corrugated galvanised iron, used not just as deck covering but also widely for the walls and lining of wood structures in general. They were transported to Chile from North America as ballast in cargo ships transporting salt.

The central, urgent issue is the degradation and advanced deterioration of the industrial installations, especially in Santa Laura and to a lesser extent in Humberstone. This is manifest especially in relation to the two materials discussed above.

The physical deterioration of these materials is produced by a daily nocturnal salty coastal mist known as *camanchaca*. This is a very dense mist that is generated by the anti-cyclone and Humboldt Current in the Pacific Ocean which travels towards the continent almost all year round. This atmospheric phenomenon condenses on all metallic structures, especially in the exteriors built with the galvanised iron; to a lesser extent it also dampens all wooden structures, many of which are out in the open and unprotected.

In addition to the high salinity of the terrain, in an area where saltpetre is extracted, this weather has become a corrosive agent degrading materials for which there is no known counterpoint or remedy, and it is progressing without respite. This is a very serious issue that has neither been addressed in the necessary depth nor with the urgency required.

It is essential to address this technical issue within the framework of the expected conservation of the site. A high priority is to be able to implement alternative solutions and carry out on-site tests and experiments, so as to later develop a comprehensive materials conservation plan for all elements physically constituting the site.

With no specific reference points or previous relevant experience, the analysis and development of treatment plans, development of new designs and the adequate replacement of deteriorated materials must be the object of on-going and constant inclusion in the conservation management of the site.

Further reading

MIGONE, Jaime and PIROZZI, Antonio: *Estado de Situación de la Conservación del Patrimonio Construido en Chile – Informe Preliminar.* Santiago: Ediciones de la Universidad Internacional SEK, 1996

17

Conservation plans

Helen Lardner

The management of cultural heritage involves caring for what is valued by today's society to enable its appreciation in the future. Conservation plans are a tool to ensure that good decisions are made about industrial heritage sites, structures, areas and landscapes, as well as their associated intangible values. A conservation or management plan is a written document that sets out what is significant about a place and provides guidelines to enable that significance to be retained during future use and development. Conservation plans should be clearly written by people with appropriate expertise, and will be composed specifically for each individual site. This chapter focuses on three key elements of good conservation plans: defining the significance or heritage values of industrial heritage; developing policies to protect this significance; and providing management strategies for the future.

Understanding significance

The first step to creating a good conservation plan is to understand the significance of the place and the way in which that significance is embodied in the place itself, its fabric, setting, use, associations, meanings, records, related places and related objects. Understanding significance involves investigating the place or landscape to identify what about its history and fabric is significant, and then secondly assessing that significance. Collecting and analysing information involves documentary research and physical investigation, as well as talking to stakeholders and those people with an association with the place. Comparison with similar sites is undertaken. This process usually culminates in a succinctly worded summary or statement which aims to express significance in terms of values or criteria.

The Nizhny Tagil Charter identifies significance as encompassing historical, technological, social, architectural or scientific values. Other documents and guidelines take a slightly more general definition of significance. For example, the ICOMOS Australia Burra Charter defines cultural significance as meaning aesthetic, historic, scientific, social or spiritual value for past, present or future generations. The assessment of significance is usually undertaken against criteria which help to analyse the values in the place. For example, criteria may include the ability to demonstrate aspects of history or rare qualities or the principal characteristics of a type of place. A site can also provide evidence of an association with a person, group or event of importance or possess particularly valued creative or aesthetic qualities. However, significance does not only lie in the physical fabric and a heritage place may have intangible values that evoke important associations relating to historic events or cultural practices for the contemporary community.

Individual countries may have their own criteria for significance, and thresholds for the level of significance may vary by region, country or internationally. These differences are not explored here. Instead the criteria for World Heritage Listing form the basis of this discussion, and examples are drawn from places on the World Heritage List because of their international application. The criteria which are more commonly applied to industrial heritage places are discussed and illustrated with examples. For the full list of World Heritage selection criteria refer to the UNESCO World Heritage website http://whc.unesco.org/en/criteria or to the *Operational Guidelines for the Implementation of the World Heritage Convention*.

The World Heritage List is made up of sites of outstanding universal value, and this is considered the highest level of significance. This threshold is established by determining that sites meet at least one of the selection criteria. In many cases, sites will meet more than one criterion. Other significant industrial heritage places may have similar values at a lower threshold, for example being important to a local community, or illustrating the development of a key industry within a country. However, the principle of assessing the significance of the place is the same.

The first criterion (i) refers to *representation of a masterpiece of human creative genius* and is often applied where a site demonstrates a major creative effort to advance a specific field or represents the peak achievement in such a field. Industrial heritage sites are usually distinguished by an exceptional technical advance, such as the Canal du Midi (1996) in France, the mill network at Kinderdijk-Elshout (1997) and Wouda Steam Pumping Station (1998), both in the Netherlands. It has also been applied to the Neolithic Flint Mines at Spiennes, Belgium (2000), which provide exceptional testimony to early human inventiveness and application as well as to the ancient Roman gold-mining area of Las Médulas (1997) in Spain.

Places which meet the second criterion (ii) *exhibit an important interchange of human values, over a span of time or within a cultural area of the world, on developments in architecture or technology, monumental arts, town-planning or landscape design*. Industrial towns may meet this criterion; for example, Sewell Mining Town (2006) in Chile is an outstanding example of the global phenomenon of company towns which contributed to the worldwide spread of large-scale mining technology. Saltaire (2001), UK, is an outstanding example of a mid-nineteenth-century industrial town, the layout of which was to exert a major influence on the development of the garden city movement.

UNESCO's third criterion (iii) distinguishes sites which *bear a unique or at least exceptional testimony to a cultural tradition or to a civilization which is living or which has disappeared*. The Cornwall and West Devon Mining Landscape (2006), UK, presents a vivid and legible testimony to when this area dominated the world's output of copper, tin and arsenic. The Four Lifts on the Canal du Centre, La Louvière and Le Roeulx (1998) in Belgium bear exceptional testimony to the remarkable hydraulic engineering developments of nineteenth-century Europe.

The fourth measure of significance (criterion iv) is applied to a site which is *an outstanding example of a type of building or architectural or technological ensemble or landscape which illustrates (a) significant stage(s) in human history.* The Canal du Midi is regarded as one of the greatest engineering achievements of the Modern Age, providing the model for the flowering of technology that led directly to the Industrial Revolution and the modern technological age. In addition to its technological innovation, the Canal is an exceptional example of a designed landscape. The same criterion is applied to Humberstone and Santa Laura Saltpeter Works (2004) in Chile, which together became the largest producers of natural saltpetre in the world, transforming the Pampa and indirectly the agricultural lands that benefited from the fertilizers the works produced.

The final criterion (v) refers to *an outstanding example of a traditional human settlement, land-use, or sea use which is representative of a culture (or cultures), or human interaction with the environment especially when it has become vulnerable under the impact of irreversible change.* An example is the Mining Area of the Great Copper Mountain in Falun, Sweden (2001), which demonstrates successive stages in the economic and social evolution of the copper industry in the Falun region.

One of the requirements in assessing significance is to understand a place or landscape in a context that would allow its comparative rarity or representativeness to be assessed. This is critical if questions of 'pioneering', 'innovation' or 'adoption of obsolete technology' are being considered. Comparative studies which establish that context are rare and may be expensive to undertake, especially when technology is adopted on an international scale. TICCIH has membership groups based on thematic sections which may be able to provide advice. Some comparative studies have been prepared by TICCIH which may help overcome this problem.

A related issue is the need to understand the integrity of a place or landscape. Changes to a place adding new fabric or removing older fabric may impact negatively on its integrity. For example, the importance of a flour mill may be altered by removing all the machinery on which its significance was founded. It is thus critical to understand the sequence of change to a place so as to identify the degree of integrity and authenticity that is present.

After defining the nature of the significance of an industrial heritage site, the conservation plan should establish the relative significance of the components of the place. These components may include buildings, structures, landscape elements, setting, archaeological remains, technology or equipment, collections, artefacts, documents and related objects. In order to make good management decisions, the extent and level of significance of parts of the site must be clear and often this material is provided graphically as well as in writing. It should be noted that not all the components of a site are of the same level of significance.

Conservation management

There is a step between assessing significance and developing management policies – this is assessing the opportunities and constraints relating to the place or landscape as these provide a framework for conservation policies to be developed. The process of identifying opportunities and constraints is one of consultation with relevant owners and stakeholders.

A c.1880 photograph of the Hoffman Brickworks Co. No. 1 Works, Brunswick, Australia. Old photographs of working industrial sites are excellent resources for conservation plans. (University of Melbourne Archives Collection)

Key constraints on industrial places are often the poor condition of buildings and infrastructure and site contamination issues. On the other hand the size and shape of industrial buildings often makes them good candidates for adaptive re-use and innovative design.

It is important when considering opportunities and constraints that appropriate professional advice be obtained. Constraints such as site contamination can often be managed with professional input and have minimum impact on the potential use of a site. Similarly the commercial reality of plans for adaptive re-use of a site may need to be tested by experienced property management, quantity estimators and other consultants. Most conservation plans will need a range of inputs, so it is essential to engage a team with appropriate expertise.

Developing policies to protect significance

The next stage of the conservation plan for an industrial heritage place is to develop policies to protect its significance. It should be remembered that the significance of each component of a site may need to be managed by different policies and techniques.

Where do ideas for policies come from? For most places there is a suite of general policies that are needed, but to prepare a relevant and implementable plan individual consultation is required. This should include owners and managers as well as relevant stakeholders (including the community and heritage authorities) and it is critical in generating ideas for management policies.

The policies need to anticipate future management issues but retain a degree of flexibility or adaptability in order to meet changing circumstances. Policies are not written in response to one issue but should establish a framework for good decisions to be made by a variety of people, for example the site manager dealing with day-to-day issues, or the owner and heritage authorities considering a proposal for change.

Typically policies would be prepared for the following matters and should be justified by linking the policy back to the significance of the place or landscape or the significance of a component. The policy can be supported by various tasks required to achieve its aim. If outlined explicitly in the conservation plan, this approach allows the process of implementation to be monitored.

- *Maintenance* – Types of maintenance tasks, the frequency they are required and the responsibility for undertaking them are important to establish.

- *Conservation works* – A condition survey can recommend repairs, restoration or reconstruction that may be needed to retain significant fabric. These works should be prioritised within a reasonable time frame.

- *Use* – Policies which establish the types of suitable uses, including possible new uses, can be very important for industrial heritage places. In some cases it may be more important to continue the historic use of the place even if it results in changes to existing fabric to allow technology to be updated and the existing use to continue. For other sites, such as mines for example, the significant activity may have ceased and the current use may be for heritage interpretation and tourism, which can introduce substantial change.

- *Code and standards compliance* – For many industrial heritage places, the need to meet authority requirements without impacting on significance can be challenging. Guidance is often required where machinery is exposed and presents a safety risk or where the provision of equitable access may mean installation of new lifts and ramps. Dealing with hazardous substances, such as waste products from industrial processes or chemical stores, can be challenging.

- *Statutory requirements* – Management decision-making processes and legal compliance should be outlined in the plan. There may be approvals needed from internal and external management as well as statutory requirements, such as heritage permits, prior to undertaking works at the site. The plan can be a tool to reach agreement with heritage authorities, to provide a degree of certainty about future planning or alleviate the need to get approvals for minor matters. The approvals and processes required to implement the conservation plan should be clearly outlined. Direction may be provided to assist in weighing up the long-term options with competing day-to-day demands on the site.

- *Risk preparedness* is a management strategy for the future of industrial heritage sites. Risks may be from natural events such as fire, flood or storm, or from site security, including theft and vandalism. A strategy to deal with these issues and to protect the significance of the site should be included in the conservation plan.

- *Managing change* – By using the significance ranking of the components of the place it is usually possible to provide guidance on opportunities and constraints in terms of making changes. For example, areas of lesser or no significance can be preferred for interventions, such as the accommodation of new buildings or facilities, over other more important areas whose significance may be more vulnerable to alterations. Impact on the setting of the place should be carefully considered as the loss of context or the loss of the visual relationship between the parts of a site may be very detrimental. On the other hand, a place which demonstrates technical advancement of significance may have areas where no new intervention is appropriate. The introduction of energy efficiencies is an area of change where the impact on significance must also be considered.

- *Subdivision or land consolidation* – For many industrial heritage places, changes to the scale of operations or as a result of the ending of its operation may impact on the amount or extent of the land required. Careful consideration should be given to the context of the place and its significance. For example, the relationship between workers' houses and their workplace may be critical to an appreciation of the significance of some sites.

- *Interpretation* – A conservation plan provides policies to assist in the interpretation of the significance of industrial heritage sites. Working sites often benefit from interpretation that explains the nature of the heritage significance to workers and visitors. For tourist sites, a detailed interpretation strategy may be produced, but products should be consistent with the interpretation policies that are established to reflect the significance in the conservation plan.

- *Protocols* – It may be necessary to develop protocols or codes of practice for industrial heritage sites to protect significance. An example may be archaeological protocols which could be required where it is likely that hidden remains may exist with research potential. Similarly, some areas of a site may be fragile or confined, and it may be necessary to have a protocol setting out the way this part may be accessed.

Providing management strategies for the future

A conservation plan must be practical and able to be implemented. It therefore needs to consider how the recommended actions can be implemented, by whom and in what time frame. To achieve this effectively, the conservation plan must identify the stakeholders to be involved in the site, for example owners, workers, government authorities, neighbouring properties and people with a significant association with the heritage place. In many cases where industrial heritage places historically had a large workforce or where the fabric may be a landmark, community members may have a strong attachment to the place. The conservation plan should establish the stakeholders and the means of communication with them.

Similarly, the financial and other resources required to meet the recommendations of the conservation plan should also be detailed. Actions described in the maintenance plan and conservation works schedule need to be prioritised, set out in a reasonable time frame and costed. For operating industrial heritage sites, the consequences in terms of the potential impacts on production may need to be quantified as these could be substantial.

A simple plan diagram can illustrate the relative significance of surviving components such as these at the Hoffman Brickworks Co. No. 2 Works, Brunswick, Australia. Hoffman Brickworks Conservation Management Plan in association with Essential Economics Pty Ltd, HLA Envirosciences Pty Ltd and Look Ear Pty Ltd, unpublished report, April 1999. (HLCD Pty Ltd)

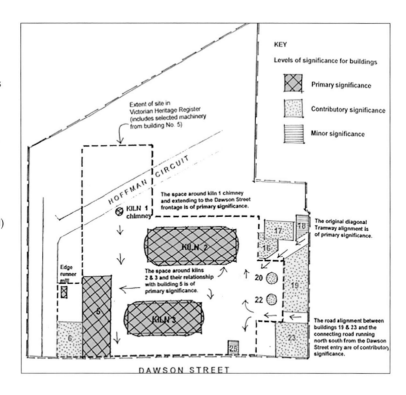

Lastly, the conservation plan must outline how policies recommended and actions proposed will be documented and outcomes monitored for the future. It is usual that the conservation plan itself will be reviewed and updated regularly.

Conclusion

Identifying industrial heritage is not an end in itself, for if industrial heritage is to have a value for current and future generations efforts must be made to conserve its significant values. A conservation plan which clearly establishes the significant values of the industrial heritage site outlines policies to protect these values and provides practical guidance on implementation and management is an investment in the future.

Further reading

CLARK, K: *Conservation Plans in Action*. Proceedings of the Oxford Conference. London: English Heritage, 1999

JOKILEHTO, J *et al.*: *The World Heritage List What is OUV? Defining the Outstanding Universal Value of Cultural World Heritage Properties*. Berlin: ICOMOS, 2008

KERR, J S: *The Conservation Plan: a guide to the preparation of conservation plans for places of European Cultural Significance*. Sydney: National Trust of Australia (NSW), 1990

WORLD HERITAGE CENTRE UNESCO, *et al.*: *Operational Guidelines for the Implementation of the World Heritage Convention*. Paris, France, World Heritage Centre, 2011

WORTHING, D and BOND, S: *Managing Built Heritage: the role of cultural significance*. Hoboken: John Wiley and Sons, 2007

18

Adaptive re-use and embodied energy

Mark Watson

Introduction

It is a paradox that building conservation is not about the past. It is about the future. The choices we make now about what to keep from the past are also about what changes to make to what we have inherited. While conservation of most building types is bedevilled by phrases such as 'conserve as found', those who try to tackle big issues such as urban renewal or sustainability have found that industrial buildings can and ought to be an opportunity for change. Economic change means that an old factory is mainly of value to its owners for what it could become, not for what it once was. And in order to judge the environmental value of that adaptive re-use the question needs to be asked: 'what if it was not re-used and a new building provided this function/service instead'?

How to measure the energy benefits in re-cycling buildings

Global climate change is attributed in large measure to emissions of carbon dioxide and other gases from the burning of fossil fuels, something that increased exponentially with the Industrial Revolution. A portion of the fuel is burned to heat indoor spaces. Therefore better-insulated new buildings are part of the solution, but very few new buildings are being built, so the pressure turns to existing buildings. Some environmental scientists have argued that the biggest problem lies in all of the old buildings that are 'hard to treat'. If only their demolition could be speeded up, they say, the planet would be a better place. But would it?

Building preservation or conservation saves energy by taking advantage of the non-recoverable energy embodied in a building, and extending the use of it. Simply put, building materials contain the 'embodied energy' already invested into them. Embodied energy means the sum of all the energy that was used to build a structure – fuel, materials and human resources. Timber, for example, seals in the carbon dioxide absorbed when the tree grew, as well as the energy that went into sawing it, while some estimate that around 5–6 per cent of CO_2 emissions derive from the global manufacture of cement. In addition, all of the building materials have been transported to their present location, at some cost in energy terms. Making continued use of this existing environmental capital means less energy used in demolition, less waste to landfill sites, and less energy needs to be devoted to bringing in new building materials. Embodied energy is only now beginning to be included in the emerging discipline of carbon counting. Operational savings – by energy-efficient insulation and by use of renewable energy – take many years to take effect. Benefits can be lost if short design lives that are typical of new buildings, and short refit cycles, increase lifetime emissions, no matter how efficient when in use. The calculated benefits from that investment cannot account for future variation in energy prices. It is hoped that energy will be derived from more 'green' sources than at present, so by then the savings in carbon dioxide in operational use will be less than today.

Savings in embodied energy achieve immediate reductions in carbon dioxide. Yet satisfactory measures of embodied energy are hard to find. In the UK, Historic Scotland has done some work on this area regarding natural stone imports, factoring transport costs into the Life Cycle Assessment, and windows, the energy of materials and ease of repair, as well as their impact on energy in use (Menzies: 2011).

Adaptable, long-life, loose-fit buildings reduce carbon dioxide emissions in the long term. The greatest reductions may then be achieved by re-using old industrial buildings, which may go through several changes of use over their lives. Standard Assessment Procedure (SAP) ratings for assessing emissions, commonly used in the UK and other countries, do not record this. Embodied energy assessment can capture this fact, and engineers and surveyors are among the professions now having to address this.

Adding the embodied energy costs of a refurbishment (in America, rehabilitation) to the operational emissions that are predicted to follow refurbishment allows an informed choice to be made about levels of intervention that might be appropriate in an existing building, or even whether to replace it by a new one.

Life Cycle Assessment (LCA) examines the total environmental impact of a material or product through every step of its life, from obtaining raw materials all the way through manufacture, transportation, use in the home and disposal or recycling. In the US the use or re-use of a building is rewarded by credits through LEED (Leadership in Environmental Energy and Design), but some argue that these do not give enough weight to re-use. The National Trust for Historic Preservation in America argued strongly in favour of better weighting in *The Greenest Building: quantifying the environmental value of building reuse.* It can take many decades for a new building to perform so well that it would be worth constructing anew instead of using an existing building, even one whose energy efficiency in use was 30 per cent less.

The assumption in LCA is that eventually a building (or its components) will come to the end of its life, so the materials put into it are described as 'from cradle to grave'. Their embodied energy will not be lost if they have been designed for disassembly and re-use. But in the building conservation world (in America, 'historic preservation') we know that buildings are capable of very extended lives beyond the design life usually assigned them. By averting the 'grave' for a long time, the embodied energy first invested in the building is used and re-used, without degradation to the environment.

If conversion to other uses is to be encouraged, the premises so formed have to be at least as good as the newly built equivalent. A historic building is not, and should not be, completely exempt from modern building codes essential to human comfort and safety. Nor should it be a conspicuously worse consumer of energy than a new building of equivalent type. So performance in use needs to be improved, particularly in warehouse conversions to residential use, as the National Trust for Historic Preservation study concluded.

An existing industrial building can often be shown to perform surprisingly well against modern codes due to factors inherent in the structure. A solid brick-arched or concrete floor, or a 'slow-burning' timber floor (American mill construction employing heavy timbers), contains much embodied energy compared to a standard joisted timber floor. A key consideration is that traditionally constructed, vapour-permeable buildings absorb and then release moisture. They are sometimes described as 'breathable' buildings, and a typical cut-off date in the UK is 1919, although these traditional types of building continued to be built after this date. Ill-considered insulation could trap moisture, reduce energy performance and shorten a building's life, as was proven in Finland. A shorter life cycle means expenditure of energy in building new replacements, which may not have time to repay their environmental costs even if they do achieve the relatively good energy efficiency claimed for them.

The need to reduce emissions of carbon dioxide increases the demands made of existing buildings in terms of thermal performance, yet their embodied energy already contributes to the war against global warming. A textile mill will usually have high thermal mass, thick walls and floors, though this is not the case with all industrial building types. It would be necessary to increase the insulation considerably of a building such as a forge that has only a single skin of corrugated iron, and is intended to be reused for sedentary office or residential functions.

On the other hand, some industrial buildings can be very heavy in their existing embodied energy. Reinforced concrete buildings fall into this category. It is particularly valuable to keep all that concrete, and therefore the embodied energy that went into it.

Examples of best practice

An embodied energy calculator such as that provided by the Chicago-based May T Watts Appreciation Society [http://thegreenestbuilding.org/teardown.html] can show how the results might vary, taking as examples a Scottish wool mill, a sugar refinery/whisky bond, the first Finnish cotton mill and finally a reinforced-concrete foundry in France.

Tower Mill, Hawick, Scotland, was built in 1851 for wool spinning, the main industry of the Scottish Borders. It fell derelict, was re-used and now contains small business premises, a café and a cinema. It comprised 2,010 m² of floor space, reduced to 1,890 m² after conversion. The result is given in MBTU, or approximately one joule, the unit used to describe the power of heating and cooling systems. There is some work still to be done on the embodied energy contained in materials (such as, for BREEAM certification in the UK, the ICE inventory). All carbon calculators involve a lot of assumptions that could be open to challenge in their detail, but essentially they give an energy value to building fabric.

Using the energy calculator we find:

Bonnington Bond in Leith, Scotland, after conversion, showing the sugar refinery built in 1865. The height of the former charcoal filter house was reduced because its internal construction was of less value, culturally and in embodied energy, than the heavy iron and timber used in the refinery. Beyond is McEwan's former floor maltings, now offices in the same phased development. (Mark Watson)

The heavy reinforced-concrete structure of the 1920s Société Alsacienne de Constructions Méchaniques foundry in Mulhouse, France, now converted to a university library. (Mark Watson)

embodied energy already invested	29,856,300
energy that would have been taken up by demolition	201,209
new work to provide equivalent buildings	20,986,377
Total MBTU	58,119,900

Net consumption to remove the building and provide the same facilities in new buildings is equivalent to 117,033 kg of carbon dioxide.

Bonnington Bond is a group of large whisky warehouses in Leith, near Edinburgh. Two buildings were first built as a sugar refinery in 1865–66, with very heavy pier and panel walls and fireproof floors. The third was a floor maltings, and the fourth building is a large steel-framed brick-clad whisky warehouse of *c.*1908.

Adaptive re-use can allow greater density of development than would otherwise be permitted. Before they could be converted a case had to be made for changing the zoning from purely industrial to a mix of higher-value office and residential uses. This succeeded, on the basis that it would give these newly listed buildings a future. The phased conversion cut slices out of the deeper buildings to introduce natural light and balconies. Applying a carbon calculator to this site is complicated by the quite substantial elements of demolition, but still more has been retained than lost:

embodied energy already invested	116,400,000
energy that would have been taken up by demolition	1,440,000
new work to provide equivalent buildings	64,990,000
Total MBTU	182,830,000

Finlayson Mill in Tampere was the first big industrial enterprise in Finland. It now has a multiplicity of uses including shops, offices, publishers, pharmaceuticals, a cinema, four different museums and some housing. If it were completely demolished instead, and rebuilt to provide these things to a similar but modern standard, that would have resulted in expenditure of 1,595,040,880 MBTU. In fact, only ten per cent of the floor area was lost and rebuilt in high-rise residential form. Keeping the remaining buildings resulted in a development 55 per cent less costly in terms of embodied energy than if everything sheltered within the complex had been built anew.

The final example is a foundry built of reinforced concrete in 1920–23 by the Société Alsacienne de Constructions Méchaniques in Mulhouse, France. Casting stopped in the early 1960s, and it closed completely around 1980. Formation of a 'ZAC de la Fonderie' from 1991 led in 2002 to redevelopment of the two aisles and a run of sand and graphite silos into a university library, beside other uses. With the insertion of five new floors within the retained framework, the surface area rose from 7,600 m² to 17,316 m². Concrete contains high embodied energy in its thermal mass.

A calculation of the embodied energy shows the gain from re-use:

embodied energy already invested	95,076,000
energy that would have been taken up by demolition	820,800
new work to provide equivalent buildings	216,623,160
Total MBTU	312,519,960

This particularly good result, demonstrating the benefits of adaptive re-use, is obtained because the area was increased by insertion of new floors, and the fact that the 'heavy construction' option in the 1920s means high input of embodied energy, and a putative higher demolition cost in taking away so much reinforced concrete. But other forms of calculation might set the baseline at zero, disregarding past investment in embodied energy, as actual savings in carbon can only be made in the future. Yet the notional demolition and new-build costs would still be substantial.

Conclusion

As operational energy emissions in use fall, embodied carbon will become the main battleground for achieving sustainable development. Industrial buildings, where high embodied energy is often locked into their heavy construction, can play an important part in reducing carbon emissions, but only if they perform a useful role. Those who cherish the industrial landscape need to welcome adaptive re-use and to seek ways to ensure that the needs of tomorrow are partly met in buildings of yesterday.

Acknowledgements

The writer is representing his personal views, not those of his institution. He is grateful to the TICCIH Congress in Freiberg, where they were first aired in 2009, and to feedback received from further evolution of this debate at NTU Athens (Chronocity Erasmus Programme), the Transylvania Trust in Cluj-Napoca, STICK in Glasgow, CILAC in Belfort and Mulhouse, and to colleagues who are doing much to advance the subject, Roger Curtis and Carsten Hermann. Thanks also to Paul Smith, Ewan Hyslop and Katie Hummelt for their helpful comments on drafts.

Further reading

CILAC, Dossier: Reconversions. L'Archeologie Industrielle en France, 2006, No. 49

CILAC, Actes du colloque de Belfort. L'Archaeologie Industrielle en France, Juin 2012, No. 60

GASNIER, M: Patrimoine Industriel et Technique. Lyon: Lieux Dits, 2011

HISTORIC SCOTLAND: Conversion of Traditional Buildings, Guide for Practitioners, 6. Edinburgh, 2007

MENZIES, Gillian F: Technical Paper 13 – Embodied energy considerations. Research Sustainability Building Management. Edinburgh: Historic Scotland, 2011

NATIONAL TRUST FOR HISTORIC PRESERVATION IN AMERICA: The Greenest Building: quantifying the environmental value of building reuse. US, 2012

POWELL K: Architecture Reborn: the conversion and reconstruction of old buildings. London: Lawrence King, 1999

STRATTON, Michael: Industrial Buildings conservation and regeneration. London: E & FN Spon, 2000

19

Post-industrial landscapes

Norbert Tempel

'Landscapes give us an informative impression about the economic and technical development of a particular society; they are, in fact, more informative as they give us a comprehensive, detailed and precise account of the state of the environment in a far better way than any museum could possibly do.'

Walter Benjamin, Passagenwerk

Introduction

As we are all aware, industrial activity changes the environment. Industrial processes have been shaping the landscape for many hundreds of years and have had far-reaching consequences for the ecology of all environmental media. Natural resources are used; soil, water and air are polluted. In fact, every industrial plant can be interpreted as a testimony to the economic reality of its time. Every mill in the past affected its environment directly and indirectly and left an ecological footprint. Today we understand that the consequences of industrial activities are not limited only to a certain region but also lead to changes of global dimensions. In this sense, it is interesting to see that in Western Europe and the United States, environmental consciousness developed in the late 1960s and continued into the 1970s at the same time as interest in the preservation of industrial monuments began to grow.

In most cases when an industrial plant is closed down or a mine is abandoned, the remediation of environmental contamination – the cleaning up of a site so that no traces are left – takes priority over heritage preservation. This way of thinking is hasty and indefensible. Industrial heritage is an essential part of human development and of history. It can tell us a great deal about economic structures as well as about the working conditions – what Marxist theory calls 'relations of production' – of its time. It gives us the chance to reflect on the use, or perhaps abuse, of our resources. It also allows us to reflect upon the pollution and destruction of our environment, social and economic changes, our changing perception of technology and the debates concerning priorities in our society. The contemporary discussion about changing energy production from nuclear to sustainable sources is a good example of this.

Plant species colonising the abandoned lignite open-cast Espenhain mine in Lusatia, Germany, awaiting recultivation in 1990. Industrial nature even includes 'picturesque' ruins of landscapes. (Durka)

The landscapes that have evolved through industrialisation are now themselves endangered through de-industrialisation, yet they are worth protecting. When de-industrialisation is seen as a 'social loss' for a particular region, then preservation becomes important.

This chapter examines the interaction between industry and nature and some special aspects of the handling of post-industrial landscapes, and considers some of the other future tasks for the preservation of industrial monuments, considering the constant conflict between economy and ecology.

The ecological footprint of industry

The geology of our earth has created immense reserves of raw materials, from fossil fuels and uranium to different minerals used in metal-producing industries and for construction purposes. The Industrial Revolution was of course based on the massive exploitation of these resources. Their extraction, however, has left behind particular landscape evidence which cannot be ignored. Often irreparable, long-term environmental damage has been done and extensive social problems have been created as a result of the exploitation of these resources. A significant proportion of the readily accessible fossil fuels has been used in the relatively short time of only 150 years. As the carbon age comes to an end we are increasingly moving to the use of 'green' energy: water, wind and sun and the exploitation of plants as biomass energy.

Economy and ecology have always played an important role in site selection, be it for a mill or a colliery. Access to energy, mineral deposits and other natural resources are as decisive for the success of an industrial venture as political, economical and social factors. The many consequences of industrial activity for the environment should, however, be acknowledged. Mineral extraction and processing as well as industrial plants produce contaminant-laden exhaust and fumes, slag and ashes, heavy metal and toxic products, acids and bases – or even radioactive waste. Even when operating normally, every industrial sector has its own distinctive emission profile that pollutes the environment – air, soil and water – but the material of the plant itself can endanger or harm workers and local people. In most cases, it is only later that the public hears about the risks and side-effects of a process which were unknown, or underestimated, or even kept secret. The global consequences of environmentally unfriendly greenhouse gases – not only caused by industry and traffic but also by industrialised agriculture – have become highly visible.

In addition there is the risk of disasters. The explosion in the pesticide plant in Bhopal, India, on 3 December 1984 – the biggest chemical catastrophe to date with several thousand victims – is one of the best known environmental disasters, followed by the terrible nuclear power plant accidents in Chernobyl 1986 and Fukushima 2011.

For economic reasons, waste that cannot be disposed of was and still is being dumped or burned, even when there are technical solutions or the possibility of recycling. This leads not only to aesthetic problems, such as waste tips. The pollutants can end up in drinking water or in the air. Entire river courses have been sacrificed – straightened, canalised, deepened or used as sewers for waste water. The abstraction of water for industrial processes and the discharge of heated cooling water disturb the ecology of rivers. Gas emissions of methane from old coal mines are not only environmentally unfriendly but remain an explosive hazard in the surroundings of former pits even many years after the mines have been closed down. Lakes that were formed by subsidence caused by mining were regarded as harmful to the image of a region – until their use as an ecological niche was recognised.

Already in the 1950s, first in England and in Wales, scientists had begun to investigate and analyse the flora and fauna of urban and industrial 'brownfields'. They soon discovered that mining waste tips and slag heaps from iron and steel production, for example, offered a special habitat to Mediterranean, coastal and moor vegetation. Moreover, these landscapes were often inhabited by a large population of different species of birds, animals and insects, thus providing an idyllic asylum for many rare species.

Meanwhile the operators of quarries, such as Europe's biggest limestone company, Rheinkalk, in Germany, pursue a clever strategy together with nature conservation groups to create ecological niches for endangered animals and plants and to market the advantages of 'second-hand nature'.

The reaction of society

Many of the consequences mentioned above were already identified and criticised in the early period of industrialisation. However, interventions by the state were limited, and economy was given priority over ecology. In these early years, the people affected sometimes tried to defend themselves by legal means but were seldom successful. Moreover, public authorities intervened only half-heartedly in favour of the neighbours of industrial plants. This continues to be true even today. As regards mining legislation, environmental aspects were not even considered in many industrial countries right up until the 1960s. And even today, in the United States the official protection of the environment, which was foreseen in the reforms of the Mining Laws of 1872, still faces massive resistance from industrial sectors.

The environmental consequences of big open-cast mining are particularly noxious. Conflicts with landscape and nature conservation during the operation are said to be reduced by sanctions (for example a certain management for cut top soil) and the obligation to re-cultivate (re-using land for agriculture or forestry) or re-naturate (creating an artificial natural condition without commercial use) respectively. Today this is explicitly required in German operational permits. In the Rhineland coal-mining district, re-cultivation of areas used by brown-coal mining can look back on a tradition of more than 200 years. Already in 1766 in a lease contract of the Roddergrube mine near Brühl, the first criteria for the rehabilitation of the mining landscape were determined. In 1784, elector Maximilian Frederic enacted the first known Act of Recultivation. In stark contrast to this we can observe that in Africa or Brazil, closed ore mines today at the most only get a barbed wire fence.

However, a typical model for renaturation is generally the vision of a second-hand landscape which should look as natural as possible. Technical elements only disrupt this vision and should be eliminated according to the considerations of conservationists and environmentalists. These pressure groups have always taken an anti-industrial attitude.

Measures to preserve areas of natural beauty and wildlife began in England, France and Germany around 1900. These were seen as aesthetic, ethical and political necessities which were defined in governmental legislation. A hundred years later, we have to confirm that the preservation of nature and the conservation of the environment have been successfully anchored in many of our legal systems. On the other hand, monument conservation, which has always had a weaker position in society anyway, now appears to be even more on the defensive than before.

Environmental awareness and industrial heritage

Zero emissions from industrial production is still an aim for the future. Engineers in the 'good old dirty times' did not waste any effort on this. Resources seemed endless, and nature patient. The starting point for the change was in 1972 with the Limits to Growth Report by the Club of Rome and the Stockholm Conference on the Human Environment, which raised concerns about environmental issues and started a wave of governmental regulation. At this time, the first citizens' action groups such as Greenpeace were formed who opposed the extension of nuclear energy. Through public pressure, some of the most obvious crimes against the environment were reduced. In the 1980s green, ecologically orientated political parties were founded. The problem of abandoned, polluted industrial areas had been recognised. It was clearly not enough just to close and tear down old environmental hazards and then sow grass; the problem was much deeper. Pollution had already leached into the aquifer and had to be disposed of, at considerable expense. To do this, elaborate procedures had to be developed and several proposals were published in the meantime. This way ecology became a giant business for planners and companies. Unfortunately, the usual method for removal of contaminants tends to erase the important traces of industrial history rather than decontaminating the land.

In the United States the expression 'brownfields to greenfields' was coined later. In 1980 the US Congress passed the Comprehensive Environmental Response, Compensation and Liability Act (CERCLA), creating a programme called the Superfund to address the country's legacy of hazardous materials left at abandoned industrial sites. Congress gave the Environmental Protection Agency (EPA) responsibility for administering the Superfund, but did not exempt the EPA or the Superfund from compliance with the National Historic Preservation Act of 1966.

Since the 1980s, historians also have been working on the environmental issues. At that time disused 'uneconomical' large-scale industrial plants such as collieries, coke oven plants, gasworks, blast furnaces, textile, glass and porcelain factories, brickworks and even transport facilities, were seen as essential witnesses to history. These mostly 'bulky' monuments have been turned into industrial or art museums, office buildings, studios, loft apartments, cultural centres, discotheques, shopping malls and so on. In Germany, the federal state of North Rhine-Westphalia paved the way with combative citizens' movements, a new Monuments Act and positive-thinking experts in their ministries and institutions.

Current procedures and future tasks

'It is unique in the world to create in such a short time a completely new artificial landscape covering such a large area.' The International Building Exhibition IBA Fürst-Pückler-Land fashioned 12,200 ha of new watercourses and 42,200 ha new land from a large brown coal open-cast mining area.

During the last few decades, the German model for the recultivation of its brown coal open-cast mines has changed from restoration for agricultural and forestry use to the creation of more varied former mining landscapes with a holistic development of habitats. At the beginning of the twentieth century, large waste heaps were regarded as an aesthetic problem for the landscape, and a lot was done to find acceptable solutions. In 1929 the forest administrator of the Lower Lusatia coal mines in Schipkau, Rudolf Heusohn, said: 'The creation of parks on dump sites and slagheaps leaves space for our imagination and sense of beauty.' Today, decommissioned open-cast mines in Lusatia are being transformed into vacation destinations of unexpected dimensions. Pit heaps of hard coal mining in the Ruhr area have also changed. They used to be deposited like pointed cones and then formed into plateaux; today they are modelled as landscape buildings and planted with grass while deposited – with the future use as leisure facilities already in mind. On top of them one can find sometimes cost-intensive works of aspiring artists or nowadays wind turbines as symbols for post-carbon energy production.

However, an honest handling of the landscape which has been transformed industrially, the conscious preservation and demonstration of traces of industrial activity as an integral part of a post-industrial landscape, are all factors which have only been realised recently.

The International Building Exhibition IBA Emscher Park in the Ruhr set international standards in the 1990s. This idea has been continued by others as we can see in the latest International Building Exhibition IBA Fürst-Pückler-Park (2000–10) in the brown coal area of Lusatia. The acceptance among the population has probably also been influenced by neologisms such as 'industrial nature' in the Ruhr region or 'industrial garden world' in the devastated area of Dessau/Bitterfeld/Wolfen.

Industrial nature is a concept that refers to the regeneration of natural vegetation on industrial sites; the invasion of abandoned or disused industrial sites by colonising species; or new plantings on abandoned, disused or remediated industrial sites. Worthless

A landscape of leisure, the Partwitz Lake was 'renatured' from the former open-cast lignite mine excavations in Lusatia, Germany, part of the International Building Exhibition IBA Fürst-Pückler-Park project (2000-2010). (Gerhard Feiler)

industrial buildings and plant often become integrated into the general picture of landscapes as landmarks, sculptures or as even 'picturesque' ruins.

In the meantime, a new trend has appeared: the increased popular interest in experiencing the value of the bizarre lunar landscapes which were created in Lusatia in the course of the mining there.

David Blackbourne argues in his well-regarded book *The Conquest of Nature – Water, Landscape and the Making of Modern Germany* (2006) that an extensive 'renaturation' should be avoided: artificial aspects in a landscape can also have their own special appeal. Anyway, renaturation and recultivation have limits due to economic and ecological reasons.

Although these new models are more acceptable from the point of view of the industrial culture there is no ideal solution – the ideas of the various players have to be balanced again and again. The production of raw materials, agriculture and forestry, nature conservation, the preservation of historic buildings and monuments, tourism and the needs of a leisure-orientated society that sees itself as post-industrial, are difficult to coordinate.

The argument that tourism creates jobs is often presented since it makes use of an 'intact' landscape in a sustainable way. With their bad image, industrial ruins are often seen as disturbing, and even wind turbines, which produce energy in an eco-friendly way, are regarded as a negatively visual intrusion. The danger of overusing a post-industrial landscape for tourism and event culture is often ignored.

Case study: Rheinfelden hydropower station, Germany

In 2010 the apparently unresolvable conflict between nature conservation and the protection of historic sites achieved an unexpected relevance in the case of the old hydroelectric power station on the river Rhine at Rheinfelden. Since the construction of the new and bigger power plant had a considerable environmental impact, an ecological balance had to be struck. The plans were approved to tear down the old power station in order to create an appropriate ecological compensation. The extremely high historical and technical value of the monument, representing a pioneering plant for the creation of electricity by water power, was not recognised, or, to be honest, was simply ignored by the authorities. With good will and a little care from all concerned the site could have become an extraordinary industrial witness to the use of green energy, with its side-effects and efforts for ecological compensation, which would have been a unique and diverse contribution. Unfortunately this unique monument was destroyed in 2010.

Conclusion

There are many questions that need to be discussed. How can extensive industrial activity be kept lastingly visible, and to what extent can this be expected of the environment and the local residents? Which industrial structures are suitable to be kept as comprehensive examples to our industrial heritage? How to keep their industrial character? How to react to the ephemeral character of most industrial buildings? How to stop 'unwanted' reactions by nature, without being harmful to the environment? Examples are waste heaps that should keep their industrial character, and which should not be turned green – yet, permanent use of herbicides would be unthinkable for ecological reasons. At the moment, many waste heaps are cleaned up, sealed and planted with grass in order to prevent the leaching of heavy metal into ground water – ecologically this is irrefutable. Have we to say good-bye to our 'much-loved' tar and silver lakes (eastern Germany chemistry belt), coloured slag heaps and tamed rivers such as the Emscher, whose riverbed is encased in concrete but not yet renaturalised? Let us stand up for the preservation and development of landscapes as 'sedimented history', may it be highly esteemed or seen as conflict history.

Further reading

FAIR, J Henry: *The Day after Tomorrow. images of our earth in crisis.* Brooklyn, NY: Powerhouse Books, 2010

HAUSER, Susanne: *Metamorphosen des Abfalls. Konzepte für alte Industrieareale.* Frankfurt: Campus, 2001

INTERNATIONAL INSTITUTE FOR ENVIRONMENT AND DEVELOPMENT (ed.): *Breaking New Ground: mining, minerals and sustainable development. The report of the MMSD Project of the IIED.* London: IIED, 2002

QUIVIK, Frederic L: Integrating the Preservation of Cultural Resources with Remediation of Hazardous Materials: an assessment of Superfund's record. *The Public Historian*, Spring 2001, Vol. 23, No. 2, 2001, 47–61

UNITED STATES ENVIRONMENTAL PROTECTION AGENCY – OFFICE OF SOLID WASTE AND EMERGENCY RESPONSE (ed.): *Revitalizing America's Mills. a report on Brownfields Mill Project.* Washington: EPA, 2006

20

Industrial ruins

Masaaki Okada

Introduction

In recent years old or obsolete structures of civil engineering facilities, industrial plants and buildings have begun to be revalued positively, either as historic or local heritage, or from the perspectives of industrial archaeology, the history of architecture and technology, or from the point of view of local development. These values generally consist of local or technical history or contemporary design. However, the values of ruined industrial structures themselves should not be limited only to the story or meaning lying behind their existence. The landscape created by the decayed or rugged surfaces could be another value of industrial heritage. How, then, do we recognise and realise such aesthetic values? What values do people discover when they visit and see industrial ruins? How are these values categorised? This chapter aims to illuminate the values of the landscapes of industrial abandonment, referring to the value of ruined landscapes found in British 'Picturesque' gardens of the eighteenth century and to Japanese traditional aesthetics of 'Wabi-Sabi'.

Present industrial ruins

Many industrialised countries experienced remarkable economic growth from the eighteenth to the twentieth centuries, with heavy industrialisation and rapid urbanisation. Now the industrial age is drawing to a close, a very considerable quantity of industrial heritage remains. Some has already been recognised as cultural heritage; much, however, continues to survive in the form of abandoned ruins.

Economic decline has occurred in many industries, creating factory ruins and abandoned mines, and similar phenomena can be found all over the world. Popular enthusiasm for the cultural values of abandoned industrial sites is, however, apparent. Railway trails are among the most significant and popular forms of industrial ruin for hiking and discovering the testimonies of the past such as platforms, bridges, tunnels or rails. The conversion of New York's elevated railway into the popular High Line provides a spectacular instance of the appeal of abandoned lines and their cultural potential. Several guidebooks introducing railway trails have been published, and walking or cycling along old railway routes is growing in popularity.

So, too, the ruins of defence works. Coastal defences, air-raid shelters or gun

Case study: Gasworks Park, Seattle

Arguably the pioneering instance of the active conservation of large-scale industrial ruins for their aesthetic value is the former coal gasification plant in Seattle, Washington. The gasworks closed down in 1956 and re-opened as the main element in the new public park some twenty years later. The decision was justified for the gasworks' 'historic, aesthetic and utilitarian value', the last such plant in the US. It has a strong 'eye-catcher' value, on a spectacular shore of Lake Union and surrounded by green turf, its *sachlich* quality perhaps enhanced by contemporary graffiti. (Joe Mabel, GNU)

Case study: Gunkanjima Island, Japan

Gunkanjima in the East China Sea is nick-named Battleship Island because of its long, ship-like profile. It is also called Ghost Island, and since 1974 it is only ghosts who have inhabited it. A hundred years earlier, the first miners came to the island to access undersea coal, an important ingredient in Japan's rapid industrialization. The population of this unique miners' village peaked in 1959, when over 5,000 were squeezed on to the island, some housed in the earliest concrete apartment blocks erected in Japan.

Tourists started making the 50-minute crossing from Nagasaki in 2009, stimulated by international photographic exhibitions of the crumbling concrete, to experience directly the atmosphere of this eerie landscape of industrial abandonment. (Jordy Theiller, GNU)

Case study: Emscher Park, Germany

The heritage-led recovery and economic revival of the great coal-mining and steel-producing region in western Germany is discussed in several sections of this book. Here it is included as perhaps the most cited example of the assimilation and integration of industrial ruins into a living environment. The highly successful decision of the International Building Exhibition (IBA) to retain many of the old steel structures, concrete stores, pipelines and waste heaps, and leave them to turn spontaneously into

a landscape of re-natured ruins, has been vindicated by the visits of hundreds of thousands of tourists, and the approach has been copied and adapted all over the world. Discussion has moved on from the wisdom of the original decision to examine how much conservation is compatible with retaining the 'cool' industrial ruin's surface, or may it in fact mar the aesthetic of decay? (Benjamin Fragner)

Case study: Clot del Moro cement museum, Spain

Masonry ruins present contrasting conservation challenges as well as aesthetic qualities to metal ones. The early twentieth-century Portland cement factory outside Barcelona suffered decades of severe weathering after it was abandoned in 1975. When it reopened as a museum thirty years later only a part was restored, in order to accommodate an exhibition on cement production and the history of the strange factory, while the remainder of the structure has been allowed to continue along the path determined by nature. Encrustment of the walls with half a century of solidified cement dust has added to the 'picturesque' character of this remote, mountainous site. (MNACTEC) platforms constructed before the end of World War II had been completely ignored in Japan until recent years. Scholars in the field of the history of civil engineering have been surveying them mainly from the view of the history of technology. Meanwhile, increasing numbers of enthusiasts of ruins have begun showing their explorations of old defence bases on their web sites as places to be discovered.

Some obsolete civil engineering sites have already been recognised for their value as technological or regional heritage, but most of them are still ruins which attract little attention, even when they have a high potential as cultural landscapes. On the other hand, there are cases of former industrial facilities such as the Kanamori Warehouse in Hokkaido or Sorimachi Lock Bridge in Ibaragi, which have been listed for their historical significance, but which are completely cleaned and restored to look brand-new so that visitors can see how they worked, or just to make them feel more comfortable. While this may be an appropriate way of encouraging visitors, at the same time there should be some other ways to respect the passage of time itself and the landscape it has created.

What values can be defined and stressed for old industrial sites?

One of the significant aspects must be the landscape of ruins. 'Ruin' is often understood in a negative way, as something dead or decadent. However, it is also possible to take ruins in a much more positive or even creative way: ruin is what industrial heritage obtains as its essential characteristics through the passage of time, i.e. the revelation of history itself.

There are enthusiasts who love ruins. If this seems too fanatical, even fetishistic, there is an existing viewpoint to help make it something enjoyable for many people. Understanding of the aesthetics of ruins may lead us to think of rich ways to show industrial heritage as even more 'real'. Two approaches to the appreciation of the aesthetics ruins can be found in Europe and in Asia.

Eighteenth-century Picturesque gardens

When we attempt to determine the value of the landscape of contemporary ruins, British landscape gardens of the eighteenth century form a worthwhile reference point. In spite of the differences of age or social background, we may abstract the value of landscapes of ruins from aesthetic attitudes which position them as a part of Picturesque landscapes.

Picturesque ruin landscapes fall into different categories. The first type produce a diversity of landscape composition, working as 'eye-catchers'. In this sense, the superficial landscape property of the ruin is applied rather than its metaphorical meaning. In general, scales, colours or textures of man-made facilities are quite different from ones of nature. This may suggest the possibility of industrial ruins to generate apparent contrasts with natural landscape.

Picturesque gardens, even man-made structures, were designed to be integrated into the natural surroundings. In this meaning, ruins are appropriate elements since they were also formed (or at least, seem to have been formed) through natural processes such as weathering, natural corrosion or physical collapse. Industrial facilities are generally formed through the process of material efficiency, of construction, economy, or of management, which are all without aesthetic intent: the 'taste of industrial architecture is paradoxically discovered as elements without aesthetic intent' (Harbinson). Furthermore, subsequent weathering processes add the atmosphere of nature to the surface of industrial ruins.

Finally, ruins in picturesque gardens reflected the elegance of ephemera. They represent metaphysically the notion of change, transition, decay or wilderness. To express sanctity or dignity, ruins often take the form of ancient Gothic architecture or Grecian temples. Industrial facilities generally have a super-human scale and may bear the transcendent or sublime image.

Japanese 'Wabi-Sabi' aesthetics

Considering the essential value of ruins, Japanese traditional aesthetics, 'Wabi' and 'Sabi', may also be quite helpful. Neither term is easy to translate into English, but 'Wabi' is generally understood as 'enjoyment of a quiet, leisurely life free from worldly concerns', and 'Sabi' as 'quiet simplicity, lonely, austere beauty'.

Wabi originated in the medieval eremitic tradition, and emphasizes a simple, austere, serene or transcendental frame of mind. This aesthetic is clearly reflected in the tea ceremony, or *haiku* (a traditional Japanese poem comprising 5-7-5 syllables). Ascetic literati valued poverty and loneliness as 'liberation from material and emotional worries'. In addition, the absence of apparent beauty could be considered as something of even higher beauty, which has substantial connection with 'Zen'. Such aesthetics make much of simplicity and incompleteness, preferring, for instance, the incomplete moon, partly hidden by clouds, to the full moon.

On the other hand, *Sabi* is the ancient poetic ideal fostered by Bashō Matsuo (1644–94). *Sabi* looks for loneliness, resignation and tranquillity, and the aesthetic ideal of the tea ceremony. It introduces 'old' or 'old-looking' things to a positive view. For instance, the 'Koryo-dynasty tea bowl' in the sixteenth century is one of the best examples to aid a proper visual understanding of Japanese 'Wabi-Sabi' aesthetics. In the tea ceremony, tea-bowls play important roles to emphasize the artistic atmosphere, and many kinds of bowls are used. In the latter part of the seventeenth century, Japanese tea enthusiasts ordered tea bowls from Korea, and these were intentionally produced to look old and crude, even if they were newly created.

This 'Wabi-Sabi' aesthetic implies a very important philosophy, the possibility of generating an aesthetic value in something old and crude, and the fact that this naturally generated value is something we can intentionally create (or is worth preserving).

Industrial heritage = industrial facility + ruin

Japanese aesthetician Atsushi Tanigawa pointed out that the value of ruined landscapes is formed by superficial characteristics: irregularity, diversity, chaos or coarseness. In terms of the aesthetics, this value can be called *sachlich* (factual) beauty which is generated by natural weathering processes, with little relation to the original use.

What is even more interesting is that *sachlich* also means 'practical'. In this meaning, industrial heritage possesses two overlapping values of *sachlich*-ness; one as a ruin and the other is as an industrial facility, generally formed with practical process such as function, efficiency or dynamics. Both in the process of its creation of form and in the subsequent weathering process, industrial heritage takes on *sachlich* forms, such as primitive, geometric, symmetrical or rectangular shapes, and with the passage of time it take on other *sachlich* forms such as crude, dirty, cracked, corrupted, warped or partially destroyed. These two *sachlich* values are substantial aesthetic properties of industrial heritage to emphasize its 'substantial' appearance. That should be taken into account in considering their preservation.

Conclusions

For the interpretation of industrial heritage, an emphasis on the history or original use of a site is one of the key elements. In order to make visitors more comfortable or to help them understand, the enhancement of places or landscapes is also to some extent effective. On the other hand, we should remember that our heritage has experienced the passage of time and that this is what makes it a valuable historic testimony. This means that the passage of time is another substantial element possessed by heritage, and therefore can be an important factor in its preservation. This emphasis can lead to the generation of different landscape values as industrial ruins.

Further reading

EDENSOR, T: *Industrial Ruins, Space, Aesthetics and Materiality*. Oxford: Berg, 2005
HARBISON, R: *The Built, the Unbuilt, and the Unbuildable – In Pursuit of Architectural Meaning*. Cambridge: MIT Press, 1993
OKADA, M: Industrial Heritage and Ruin Landscape. *JSCE Newsletter of Committee on Historical Studies in Civil Engineering*, No.37, 2009
TANIGAWA, A: *Aesthetics of Ruins*. Tokyo: Shueisha, 2003

21

Conservation and
community consciousness

Hsiao-Wei Lin

Introduction

Most regeneration projects in the area of industrial heritage are concerned with the functional and social elements of the sites in question. The decline of industry often has a strong impact on local regions, as people lose their jobs, factories are abandoned, towns decline, and deserted industrial landscapes are left behind. Regenerating the industrial heritage requires a strong community consciousness to sustain its long-term operation. In western countries, different trust organizations often lead the major conservation and re-use work. Three well-known examples from the United Kingdom would be the Ironbridge Gorge Museum Trust, the New Lanark Conservation Trust and the Blaenavon Partnership, which all involved a broad range of experts, scholars and local communities in the revival of their local areas. However, in Asia, non-governmental organizational development is still not as popular as in the West. How, then, has the emergence of community consciousness been fostered? The example of a small paper-making village, Jyy-Liau-Uo in Taiwan, its cultural landscape and conservation process, provides a positive example for the conservation of cultural and industrial heritage by fostering local community consciousness within a cultural landscape and family history.

In the three examples cited above, the participation and identity of the local community played an important role in the research, re-use and maintenance of the sites. Moreover, the cultural landscape of industrial heritage demands a sustainable way of living. The conservation of Jyy-Liau-Uo Paper Village and its re-use plan have been proceeding since 2007 and demonstrate the process of the conservation for a declining paper village, the development of local community consciousness, and how they re-use their industrial characteristics. It will evaluate the related issues of traditional industrial heritage on cultural landscape, regional regeneration and civic participation.

Background

The geographical characteristics of Taiwan form the base of diverse biological and ecological features. Industrial development was generated by various resources of farming and mining products, and technologies were brought in by different political powers at various stages. Much of the preserved industrial heritage, such as tobacco workshops, sugar factories, salt fields and forestry, represent the interaction between inhabitants and the land. Under the challenge of the global economy and the decline of local industry, community involvement has turned to be the driving force and foundation of conservation work in the past ten years in Taiwan.

The Movement of Local Community Empowerment started in 1994. It is not only a social movement but has also become the major force for the conservation of cultural as well as industrial heritage. For example, the Council for Cultural Affairs in Taiwan has promoted the Policy of Local Cultural Museum (PLCM) since 2001. As of 2009, there are 278 local cultural museums established all over the island. Among them, more than 48 museums are related to industrial heritage, especially traditional industries such as mining, coal, tea, salt, ceramics and so on. As one of the major subjects of local cultural museums, the conservation and interpretation of industrial heritage plays an important role in the regeneration of declining industrial areas within a global context. The conservation project of Jyy-Liau-Uo Paper Village, based on a 200-year-old history of making paper, provides a model for regional regeneration through cultural and industrial heritage.

The conservation process

Empowerment of local community consciousness is a major concept for the conservation of small industrial sites like the Jyy-Liau-Uo Paper Village. Since 2007, the residents of Jyy-Liau-Uo have co-operated closely with the research term of Chung Yuan Christian University and other professionals. From 2007 to 2009, the researchers organized an historical and environmental survey, a regeneration plan for the paper-making industry, and community training courses together with local residents. These resulted in the establishment of the Liu Chuan Lao Paper Making Cultural Society, the construction of new paper-making workshops and regular community participation in guided tours. The village of 96 people is transforming its traditional industrial heritage and becoming an educational site for paper making with an ecological tour based on its 200-year history. Moreover, in 2011, a serious effort was put into realizing the site as a centre for environmental education. A documentary film about the history, tradition, paper industry and environment of the village was made. An educational pack and guide maps have been developed together with the community and the nearby primary school. In addition, its website and blog attract many people to come and visit this site.

Beside the involvement of the professional team, two local community organizations, the Worship Society of Liu Chuan Lao and the Liu Chuan Lao Paper Making Cultural Society, provide major support for the conservation of the village. The Worship Society of Liu Chuan Lao is a typical Chinese family-based society which has a long history going back to 1880 and every descendant of Liu Chuan Lao must be a member. The Society is therefore the spiritual centre of the Liu family and controls the public estate resource of Jyy-Liau-Uo. The Worship Society of Liu Chuan Lao has given strong support to the new conservation development. It provides common land to build the paper-making workshop and covers some routine expenses. The new organization is the Liu Chuan Lao Paper Making Cultural Society which was established after the community training course in 2008. The aim of the society is to conserve and sustain the paper-making culture. It is the major operational body for the management of guided tours and community events for the workshop. Over the years, the members of the society have learned about conservation and are able to lead the workshops, organize exhibitions and guide tours of the village. Together with the support from the professional team, they aim to make this village an educational site for paper-making, ecological and cultural tours. In fact, its development shows the path for the regeneration of rural villages through their cultural and environmental heritage.

Good practice in community-led regeneration

During this conservation and regeneration process, several steps can be identified which are useful for some rural traditional industrial heritage development.

Survey on the history and people

The principal residents of Jyy-Liau-Uo are descendants of Liu Chuan Lao and are also the land owners. The arrival from China of Liu Chuan Lao (1764–1836), who chose this valley for farming and making bamboo paper, is recorded on a land rental document dating from 1805. His property was large enough to be divided between six descendants, and some common area along the stream is managed by the Worship Society of Liu Chuan Lao. Their close family relationship can be seen on the nearly 2,000 participants of seven generations joining the annual spring worship, although only 38 families and 96 people normally live in the village. A thorough survey of their family history built up the confidence of community people to share their knowledge and story to guests and they are proud of their own history. The support from the Worship Society of Liu Chuan Lao and the newly established Liu Chuan Lao Paper Making Cultural Society is a strong base for this process of conservation and transformation.

A long-term community training course

Between 2007 and 2011, a series of community training courses have been introduced to the community. These include the subjects related to finding family history, drawing a community map, the re-use of cultural heritage, paper and bamboo handcrafts, ecological workshop, guiding skills, related site visits and so on. The aim is to generate a common vision for the long-term development of the area. In fact, through these courses, the community decided to set up the Liu Chuan Lao Paper Making Cultural Society for the operation of the site. In addition, the outcome of the courses is reflected later in the content of educational packs and leaflets. Nowadays, during the weekends and weekdays, the community residents lead the guided tours and paper-making activities.

Discover the natural character of the site

Discovering of the natural character of the site helps to understand the local development history and appreciate the cultural landscape. *Uo*, '窩' in Chinese, means a typical valley topography with one point of access. The natural resources of this valley attracted the Liu family to settle here. Jyy-Liau-Uo is between 96 to 190 metres above sea level and is rich in bamboo plantations and there are three natural springs, making it an ideal location for paper production. It also developed a water supply system with bamboo pipes for making paper and farming. This traditional industrial settlement shows a good use of natural resources and human activities. The springs provide basic water

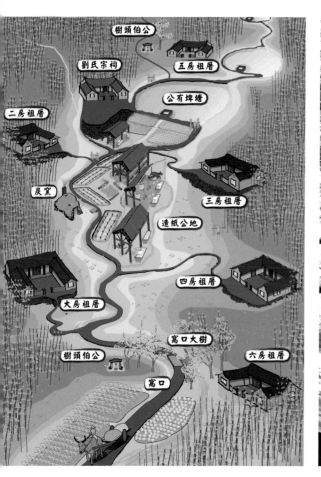

Guided tour maps like this one were prepared by villagers working with the professional team. The route forms the spinal column of the workshops, guided tours and community events which seek to replace the old paper-making economy. (Hsiao-Wei Lin)

The present natural and cultural scenery of the paper-making village, Jyy-Liau-Uo in Taiwan. (Bo-Chi Chan)

for agriculture and producing paper. Ponds and a drainage stream were formed along the main road through the valley. In addition, there were some typical plants (such as spiky *Oldham Scolopia*, Thorny Bamboo) which were planted as a fence to divide the boundary of the village area and defend them against intruders. There are also ancient trails for transporting goods from the valley to the neighbouring town and which now are popular for hiking.

Read the industrial cultural landscape

The land-use of this settlement is an integrated demonstration of cultural landscape with living, production and farming functions. Production of paper is a labour-intensive and seasonal job. Most villagers would be involved with the related works. Bamboo must be cut in the spring then soaked in water with lime powder for two months. Then it can be used to make paper. During the two-month break, farming of vegetables and fruits generates income and creates a beautiful farming landscape in the village. Paper production and farming are gathered in the central flat area along the main road and stream as a working zone. Houses are situated on the gentle slope area as a living area. The surrounding mountain provides the bamboo for paper production.

Due to the topographical limitations, transportation and most of all family traditions, the land, and also the trees, are kept by Liu families. The whole landscape is therefore able to avoid large-scale developments and retains its traditional character and cultural landscape.

Define industrial and cultural heritage

The remains of the paper industry form the special character of Jyy-Liau-Uo. Paper production was introduced from China to Taiwan in the 1880s. In the early stages it was located in the centre of Taiwan and used bamboo as the raw material. This paper product was for worship ceremonies. The paper made in Jyy-Liau-Uo is also bamboo worship paper, and production continued until the 1950s. Tools such as press stone wheels still lie in the Jhih-Liao-Wo. A pond from a natural spring still functions for agricultural activities. In addition, the surrounding bamboo forest is the best explanation for the origins of the paper industry here. In fact, Jyy-Liau-Uo is special because its surrounding settlement demonstrates a long history of migrants who lived here and produced with its natural resources.

Today, there is a community-built Chuan Lao Pavilion (1995) which collects some of the old paper-making tools, a community paper workshop for exhibitions, guided tours and paper activities, and a wheel pavilion with a reconstructed wooden grinder, and a paper press made by the community to demonstrate the production processes. Although they are not historical buildings, they have become the symbol of a community centre for hosting related cultural events. They represent the emerging local community consciousness within its cultural landscape of the industrial heritage and family history.

In addition to the remains of industrial heritage, there are five traditional family houses. Some of them have more than one hundred years of history. There are also temples to worship gods and Cai Lun, the inventor of ancient paper. These religious traditions date from the 1800s.

Conclusion

Conservation of the industrial heritage has often been focused on large sites and their redevelopment through adaptive re-use, urban regeneration, museums or tourism. However, how do we contend with those small and traditional industrial heritage sites which are not as attractive as the more imposing ones? The conservation process of Jyy-Liau-Uo Paper Village certainly provides a positive example of industry-based renewal for fostering local community consciousness. This site and its conservation process have provided the context for a good co-operation with a professional team and the empowerment of the local community. The uniqueness of the strong family ties and traditional attitudes to the land is the base for this industrial cultural landscape. This close relationship between the people and the land is of precious value in today's industrialized world. The continuing lifestyle and land-use represent the essence of cultural landscape.

The experience of this project illustrates important issues of industrial heritage: why do we conserve the industrial heritage? What is heritage? How should we conserve it?

The combination of natural and cultural resources in Jyy-Liau-Uo represents a validity of societal context in terms of the regional development of a small-scale industrial heritage. This movement provides emotional support and an economic return for the declining traditional industry. It fulfils the mental and strategic levels of conservation work for the region.

The heritage of Jyy-Liau-Uo includes the complete setting which formulated the industry. It echoes the conservation concepts of authentic and contextual conservation of the Nizhny Tagil Charter. The focus of the industrial heritage of Jyy-Liau-Uo is not only on its materials, tools, and building artifacts, but also on family values, environmental protection and community empowerment.

Finally, the methodological and operational approach of this site linked different professionals and community. The close co-operation during the process of survey, re-use planning and community course and community participation shows an impressive outcome of the local cultural tourism development. Jyy-Liau-Uo now has its own website which is operated regularly by community members. It is developing toward an educational site for industrial heritage, ecological and cultural tours with community empowerment.

Further reading

ALFREY, Judith and PUTNAM Tim: *The industrial heritage – managing resources and uses*, London: Routledge, 2003

LIN, Hsiao-Wei and Chun-Ming HUANG (eds): *Introduction to Taiwan's Industrial Heritage*, Taichung: Headquarters Administration of Cultural Heritage, Council for Cultural Affairs, 2011

LIN, Hsiao-Wei: *Report of 2011 Regional Cultural Heritage Strategic Planning in Jhih-Liao-Wo Paper Making Village, Hsinchu County*. Jhubei: Cultural Affairs Bureau of Hsinchu County Government, 2011

22

Industrial Heritage and the World Heritage Convention

Peter Stott

Introduction

The Convention concerning the Protection of the World Cultural and Natural Heritage, better known as 'The World Heritage Convention,' is an international treaty to recognize, promote and protect the world's natural and cultural heritage considered to be of 'Outstanding Universal Value'. Each year, natural and cultural sites which meet this standard are added to the World Heritage List by the 21-government World Heritage Committee, an executive body elected on a rotating basis every two years by all countries that are signatory to the Convention meeting in General Assembly. As of November 2011, 188 nations ('States Parties') had adhered to the Convention, making it the most widely adopted international environmental treaty. The World Heritage List itself currently consists of 936 natural and cultural sites, ranging from the Taj Mahal in India to the Grand Canyon in the United States; from Australia's Great Barrier Reef to Chartres Cathedral in France.

The List is often referred to as 'UNESCO's World Heritage List' because the United Nations Educational, Scientific and Cultural Organization (UNESCO), based in Paris, was instrumental in the establishment of the Convention and today, through UNESCO's World Heritage Centre, provides the Secretariat for the Committee. The concept of the List, itself, however, derives from a United States proposal in 1965 for an international list to identify and protect cultural and natural heritage similar to the UN List of National Parks and Equivalent Reserves adopted by the United Nations a few years earlier. At a 1972 Expert Meeting hosted by UNESCO, the List concept was merged with UNESCO's proposal for a 'Red Cross for monuments', and the resulting international instrument was adopted by the UNESCO General Conference later the same year.

Guidelines for inscription

Fifteen countries were elected to the World Heritage Committee in November 1976, which held its first meeting at UNESCO headquarters in Paris the following June. Its principal order of business was the adoption of its working methods. In addition to a

Rules of Procedure for the conduct of Committee sessions, the Committee also adopted its *Operational Guidelines for the Implementation of the World Heritage Convention*, today the definitive guide for anyone wishing to understand how sites are inscribed on the List. The key feature of the first *Operational Guidelines* was the adoption of natural and cultural criteria which would interpret how 'outstanding universal value' should be evaluated. The criteria were developed by the two 'Advisory Bodies' named in the Convention to evaluate properties for the Committee: the International Council on Monuments and Sites (ICOMOS) and the International Union for the Conservation of Nature (IUCN). IUCN proposed four criteria for natural properties; ICOMOS developed six criteria for cultural properties. These criteria have been modified by the Committee over the intervening years. However, to understand the Convention's application to industrial heritage it is important to appreciate how the cultural criteria might be applied. To be inscribed on the World Heritage List, cultural properties must meet at least one of the following criteria and

(i)   represent a masterpiece of human creative genius;

(ii) exhibit an important interchange of human values, over a span of time or within a cultural area of the world, on developments in architecture or technology, monumental arts, town-planning or landscape design;

(iii) bear a unique or at least exceptional testimony to a cultural tradition or to a civilization which is living or which has disappeared;

(iv) be an outstanding example of a type of building, architectural or technological ensemble or landscape which illustrates (a) significant stage(s) in human history;

(v)   be an outstanding example of a traditional human settlement, land-use, or sea-use which is representative of a culture (or cultures), or human interaction with the environment especially when it has become vulnerable under the impact of irreversible change; [or]

(vi) be directly or tangibly associated with events or living traditions, with ideas, or with beliefs, with artistic and literary works of outstanding universal significance. (The Committee considers that this criterion should preferably be used in conjunction with other criteria).

Although it is today less easy to recognize, cultural criterion (iv) was designed for industrial heritage. Ernest Allen Connally, Secretary General of ICOMOS at the time, was personally responsible for much of the wording. (Connally had been the first chief of the Office of Archaeology and Historic Preservation in the US National Park Service, the parent agency to the National Register of Historic Places, and there are noticeable similarities between the National Register and World Heritage criteria.) In notes for an unfinished manuscript on the history of the World Heritage Convention, Connally wrote that criterion (iv) 'was expressly constructed to provide for inscription on the World Heritage List of transcendentally significant structures that would not classify as buildings. We were thinking primarily of engineering structures, such as bridges, tunnels, canals, etc. ICOMOS [Connally wrote] was quite aware of the new discipline of industrial archaeology which had taken rise in the 1950s.' As adopted by the Committee

The second 'industrial' complex to be inscribed on the World Heritage List was the Royal Saltworks of Arc-et-Senans (1775). Open-pan salt production techniques probably counted less for its inclusion than the monumental architecture, characteristic of Ancien Régime industrial ventures. (Peter Stott)

in 1977, properties meeting criterion (iv) should 'be among the most characteristic examples of a type of structure, the type representing an important cultural, social, artistic, scientific, technological or industrial development'.

The key word was 'structure'. This intention was lost when the Committee revised the criterion in 1984, substituting the words 'building or architectural ensemble' for 'structure'. The concept was reintroduced in 1995 with the phrase 'technological ensemble'. Although most nominations justify outstanding universal value by reference to more than one criterion, despite the changing phrasing of the criterion, nominations for industrial heritage are invariably justified under criterion (iv).

Industrial WHS

Curiously, the first two industrial properties entered on the World Heritage List were both representative of European salt production: the Wieliczka Salt Mine (Poland, 1978) and the Royal Saltworks of Arc-et-Senans (France, 1982 – expanded in 2009 under the revised name 'From the Great Saltworks of Salins-les-Bains to the Royal Saltworks of Arc-et-Senans, the production of open-pan salt'). It could be argued that while both recognized the industrial technology of salt, both nominations were also aided by their aesthetic appeal – the salt sculptures left by workers at Wieliczka and the monumental architecture of Claude Nicolas Ledoux at Arc-et-Senans. Three years after Arc-et-Senans, the first two Roman aqueducts were entered on the List: the Pont du Gard (France) and the Roman Aqueduct at Segovia. (Spain had proposed the aqueduct by itself, but ICOMOS recommended that the nomination be expanded to include the town, and the site was inscribed as the Old Town of Segovia and its Aqueduct.) Ironbridge Gorge, the icon of industrial archaeology, was among the first group of nominations proposed by the United Kingdom in 1986 after its ratification of the Convention two years before. Today, with seven industrial sites on the List, the UK leads in its recognition of industrial heritage, followed by Germany with four properties, and France, India, Netherlands, Sweden and Spain with three sites each.

After 1986, the number of sites representing industrial heritage expanded rapidly. Ironworks, mines and mining towns were often represented among the annual inscriptions. Two years after an expert group meeting held on the Rideau Canal in Canada in September 1994, and the publication of TICCIH and ICOMOS' *The International Canal Monuments List*, the first canal, the Canal du Midi (France) was added to the List. (The Rideau Canal itself would not be inscribed until 2007.) The first railway, the Semmering Railway (Austria) appeared on the list in 2009, followed only a year later by the first of a series of Indian mountain railways, the Darjeeling, a nomination sponsored by the Indian Railway Ministry that would become a significant multiple property or 'serial' nomination of railway lines in different parts of India. The range of industrial and engineering heritage continued to expand in the first decade of the twentieth century with sites inscribed for radio communication (Varberg Radio Station, Sweden); irrigation systems (the Dujiangyan Irrigation System, China; Aflaj Irrigation System of Oman); a transporter bridge (Vizcaya Bridge, Spain) and a ten-country chain of historic geodetic survey points (the Struve Geodetic Arc). Depending on how industrial heritage is counted, approximately fifty properties since 1978 have been inscribed specifically to represent industrial and engineering heritage.

Since 1980, the Committee has requested that, prior to nomination, properties should be included on the country's 'Tentative List', an inventory of properties meeting the criteria which the State intends to propose for inscription. In theory, Tentative Lists can provide the Committee and the Advisory Bodies with a global overview of the range of property types against which to compare current nominations; in practice a variety of political and institutional constraints usually limit the ability of countries to fulfil the Committee's broader agenda. Nevertheless, while the Tentative Lists (available online through the World Heritage Centre's website) are not vetted by ICOMOS or IUCN for their appropriateness, they do provide a general indication of the future direction of the List.

As the World Heritage List has become better known, aided certainly by the World Heritage Centre's use of its website beginning in 1996, so political pressure for inscription has grown exponentially, not only on the Committee and its Advisory Bodies, but on the national ministries or government agencies responsible for making the nominations, pressured by local municipalities and legislators. Tourist dollars are seen as the prime advantage of World Heritage inscription, and outside observers have increasingly questioned whether the list is truly representative of the world's outstanding heritage and has not been diluted by the inscription of lesser-quality sites. While the World Heritage Fund, to which every State Party must contribute, can provide limited funds for training or projects (often seed money) for some World Heritage sites in less-developed countries, it can in no sense be considered a raison d'être for inscription.

Safeguarding world heritage

Protection afforded to sites by the Convention has grown as the Convention has matured. Initially seen as a largely honorary designation with few requirements beyond meeting the criteria, over time the Committee has increasingly been concerned that sites proposed for inscription should have adequate regulatory or legislative protection and a management system in place at the time of inscription. These requirements are outlined in the *Operational Guidelines*, but both protective measures and management systems vary according to the ability of the national authority to develop and implement them. In some instances, management plans put in place for the purpose of satisfying the requirements at the time of inscription, have been allowed to lapse. In theory, these deficiencies should be recognized in the Periodic Reports that States Parties are required to submit on the state of conservation of sites in their own country, but as these reports are prepared by the State Party itself, management deficiencies at sites can be overlooked.

The Committee has relatively few sanctions it can apply to correct conditions at sites. At each Committee session, the Secretariat and the Advisory Bodies present reports on the state of conservation of sites either reported to it, or reports that the Committee itself has requested. The principal 'sanction' available to the Committee is inscription of a site on the List of World Heritage in Danger. The Committee tries to view this step as a positive measure, but its use is controversial. Between 1979 and 1991, the nine inscriptions on the Danger List were all at the request of the States Parties concerned who all saw the designation as a vehicle for awareness-raising and a tool to stimulate increased funding. Following the shelling of the World Heritage city of Dubrovnik, Croatia, by the Yugoslav army in 1991, the Committee began to take a much more aggressive approach and decided that in certain cases, its most effective assistance to a property could be 'the message sent by inclusion of a site on the List of World Heritage in Danger' without such a request being made by the State Party in which the site was located. In 1992 the Committee inscribed seven sites on the List of World Heritage in Danger, four without the consent of the State Party. The United States, which chaired the Committee that year, championed the Committee's prerogative to make such inscriptions unilaterally. From the start, too, it had been convinced that 'inscription on the List of World Heritage in Danger should not be seen as a sanction, but as the acknowledgement of a condition that calls for safeguarding measures, and as a means of securing resources for that purpose'. To prove its point (and with behind-the-scenes encouragement), it did not object when the Committee inscribed both the Everglades and Yellowstone National Park on the List in Danger in 1993 and 1995, respectively. However, few other countries on the receiving end of such designations felt the same way. Debates over this tool became increasingly rancorous, and today, without such a request from the State Party concerned, inscription of a site on the List of World Heritage Danger is rare. As of February 2012, there are 34 properties on the list of World Heritage in Danger, including one industrial heritage site, Chile's Humberstone and Santa Laura Saltpeter Works, inscribed on the List in Danger in 2005, simultaneously with inscription on the World Heritage List itself. The fragility of the buildings, many constructed with local materials and light-weight construction, and a 40-year absence of maintenance, was identified as a clear threat to the site, according to ICOMOS. Nevertheless, the Committee agreed with the Advisory Body evaluation that the Humberstone and Santa Laura sites were clearly of outstanding universal value.

The four hydraulic boatlifts on the Canal du Centre, La Louvière and Le Roeulx (1888-1917) in Belgium are testimony to the remarkable hydraulic engineering developments of nineteenth-century Europe and were inscribed in 1998. The elevators are double, consisting of two vertically mobile caissons, hydraulically linked in such a way that one caisson rises as the other descends. (Peter Stott)

Sanctions

The ultimate sanction the Committee can apply is removal of a site from the World Heritage List itself. Although there is not the same debate about the Committee's right to take this action, until 2007, the Committee had never taken such a step, and many wondered whether it would ever have the political courage to do so. However, the step was made easier by a voluntary request for delisting by Oman in 2007. After unsuccessful efforts to reverse the decline of the Arabian Oryx in its native habitat, Omani authorities decided that only a captive breeding program would be successful. Accordingly, the authorities reduced the size of the site by 90 per cent and requested that the Committee remove the Arabian Oryx Sanctuary from the World Heritage List. This action became a key precedent for the second delisting two years later, when after several years of discussion, the Committee and German authorities came to an impasse over the impact of a new bridge over the River Elbe on the World Heritage site of Dresden Elbe Valley. After a long debate, the Committee concluded that its own credibility as well as the credibility of the List were at stake. The Committee ultimately decided that the site should be delisted. As a result of these two delistings, the Committee has an additional tool in its array of sanctions, one that many thoughtful observers believe is long overdue.

Further reading

JOKILEHTO, J, comp., *et al.*: *The World Heritage List: Filling the Gaps – An Action Plan for the Future. Monuments and Sites XII.* Paris: International Council on Monuments and Sites, 2005

JOKILEHTO, J: *The World Heritage List. What is OUV? Defining the Outstanding Universal Value of Cultural World Heritage Properties. Monuments and Sites XVI.* Paris: International Council on Monuments and Sites, 2008

PRESSOUYRE, L: *The World Heritage Convention, twenty years later.* Paris: UNESCO Publishing, 1996. (Originally published 1992 as La Convention du Patrimoine Mondial, vingt ans après)

UNITED NATIONS EDUCATIONAL, SCIENTIFIC AND CULTURAL ORGANIZATION: *World Heritage: Challenges for the Millennium.* Paris: UNESCO, 2007

23

World Heritage, concepts and criteria

Michel Cotte

Introduction

As an historian of technology, and as one of the ICOMOS advisors for the implementation of the UNESCO World Heritage List, I intend to give an up-to-date overview of the position held by the heritage of technology, industry and science on the List, together with the latest trends in the criteria and regulations regarding listing and the definition of the 'Outstanding Universal Value' when applied to our present field of study.

The World Heritage Convention

The World Heritage Convention was signed in 1972. It developed from the merging of two separate movements. The older trend focused on the preservation of cultural sites with exceptional value and acknowledged international significance. The event that aroused particular international concern was the decision to build the Aswan High Dam in Egypt, which would have flooded the valley containing the Abu Simbel temples. During the early 1980s, the world heritage movement turned towards the conservation of exceptional natural sites. It became its most significant feature, as the Convention links together in a single document the concepts of nature conservation and the preservation of cultural properties. The Convention recognizes the way in which people interact with nature, and the fundamental need to preserve the balance between the two. The heritage of industry, technology and science, being basically an interaction between human beings and nature, could, at least in theory, be well suited to the List, and even be pivotal.

The foundation of the process is the recognition of the 'Outstanding Universal Value' (OUV) of the place as defined by the Convention and specified through the Operational Guidelines: 'Outstanding universal value means cultural and/or natural significance which is so exceptional as to transcend national boundaries and to be of common importance for present and future generations of all humanity. As such, the permanent protection of this heritage is of the highest importance to the international community as a whole. The Committee defines the criteria for the inscription of properties on the World Heritage List.' To satisfy the OUV, cultural properties must meet one or more of the six cultural criteria defined by the *Operational Guidelines*.

Concepts and criteria

The background for World Heritage listing of the heritage of technology, industry and science depends mainly on three sets of factors. The first one is the progressive and general changes in the application of the World Heritage Convention and the definition for criteria (ten since 2004, six for cultural heritage and four for natural heritage); next come the thematic issues raised by the technology, industry and science heritage actors and lobbies (see below, for instance, and the focus which is currently put on astronomy and astronomical equipment); finally, the impulse towards a more 'representative, balanced and credible World Heritage List', which is presently one of the main objectives of the World Heritage Centre, contributes to the movement by setting a chronological order for themes' implementation, but every State Party member of the Convention remains free of its proposals for inscription on the World Heritage List.

The result of their interaction is a process of three main steps in the history of the Convention implementation. It first followed the main trend of the early decades of the Convention, which focused first on 'monuments', then on collections of monuments or 'ensembles', and later on urban values and city planning. In this way, outstanding technical equipment built for industrial purposes or for civil engineering was perceived as a 'monument', and its architectural and urban value, associated with the history of industry, would justify World Heritage recognition. From another point of view, the recognition of the workers' housing estates as exceptional 'ensembles' was a possibility, involving industry, urban planning, architecture and social history.

A second direction was set by canals, understood as a paradigm for transportation corridors and organized routes for human mobility and commercial exchange. This thematic field, which we can sum up as 'civil engineering heritage', developed in the mid-1990s. Besides canal networks it includes bridges, waterscapes and hydraulic equipment, and finally railway lines. Such a thematic approach is indeed promising, but is most likely underestimated by both State Parties and industry historians and experts who do not promote this category of properties for possible nomination.

The 'cultural landscapes' concept was a further issue discussed in the same years and recognized by the World Heritage convention in 1992. The Committee acknowledged that cultural landscapes represent the 'combined works of nature and of man' designated in Article 1 of the Convention. They are illustrative of the evolution of human society and settlement over time, under the influence of the physical constraints and/or opportunities presented by their natural environment and of successive social, economic and cultural forces, both external and internal. Cultural landscape allows a comprehensive understanding of a site, promoting the assessment of relationships between several features: nature and culture, monument and context, built ensemble and environment, tangible and intangible heritage, networks and flows, social and economic significance, and so on.

Mines and mining landscapes were among the earliest concerns to industrial archaeologists but few were able to fall into this category. Industrial landscapes are particularly subject to continuous change, through phases of industrial expansion through to today's process of deindustrialization, so the 'relic landscape' is frequently tainted with non-integrity. Consequently, the understanding of landscape as a concept is not always clear or complete, in terms of attributes, and the demonstration of their 'Outstanding Universal Value' as a unique or exceptionally significant industrial landscape can therefore be compromised. They do not often meet the criteria for the

'Outstanding Universal Value' which is the essential condition for inscription. Industrial landscapes usually fall under the second category which is the 'organically evolved' landscape. This results from an initial social, economic, administrative, and/or religious imperative which developed its present form by association with and in response to its natural environment and social or economic changes. 'Organically evolved' landscapes reflect that process of progression in their form and component features; they are still alive, especially when they preserve the sense and authenticity of heritage in a working site. Continuing landscapes form a subcategory which retains an active social role in contemporary society closely associated with traditional ways of life, and in which the evolutionary process is still in progress. At the same time they exhibit significant material evidence of change over time.

On the other hand, the question of people's relationship with nature in the case of industry should be stimulating and help us think about industrial heritage as a whole, including not only tangible heritage and the landscape marks of industrial development but also its aftermath, invisible impacts such as pollution, health hazards, consequences on biodiversity, climate change and so on.

What is today obvious is that the heritage of industrial and technical processes as such is an underrepresented theme on the List. There are only a very few consistent and clear examples, with a disproportionate number in a few European regions. Attempts for improving this were actually made, for instance through some reference sites already on the List, and through 'tentative lists' of sites by the State parties. These initiatives are trying to combine all the tools and criteria offered by the *Operational Guidelines for the Implementation of the Convention* for the World Heritage List, and the results are somewhat contorted and complex approaches to the sites. Sometimes the description is confused, missing what is actually the core of the industrial, technical and scientific heritage, as a historical process of human relationships with nature, and leading to persistent misunderstandings. The fact is that in its categories (cultural landscapes, ensembles or monuments taken in consideration as isolated features), its evaluation criteria (such as 'firsts', 'authenticity' and 'integrity', all keywords in the classical approach for the protection of historical monuments), the World Heritage Convention does not easily include the heritage of technology, industry and science. In other words, architectural, urban or archaeological approaches to assess what is unique or exceptional in the World Heritage context continue to be preferred over scientific, technical and industrial achievements.

A thorough epistemology-oriented research

It seems clear that a better vision is required of what constitutes the heritage of technology, industry and science. The international UNESCO workshop held in London in January 2008 added a significant text officially associated with the World Heritage documentation: *Science and technology, an expert workshop within the framework of the global strategy for the global, balanced and representative World Heritage List.* The first sentences explain:

> The outcome of this meeting shall contribute to the development of guidelines and criteria for the review of sites of interest for the heritage of *science and technology* on the World Heritage List.

The pursuit and application of knowledge underlie all human achievements, many of which have been recognised on the World Heritage List, as for example agriculture systems, industrialisation and achievements of architecture. One of the areas relating to science and knowledge, which are under-represented on the World Heritage List, is *the natural sciences* (physical sciences including astronomy and chemistry, and biological sciences) and the development of *their application through engineering and technology*. [Author's italics]

Our comments are obvious and will be short.

- the absence of the word 'industry' but the use of the word 'technology',

- the close association of science and technology as an outcome and application of science coming from the traditional Anglo-Saxon approach to these questions. For instance, the list of inscribed sites published in preparatory documents for this seminar includes railways, canals, transport heritage … as the heritage of applied science and technology.

Workers' housing at Crespi d'Adda, Bergamo, Italy. Recognition of industrial housing estates as exceptional 'ensembles' involving urban planning, architecture and social history resulted in several planned settlements being inscribed on the List, including New Lanark in Scotland. (Luigi Chiesa, GNU Free Documentation License)

Oil pots on a horizontal steam engine preserved at the Dunedin Gasworks Museum, New Zealand. Industrial sites challenge many conservation concepts, often including dynamic processes at different scales such as machines and tools, the relationship of man with machines, flows of material and energy, social planning and management of the production process. (Neil Cossons)

It is unfortunate that the technical studies undertaken by TICCIH and published by ICOMOS, for instance on canals and railways, do not include epistemology, nor have they been extended to such essential sectors as textiles, iron and steel, public utilities or the automobile industry. Matters of method and epistemology are related to the heritage of technology, industry and science in the World Heritage perspective.

The importance of process

The definition of the heritage of technology, industry and science in the context of the World Heritage Convention relies not only upon factual description but also upon epistemology and studies in the field. For instance, the usual concepts of 'integrity' and 'authenticity' should be given an adapted definition for industrial, technological or scientific heritage, because the nature of this heritage involves a relationship with time which differs from what it could be within the frame of a more classical approach to heritage. Time is here a variable quantity understood in a scientific and/or historical sense. The understanding of such recent heritage is closely linked with the knowledge of science and technology and a comprehensive appreciation of their historical context. The 'scientific paradigm' or 'socio-technical system' at a given time and date is a question that cannot be ignored. Moreover, it is knowledge which is essential to the appreciation of industrial, technological or scientific heritage. In a given location, scientific and/or technical features may change because innovation is an imperative requirement in the field under review. This means that a *longue durée* approach of each particular branch of history embedded into the flow of development is required. Keywords for science and technology heritage and maxims for their history are therefore innovation, the possibility for change, adaptation, the progress of knowledge, and the like. These are specific, just as 'enduring' is a fundamental value on which authenticity and its assessment relies in other fields of historical and cultural heritage. The difference is a profound one. The appraisal of those values needs a renewal of the assessment method which involves new references for the analysis of World Heritage, this being true for a good many sites, some of them listed already, as well as from a theoretical point of view.

A 'good' application dossier, in such a perspective, will show both an actual understanding of what is the specificity of the site under review in its scientific and technological context and in the broader history of science and technology, and an intimate knowledge of the World Heritage Convention's general goals, methods and limits.

The essential feature of industrial and technical heritage is a productive process seen in its proper place and local context. It has much less to do with architectural, urbanistic or landscape values, whatever prominent roles they may be playing. Understanding such sites means a comprehensive analysis of a dynamic process running at different scales: machines and tools in function, the relationship of man with machines, the flows of material and energy, the experimental use of instruments, social planning and management of the production process, and so on. Integrity of structure is of course an important issue, but it is not enough, and we must pay attention to the functional integrity of the process and site, which is at stake when the business has definitely stopped trading or the scientific equipment is redundant. The legal distinction between unmovable and movable property sounds out of place in the realm of technology and science, but it is a key issue in World Heritage Convention terms. The Convention is devoted to 'properties' in a juridical sense and not to 'movable' items. There is also a powerful dividing line between site and collection, heritage and museum, infrastructure and rolling stock, and so on.

We need also to pay attention to the fundamental issue of intangible heritage as a central feature and treasure of science and technology. The World Heritage Convention does not recognize intangible heritage for its own value. It must be clearly associated with tangible features which themselves have an exceptional or unique significance. It is a delicate challenge both to identify properly what defines materiality of the place, related to the Convention guidelines, and to show clear and understandable relationships with science, technology or the practical know-how of craftsmen. Of course, there is also a more recent World Heritage Convention about intangible heritage, but it has not yet been sufficiently applied to scientific or technical values. It could certainly offer an alternative way towards recognition for the heritage of industry, science and technology, but a careful examination of its capacity under this respect is still to be done.

Conclusion

What is probably the core of the difficulty in achieving industrial, scientific and technological heritage recognition is that it belongs to different or opposing fields: intangible versus tangible heritage, movable instruments and tools versus unmovable properties, static issues versus dynamic processes, and so on. In fact, the value and interest of this heritage is precisely the fact that it is related to all these categories and the dynamic relationships between them. Several dossiers could be submitted to the World Heritage Committee by the State parties and they may offer some opportunities to promote the industrial, scientific and technological heritage in a proper way. On the other hand, ICOMOS has a duty to develop co-operation with international specialized organizations as it does for industrial heritage with TICCIH – the *Joint ICOMOS-TICCIH Principles for the Conservation of Industrial Heritage Sites, Structures, Areas and Landscapes* adopted by the 17th ICOMOS General Assembly on 28 November 2011 is a landmark – and previously for the archeo-astronomical and astronomical heritage with IAU. Discussion and facilitating cross-disciplinary interaction are the ways to build a common practice and a more efficient selection methodology for the future.

Further reading

World Heritage: Science and Technology. An Expert Workshop within the Framework of the Global Strategy for a Balanced and Representative World Heritage List, UK National Commission for UNESCO, London, 2008

RUGGLES, C and COTTE, M (ed.): *The Astronomical and Archeoastronomical Heritage in the perspective of the World Heritage Convention.* Bognor Regis: Ocarinabooks, 2011

WORLD HERITAGE CENTER: *Operational Guidelines for the Implementation of the World Heritage Convention,* e-edition, November 2011

24

Thematic World Heritage Studies

Stephen Hughes

Introduction

By identifying gaps in the functional, industrial, engineering, commercial and technological areas, the World Heritage Studies produced by TICCIH in collaboration with ICOMOS have contributed to the implementation of the World Heritage Committee's Global Strategy for a balanced World Heritage List. The Global Strategy has been in use for eighteen years, so it is an appropriate time for a review of what has been achieved. Almost half of the eighteen studies so far produced as part of this strategy concern the functional and social elements of the industrial heritage. These, and an earlier general industrial archaeological list, have provided the context for the acceptance of almost all industrial archaeological sites nominated by national governments for inscription on the World Heritage List in the current century.

The Global Strategy was adopted by the World Heritage Committee in 1994. Its aim was to ensure that the List reflects the world's cultural and natural diversity of outstanding universal value. Industrial archaeology was felt to be one of the areas under-represented on the List, and negotiations at that date between Professor Henry Cleere, World Heritage Co-ordinator of the International Committee for Sites and Monuments (ICOMOS), and Professor Louis Bergeron, President of The International Committee for the Conservation of the Industrial Heritage (TICCIH) resulted in TICCIH being recognised as specialist advisor on Industrial Heritage to ICOMOS.

Seven such Industrial Archaeology studies have been now been prepared for the World Heritage Office of ICOMOS and can be found on the ICOMOS website.

International industrial archaeology studies

Pressure from non-European governments to ration the number of European palaces, cathedrals and castles appearing on the World Heritage List helped to prompt a search for areas where European developments were truly of international importance.

In 1986, the proposed nomination of the late eighteenth-century textile mills at New Lanark in Scotland in the United Kingdom, associated with the social experiments of

Robert Owen and David Dale, failed at the first attempt because of a lack of comparative data. There was an ensuing confusion when other European governments considered they had comparable sites concerning early attempts at model social engineering, as with the Guise model worker community at Aisne and also other worker communities such as those at Le Cruesot and Mulhouse.

Other nomination attempts failed because of a lack of cognisance of how the World Heritage Criteria would be applied to specific types of industrial monuments, as was the case of Thomas Telford's and Robert Stephenson's technologically pioneering bridges across the Menai Straits in Wales, United Kingdom. The States Party had failed to appreciate that both bridges would fail to be selected for World Heritage status on grounds of 'authenticity' as it was the original form of the iron structures that made the structures of primary international importance and in both cases this element of the sites had been replaced. An alternative suggestion was that the Conwy Bridges, retaining these critical features and attached to one side of an existing World Heritage Site, be nominated instead and this is what the TICCIH Board recommended to the World Heritage Committee as part of the first Industrial Monuments List in 1994.

The significance of such international comparative work can be indicated by what happened to the original industrial archaeology study and list. TICCIH organised an International Industrial Landmarks exercise with a request for a list of five sites, or landscapes, from each country. Great Britain, where the first industrial revolution of the modern era started, can be taken as an example of how this process was activated. The Association for Industrial Archaeology (AIA), meeting at Ironbridge in 1993, helped select five examples from each of Scotland, England and Wales which were later refined by national groups within the United Kingdom. From Wales they were Blaenafon ironworks and Landscape, the international iron-making capital of Merthyr Tydfil, the intact Stephenson and Telford tubular and suspension bridges at Conwy, Dinorwig Slate Quarries, and Parys Mountain Opencast Copper Mine. In England the sites and landscapes included Cromford Cotton Mills and associated mill communities, Chatterley Whitfield Colliery, Albert Dock at Liverpool, the Cornish tin- and copper-mining area around Penwith, and Kew Bridge Engines in London. In Scotland the list included the Forth Rail Bridge, Dallas Dhu Whisky Distillery at Forres, New Lanark Cotton Mills, Lady Victoria Colliery at Newtongrange and Biggars Gasworks. Similar exercises were carried out in countries across the world.

The author, as TICCIH National Representative, co-ordinated this work in the United Kingdom and consulted authorities and experts throughout the country in compiling dossiers on each of these sites and sending them to Guido Vanderhulst, then the Secretary for TICCIH Industrial Heritage Landmarks, based in Brussels.

The list of those they considered the most important (which were not already World Heritage Sites) was forwarded to the World Heritage Office of ICOMOS during 1994. At ICOMOS, the work was organised by Professor Henry Cleere, then World Heritage Co-ordinator. At the end of 1994, the list of 33 recommended industrial archaeology sites went forward to the World Heritage Committee.

The Board of TICCIH considered that British sites were of fundamental importance because of their part in the world's first industrial revolution, with its profound international influence. Therefore no fewer than nine structures and landscapes that formed part of that process were situated in Great Britain, that is over a quarter of the final number of sites submitted to the World Heritage Office. These included Blaenafon ironworks, New Lanark Mills and village, Cromford Mills and associated mills and villages, and Albert Dock in Liverpool, all of which were subsequently successfully inscribed on the World Heritage List in the period 2000 between 2004.

Internationally, all subsequent industrial archaeology nominations for the World Heritage list have also been based on inclusion in the framework in the 1994 general list prepared by TICCIH, or the subsequent single-industry lists, with the exception of the British nomination of the Saltaire Woollen Mills and worker settlement.

The international recommendations arising from this first general Industrial Archaeology TICCIH list, outside Britain, included the four nineteenth-century canal lifts on the Canal du Centre and their surroundings (Belgium: 1998); the Verla Groundwood and Board Mill (Finland: 1996); the powered pumping-stations of the Netherlands including the wind-powered installations at Kinderdijk-Elshout (1997) and the Wouda Steam Pumping Station of 1920 at Lemmer in Friesland (the largest steam-powered pumping engine ever built: inscribed 1998); the Zollverein Coal Mine Industrial Complex at Essen in the Ruhr (Germany: 2001) and the Mining Area of the Great Copper Mountain in Falun (Dalarna, Sweden: 2001). The blast-furnaces at Völklingen in the Saarland of Germany were inscribed at the same time as the TICCIH Board completed the list with the furnaces on it.

In all, one third of the 33 sites and landscapes on the 1994 TICCIH list of outstanding industrial monuments have subsequently been inscribed as World Heritage Sites. Nine on that list were in the United Kingdom (counting Telford's Conwy Suspension Bridge and Stephenson's Tubular Bridge as separate inscriptions, and including the endangered landscape of the Merthyr Tydfil ironworks), eight in Germany, three each in Belgium and the Netherlands, two each in France, Sweden and Denmark and one each in Japan, Russia and Finland. Internationally, the sites and landscapes yet to be inscribed from Germany include the Potash Mines at Bleicherode, Thuringia; the AEG Turbinehall in Berlin; the sugar refinery at Oldisleben, Thüringen; the warehousing in Hamburg Harbour; the Göltzschal Railway Viaduct at Mylau in Saxony and the Freiberg Brassworks Mining and Cultural Landscape, Halsbrücke.

In Belgium, the early nineteenth-century coal-mining town and mine of Bois du Luc in Wallonia, the Noeveren Brickworks industrial landscape at Boom and the Tour et Taxis goods interchange station in Brussels were noted as being of importance in 1994. In Holland, the multiple Cornish beam-engines of the Cruquius Steam-powered Pumping Station were commended, along with the other two sites and drainage landscapes that have since achieved recognition as World Heritage Sites. A second site commended from Sweden was the Dannemora Iron-ore Mines and Settlement in Uppland, as were the enlightened socialist settlement of the Guise factory at Aisne in Picardy and the Menier Chocolate Factory at Noisel, in France. In Denmark, the Nivaagaard Brickworks at Niva in north Copenhagen and the Carlsberg Breweries in Copenhagen were also noted for their international importance. Finally, but not least, the Nizhny-Tagil Museum Steelworks in the Sverlovsk Province of the middle Urals of the Russia Federation was recognised for the fact that it was one of Peter the Great's early eighteenth-century multi-blast furnace ironworks with its associated developed workers' settlements.

The 1994 General Industrial Archaeology list has underpinned the formation of the 'Tentative Lists' of proposed World Heritage Sites formulated by each national government. This has been especially true in Europe where the World Heritage Office has advised States Parties that this is the area that the rest of the world perceives as being of profound importance in world history.

TICCIH/ICOMOS comparative thematic studies

There is a natural tendency for all governments and nations to think that their own monuments are the best in the world, but it is equally difficult to achieve a balanced, objective assessment of the relative merits of various candidates that is acceptable to all parts of the international community. The 1994 general list of industrial monuments was felt to be too broad in its scope and so in 1996 TICCIH coordinated the first of a series of single-industry comparative thematic studies in which criteria were developed so that informed comparisons could be drawn between widely dispersed sites from around the world.

The thematic studies are usually arranged in two sections: first an assessment of the criteria that are deemed to be most relevant to the subject area under study, followed by a list of some of the most significant monuments and landscapes of the studied type to which the criteria can be applied. The first section has latterly been considered to be the more relevant by the World Heritage Centre of ICOMOS.

The first of the World Heritage Studies, *The International Canal Monuments List*, was prepared by the author in 1996 after a UNESCO Canal Experts Meeting hosted by Parks Canada. It was more prescriptive than later studies in giving a very long list of categories of structures and canal lines related to waterway construction and use that could be nominated for World Heritage Status. This first World Heritage Study used widespread international consultation to assess which of the canal monuments might be the most important and so to be most worthy of World Heritage Status. However, national governments, the States Parties, determine which sites and landscapes should actually be put forward for nomination.

Subsequent thematic World Heritage Studies have not had international experts scoring sectional lists of possible prospective World Heritage sites. Instead, the sectional establishment of criteria is followed by a section of nine significant examples of the criteria applied to prominent sites and landscapes drawn from within the theme being covered. These examples are not prescriptive, and the criteria established can equally be applied to other outstanding sites from across the world nominated by the national States Parties. It is important, and indeed expected by the World Heritage Centres of ICOMOS and UNESCO, that examples of the sectional criteria are applied to sites spread across the world and not confined to any one continent.

Formal nomination documents such as those for Blaenavon and the Derwent Valley Mills have cited the 1994 general studies, and the subsequent single-industry studies, as contextual information to ensure that their nominations were accepted by the international community.

The studies concerned with functional archaeology and industrial archaeology are *The International Canal Monuments List* (1996); *Context for World Heritage Bridges* (1997); *Railways as World Heritage Sites* (1999); *Les villages ouvriers comme éléments du patrimoine de l'industrie (Workers settlements as part of the industrial heritage – 2001)*; *The International Collieries Study* (2003), *Les paysages culturels viticoles (Wine-growing Cultural Landscapes – 2004)* and most recently a study of *Heritage Sites of Astronomy and Archaeo-astronomy in the context of the UNESCO World Heritage Convention (by*

The Ottawa Locks of the Rideau Canal (1832) descending into the Ottawa River in Ottawa, Canada, with Alexandra Bridge (1900-1901) in the mist in the distance. TICCIH's guidance for selecting canals followed a meeting at the Rideau Canal in 1994. The canal was inscribed on the WHL in 2007. (Peter Stott)

ICOMOS and IAU, 2010). Sometimes governments have made almost immediate use of these studies to achieve the inscription of monuments, as did France and Belgium with the Canal du Midi and Canal du Centre, Germany with Zollverein Colliery, and Hungary with vineyards.

Future work and methodology

The methodology for carrying out the TICCIH/ICOMOS thematic World Heritage studies has now become well established. Those preparing national nominations within the field of industrial archaeology in countries as diverse as China, Canada, France and Britain have acknowledged how useful these studies have become in providing guidance that rises above inevitable national perceptions in helping establish relevant elements of Outstanding Universal Value and in writing the significant International Comparative Significance sections of nomination documents. Equally, the assessors of

The seventeenth-century Qingming Bridge in Wuxi on the Grand Canal in China, on the Tentative List for UNESCO's consideration. (Stephen Hughes)

the ICOMOS and UNESCO World Heritage Centres, and the field and desk mission experts evaluating nominations, expect those preparing World Heritage Site nominations to have referred to the relevant thematic World Heritage Studies and for the estimation of Outstanding Universal Value (OUV), and the assessment of Significance in the International Comparison section, to be linked to it.

Conclusion

TICCIH engaged with the UNESCO/ICOMOS initiative to produce criteria to enable the inscription of the under-represented areas of twentieth-century heritage. Further studies on the textile industry, as well as largely twentieth-century technological studies such as automobile production, hydro-electrical power-stations, power-stations generally, water-supply and other utilities, telecommunications, steel and concrete multi-storey constructions and motorways, should be prioritised. TICCIH, in consultation with the ICOMOS World Heritage Office, needs to refine the facilitating structures already established into a coherent programme that can be advanced harnessing the considerable resources established by its international networks.

Further reading

HUGHES, S: The International Collieries Study: Part of the Global Strategy for a Balanced World Heritage. *Industrial Archaeology Review,* November 2004, Volume XXVI, Number 2, 95–111

HUGHES, S: The International Canal Monuments Study: Part of the Global Strategy for a Balanced World Heritage List. *Patrimoine de l'Industrie: Industrial Patrimony,* 2007, Volume 18, 19–32

ICOMOS, *Thematic Studies for the World Heritage Convention.* Paris, 1996–2010. Available on ICOMOS website

Part IV

Sharing and enjoying

25

Industrial museums

Massimo Negri

Introduction

The impact of the notion of 'industrial heritage' on the cultural and social scene from the 1970s onwards generated a profound revision of the traditional tools for the interpretation of heritage in general, and especially as far as museums are concerned. Museums have always been among the foremost means for the interpretation of objects documenting our past at any time and in any sector. They create the necessary prerequisite for any interpretation programme, firstly to guarantee the future of objects by means of a set of procedures aimed at their best possible conservation, and secondly to make them accessible to the public by exhibiting them with more or less sophisticated tools of interpretation. Industrial, scientific and technological items do not 'speak for themselves' as works of art are supposed to do (not always true, especially with contemporary art). They need to be put in a physical and conceptual framework which renders them intelligible and makes comprehensible the variety of possible meanings which any object brings with it. The changes in these intellectual and practical processes have driven and continue to direct the development of museums in our society.

Science and technology museums

For many years, industrial heritage remained confined to the model of museums of science and technology generated over the last two hundred years by the Conservatoire des Arts et Metiers in Paris (1794), the Science Museum in London (1857), the Munich Deutsches Museum (1903), the Tekniska Museet in Stockholm (1921) and Milan's Museo Leonardo da Vinci (1953), just to mention a few traditional examples of great popularity. But the more comprehensive idea of industrial heritage caused a crisis in this established model, for various reasons. One is cultural. Industrial archaeology and industrial heritage have been characterized from the outset by a strong interdisciplinary approach. Individual items have been studied, evaluated and interpreted from various points of view: the history of technology, social history, business history, the history of design and form, cultural history in the broadest sense of the phrase. Industrial heritage has always shown its potential as a subject for specialists, as well as a subject for the broader public, even for those unfamiliar with modes of production, machinery, railways or canals. In other parts of this book, these aspects are examined in more detail. Here it is important simply to stress that industrial heritage has initiated a more comprehensive approach to interpretation in the methodologies adopted by museums.

Could one define it as an anthropological approach? Yes, this is a legitimate definition, with all its limits. Another less intellectual and more practical factor, but of the same importance, is the question of the size of the artefacts of industrial heritage. How to make a museum exhibit of a bridge still in operation, or of a canal, a forge, a row of working-class houses? Or a working steam engine? This was a challenge rarely dealt with by traditional museums. In most cases, the task was attempted by using dioramas, using smaller-scale replicas, by exhibiting parts of the whole, simply by using pictures, or by means of so-called demonstrations. It is meaningful that the first recipient of the European Museum of the Year Award in 1977 (a programme specifically devoted to innovation in the field of museums in Europe, founded by Kenneth Hudson, a leading figure in making industrial archaeology a popular subject) was the Ironbridge Gorge Museum in England, where all the dilemmas involved in the creation of a museum whose main piece was a bridge still in use were solved in a brilliant way (although it raised some perplexity in continental Europe). And equally meaningful was the museological revolution started by the ecomuseums, with the opening of the Ecomusée de la Communauté Le Creusot Montceau in France in 1972 in an area rich in industrial remains. Ironbridge and Le Creusot Montceau represent two different approaches to similar problems, namely conceiving of a museum embracing a 'collection' made up of open-air structures preserved and interpreted *in situ*, a large area of land with its combination of natural and industrial landscapes, and even an entire community with its way of life, its memories, its contradictions.

Musil, the Museum of Industry and Work of the Micheletti Foundation in Rodengo Saiano, Brescia, Italy, provides open access to the collection of artefacts from both the local and national manufacturing industry. (Fondazione Micheletti)

Museums of influence

Since then, museums dealing with industrial heritage have come to play a substantial role, both in terms of quantity and quality, in the continual proliferation of museums throughout the world, and especially in Europe where their number has more than doubled in less than fifty years.

It is not easy to orientate ourselves in this tumultuous process, especially in search of outstanding examples, those institutions which Hudson so effectively defined as *museums of influence*.

A possible tool for such an effort is the Luigi Micheletti Award, which is devoted solely to the recognition of excellence in the museum field and is specifically addressed to industrial and technical museums. It was established in 1996 by the Micheletti Foundation, based in Brescia in Italy, an area of ancient industrial tradition in the iron sector. It is now run jointly by the Micheletti Foundation with the European Museum Academy. After sixteen years of activity, with hundreds of candidates, it is a special observatory for identifying emerging trends in this field.

The earliest and the latest winners are indicative of the variety of museological uses of industrial objects as a cultural resource for permanent exhibitions. First was the DASA, a very special museum in Dortmund, Germany, devoted to safety at work. The only one in Europe (and perhaps the world) focused on such a theme, it is a large museum housed in a building expressly built for the purpose where the protagonists are 'men at work', as the subtitle of the museum expresses it. There are industrial objects here, a lot of industrial history and especially industrial 'atmosphere'. Industrial tools are shown in their most direct relationship with people and the working environment (in the most extensive sense of the phrase). More precisely, at the DASA the working human being's milieu is analyzed, represented, even imagined in its future possible evolutions. More than fifteen years after its opening, the DASA is still unique, original and provocative, and it exemplifies the large variety of possible interpretations of industrial objects in museum terms.

The Textile and Industry Museum (TIM) in Augsburg (again in Germany), the 2011 winner, can be considered to be at the opposite end of a possible 'curve' of museum development: an old industrial complex which dates from 1836, carefully converted with precise attention paid to the reinterpretation of an industrial collection with a special accent on social history. The style of exhibiting is sometimes closer to contemporary art than to the classical museography of industrial collections. But it is also a place where an old industrial tradition is revisited with a contemporary eye, without any indulgence toward the industrial nostalgia which characterized many of the first generation of museums dealing with industrial archaeology.

The Micheletti Award enlarged its scope in recent years, orientating its interest much more on museums of science and on science centres, on one side, and on contemporary history on the other. But the backbone of the award has remained industrial heritage museums. Two recent winners and the complex of industrial heritage sites in the Ruhr illustrate the variety of problems industrial museums have had to face. The Herring Museum (2004) in Iceland is a community-oriented museum based on the efforts of volunteers, who have restored, maintained and revitalized ships, equipment and the fishing harbour of Siglufiordur, once a major centre for the processing of herring. The museum includes the main features of an ecomuseum ('a mirror where the community reflects itself' in Hugh de Varine's words) and at the same time tries to find a compromise between the inevitable nostalgia for the past and the re-use of memories as a resource for the present.

Brunel's SS *Great Britain* (2007) in Bristol, UK, is a museum focused on one large ship, an artefact emblematic of the first industrial revolution. Designed by the Victorian engineer Isambard Kingdom Brunel, it is considered one of the most significant historic steamships as the world's first screw-propelled, iron built passenger liner. Salvaged from the Falkland Islands in 1970, she now lies in the original dry dock from which she was launched in 1843. Conservation plans were based on a decision to preserve all the fabric of her working life, rather than identifying a single point in time for the restoration. To create a dry, stable atmosphere, a horizontal glass plate running from the edge of the dock to the waterline of the ship seals the contaminated lower part in a dry atmosphere, at the same time creating the illusion of floating, an effect that is enhanced by a shallow flow of water across the glass surface. The adjoining museum occupies an adapted historic workshop and houses original objects and large interactive displays. Visitors step through 'Time Gates' that mark the four key stages back through the ship's dramatic working life until they reach 1843 and her launch and are ready for their voyage on board. The ship itself provides an emotional experience. Visitors are provided with a free automatic audio companion and are asked if they would like to travel first-class, steerage class or – for children – with Sinbad the cat. Once on board, visitors can roam freely through the cabins and public spaces and hear documented stories of those who travelled and worked on the ship.

The issue of the size of industrial heritage has already been raised. The physical dimensions of industrial heritage objects, especially large machines or complexes of machinery such as ironworks, blast furnaces and so on, present complex problems in terms of defining a conservation policy as well as choosing an effective interpretation path. The museums and preserved historic industrial sites located in the Ruhr area of western Germany provide an outstanding example of the spectrum of possible solutions to these problems, and the range of possible interpretative options: how to present large buildings and gigantic industrial installations as in the Ruhr Museum at Zollverein in Essen, or the great complex of the Volklingen ironworks, dating from 1873. This closed in the 1980s and is now a very original museum. A science centre focused on iron-making, the Ferrodrom, provides the door to visit the now-abandoned old productive plants; a large power hall hosts temporary exhibitions; and the whole site is used for concerts and performances. This gigantic piece of industrial landscape thereby becomes a stage for cultural events of post-industrial life.

Museums of renewal

But the most important cases of large-scale interpretation involve the regeneration by museums of derelict former industrial areas. The first example of a clear and comprehensive programme of urban renewal of an historically-important industrial centre is the pioneering intervention carried out in Lowell, Massachusetts. But the positive impact of an actual museum in the urban context is the Museum of Science and Industry (MOSI) in Manchester, UK. Founded in the early 1980s in the Castlefield district, a typical derelict industrial neighbourhood, within a few years a radical improvement was evident. The museum includes several historic buildings, a segment of railway line, a station (the terminus of the world's first inter-city passenger railway, the Liverpool & Manchester), and other important structures from the history of the Industrial Revolution. Moreover, MOSI is always renewing itself, offering fresh visions of the old and more recent industrial past. For example, the museum restored 'Baby', one of the first computing machines with resident memory, created by Manchester University in the 1950s, while its Collection Centre enables visitors to understand that part of the museum's work which is usually kept behind the scenes.

In this context, the town of Tampere in Finland goes in the same direction. Here, a varied industrial townscape in Finlayson, the heart of the town, has a dense urban 'texture' of industrial buildings, a wide variation in terms of styles and formal solutions, and is of a comparable size to Castlefield, to note only some of the most important similarities. Tampere's is well represented in its museums and cultural institutions where stories of its industrial past, in all its multi-faceted aspects, are told in a modern and very effective way. Nowadays, Finlayson is a key feature in the contemporary identity of the city. A strategic choice made by local public authorities is still bearing fruit with the creation of an innovative museum environment which is closely connected to the historic industrial setting characterizing this part of the city. In this sense, the Museokeskus Vapriikki is a museum centre of considerable substance which clearly interprets the spirit of Tampere, providing a powerful tool for 'cultivating a feeling for the industrial past', as Kenneth Hudson titled one of his last lectures.

The Museum of Science and Technology of Catalonia (MNACTEC) based in Terrassa, Spain, but articulated in a geographically dispersed network of sites, museums and interpretation centres, was a pioneering case of a museum model capable of governing an entire territorial system. It created the necessary flexibility by establishing different levels of membership in a sort of experimental 'federation' of museums and sites. The headquarters in Terrassa had the great merit of saving a masterpiece of industrial architecture, using it for a variety of permanent exhibitions. Around this hub was established an innovative 'web' concept whose knots were small museums or old industrial sites made accessible and understandable to the public. This complex of sites is a real work in progress, with always something new for the public. It is an experiment which has inspired similar projects but none comes close to the original model.

The outstanding effects of industrial heritage on the development of interpretation techniques cannot be fully documented on this occasion, but before ending, attention needs to be directed towards two areas that cannot be ignored. First, there is the vast area of company museums. These have gone beyond the original idea of a collection addressed mainly towards employees, like the original Siemens Museum, founded in Berlin in 1916 to collect the company archives; it has evolved over decades into a public space for discussions about technology and science (now the Siemens Forum, in Munich). Many company museums have proved able to take on wider responsibilities, going beyond the limited mission of attracting the attention of potential clients or collecting individual company histories. The Museu da Água in Lisbon is one example. It was founded to preserve the great aqueduct, which brought water to Lisbon, dating from the eighteenth century. The Museu Agbar de les Aigües of the Barcelona water company Agbar provides another case where the conservation of industrial heritage goes together with the pursuit of a company mission.

The other area of interest which merits attention is provided by those cases of 'contamination' among different museological categories that are built up around historic

The Quincy Smelter copper works in Michigan operated from 1903 to 1971. It is now part of the Quincy Mining Company National Historic Landmark district and a contributing site to the Keweenaw National Historical Park. National Historical Parks interpreting preserved industrial areas have been created around the textile mills of Lowell, Massachusetts, at the America's Industrial Heritage Park project in Pennsylvania, focusing on the steel industry, and the Motor Cities National Heritage Area centred on Detroit. (Bode Morin)

industrial sites transformed into museum centres. A recent example is Santralistanbul, founded in 2007 in Istanbul and based in an old electric power plant from the first decades of the twentieth century. The original plant has been restored and preserved *in situ* and is fully accessible to the public as a fascinating Energy Museum. Moreover, the museum's facilities are integrated into a large space for contemporary art exhibitions and the performing arts. Finally, the whole area is used as the campus of a private Turkish university in which workers' houses have been transformed into student accommodation. The museum's structures are spread over 118,000 square metres and it has become an essential cultural and leisure resource for the city. This is an excellent example of a good balance between conservation and innovation based on the clever re-use of an important historic industrial site.

Further reading

HINNERICHSEN, M (ed.): *Re-using the Industrial Past by the Tammerkoski Rapids.* Tampere: City of Tampere Museum Services, 2011
HOUTGRAAF, D: *Mastering a Museum Plan: Strategies for Exhibit Development.* Leiden: Naturalis, 2008
HUDSON, Kenneth: *Museums of Influence.* Cambridge: Cambridge University Press, 1987
NEGRI, A & NEGRI, M: *L'Archeologia Industriale.* Messina-Firenze D'Anna, 1977
NEGRI, M (ed.): *New Museums in Europe 1977-1983.* Milan: Mazzotta, 1984
NEGRI, M: *Manuale di Museologia per i Musei Aziendali.* Rubbettino, Soveria Mannelli, 2003

26

Care of industrial and technical collections

Johannes Großewinkelmann

Introduction

In principle, all forms of human activity, however banal or trite, are worthy of being remembered and included in the work of museums. In consequence, all the objects used in such activities also merit preserving: they provide insights into human life as it was experienced before the object became a museum piece. To a significant degree, memories are linked to material things; and by means of objects the history of former lives can be recalled. The physical destruction of objects is the destruction of memory.

The collecting of objects by industrial museums for establishing a material memory remains an open process which, under specific conditions, ventures in new directions. Many objects that testify to the industrial past are collected without a specific exhibition theme in mind, and are conserved so that our children may formulate questions regarding the past, questions we do not yet feel the need to ask. Only in this way can objects provide information for future generations who lack distinct memories of their own of the disappearing 'industrial era'. For while many industrial museums are still working off the development of the industrial society and its structural change, the process of creating museums has already been left behind by today's deindustrialization. Are industrial museums part of the industrial process, which has reached its final stage? More precisely, have the collections of industrial museums reached their final objectives, and are now only pursuing cosmetic adjustments?

Industrial museums

At the end of the 1970s, the Landschaftsverbände Westfalen-Lippe (LWL) and Landschaftsverband Rheinland (LVR), regional authorities in Westphalia and the Rhineland in Germany, founded a series of industrial museums at authentic industrial sites. They benefited initially from the experience of local people still working in industry, and the first collections and exhibitions were generally in close contact with the vivid memories of the local environment. Later on these industrial museums put more emphasis on general socio-historical arguments next to regional historical references when assessing industrial installations and facilities for the working population.

Industrial museums thereby established themselves as a new means to present and interpret the living and working environment with the utmost veracity and comprehension at authentic locations, based on production and technology and the working environment of the industrial era as well as its ways of life and cultural aspects.

For this, original buildings were conserved and original objects collected and combined with supporting interpretation and practical demonstrations. Accordingly, the collections in industrial museums grew in size, sometimes stimulated by the euphoria of starting something new. In most industrial museums in Germany, the collections suffered – and still suffer today – from the fact that only a small portion was included in an inventory and was rarely documented.

In the 1980s and early 1990s the *Industriekultur* movement no longer limited itself to industrial museums but developed into a tourist movement. As well as maintaining valuable monuments, projects included urban planning and landscaping, followed by the integration of industrial areas with all their ecological, economical and social developments. Well-known examples are the IBA Emscher Park, the Landschaftspark Duisburg-Nord, the Regionale 2006 im Bergischen Städtedreieck and the Internationale Bauausstellung Fürst-Pückler-Land in Lusatia.

Industriekultur, understood as a concern for all aspects of the cultural history of the industrial era, combines the history of technology, culture and social life and encompasses everyone in the industrial society, their daily lives as well as their living and working conditions. But treatment of the material remains of the industrial society did not really move in a positive direction under the premises of marketing the industrial culture. Consideration of the human factor as the most important part of the history of industry became more sensitive, but the treatment of the remains of industry increasingly lacked awareness. This is evident in the treatment of industrial monuments, machines and the inventory of complete industrial works. If the remains of the industrial society are consumed instead of being used as an important cultural resource, then nothing will remain for history.

Collections of industrial objects

There is an enormous spectrum of types, sizes and fields of industrial collections. As well as core areas such as technology, sociology and daily working life, they also cover national and regional themes as well as narrow collections dealing with specific industries or companies. Many industrial museums combine more than one of these core areas. Some of the problems presented relate to collections at authentic industrial sites and cover technical and social issues as well as regional history.

Technical historical collections

Early industrial museums such as the Deutsche Bergbaumuseum in Bochum were strongly influenced by the technical historical roots from which they originated. In museums of this type, 'the engineers' perspective' or a technology-oriented focus on industrial history had an enduring impact on their collections. The objects in these collections were frequently treated as purely technical artefacts which have lost all their original historical connections once installed in a museum. Conservation and restoration often put a high gloss on the machinery, tools and technical artefacts, destroying their patina and the aura of something original and authentic. These collections sometimes maintained very large pieces of machinery under favourable conditions of conservation, which has to be considered as beneficial. But the objects differ little from those kept in so-called 'science centres' from which industrial museums clearly want to distance themselves.

Collections of social and daily life

At of the end of the 1970s, *Industriekultur* was no longer defined just by machines and buildings but had incorporated the socio-historical aspects of people's living and working conditions during the industrial era. For presenting socio-historical interrelationships, exhibits and documents other than machines and tools are needed. These come from the workers' or owners' private living environments but also from political parties, trades unions, churches and other areas of society. For this purpose, collections absorbed ephemera, including catalogues, company signs and advertising, payroll books, archives, diaries, correspondence and photographs.

A discussion of industrial collections would be incomplete if it did not cover the use of the products manufactured by industry. Because of the far-reaching changes brought by the Industrial Revolution, not only are the results of the manufacturing process of interest but also how they were handled and used. The interrelationship between development and design, manufacturing and marketing, as well as their usage, results in the definition of a product culture.

Regional history collections

Setting up a collection always requires sensitivity to the regional background of industrialisation. Collecting in a region, where the pioneers significantly affected the development of trade, demands a concern for inventors. Only in such a way can the

The battery locomotive with wagons at the station of the haulage adit of the Weltkulturerbe Erzbergwerk Rammelsberg. The daily use of the original train to transport visitors to the underground exhibition areas, the need for frequent repairs and the replacement of worn parts, as well as corrosion damage caused by accumulated condensate, are impeding the long-term conservation of this unique industrial historical object. (World Culture Heritage Rammelsberg)

technical historical potential of a region be successfully demonstrated. Merely collecting patented objects and technical drawings, however, would not suffice. The many technical improvisations and custom-made products show the flexible use of technical devices and manpower and provide a view of the specialities of skilled labour which underlay the regional process of industrial development. Regional varieties of industrialisation and structural characteristics are more or less presented in most industrial collections.

Collections at authentic locations

'Industrial culture can best be experienced at conserved original sites with original objects. The maintenance of authenticity has to be strived for when restoring and utilising industrial monuments.' This strong commitment to the authentic location was emphasised in the 'Charta Industriekultur NRW 2020'. The collections of industrial museums which refer to an authentic location try to maintain and carefully present the objects in the precise condition in which the curator found them. The Müller cloth mill in Euskirchen, a site of the Landschaftsverband Rheinland industry museum network, or the Weltkulturerbe Erzbergwerk Rammelsberg in Goslar, are two examples of industrial historical collections closely related to their authentic locations.

However, the process of converting a location into a museum on the site of industry starts a decisive change of meaning. The industrial plant no longer obtains its purpose from being used but from being a cultural medium of memory.

Problems facing industrial collections

Only a few problematic aspects of collecting objects of cultural value can be pointed out here, along with the challenges faced by industrial museums. Few museums have developed the collection policies which could help them face in a controlled manner the accelerating stock of objects that has been made available by the structural change of industry. They often lack buildings suitable for their very varied collections. Technical objects are stored with no system or sorting and sometimes just unloaded into yards and exposed to atmospheric conditions. While the bigger industrial museums managed to attract attention by spectacular and expensive exhibitions, the condition of their collections has deteriorated. Only from the mid-1990s has there been a gradual improvement in the conditions for storage with more qualified personnel. Financial restrictions mean that the work of conservation and restoration has lagged behind the museums' other duties. This work is made more difficult by the complexity of the materials and the vast number and short lifetime of the industrial society's products, problems which still have to be solved for the maintenance of the huge stocks of industrial historical collections.

In view of this situation, many industrial museums made a virtue out of necessity. The worst way to keep objects is outdoor storage, but with industrial museums with many large exhibits this is, however, not likely to change. Based on this situation, during the last few years protocols have been written to guide conservation. The Canadian Conservation Institute protocol, for instance, includes measures for handling large exhibits stored in the open air. Long-term planning of museums should aim at storing all exhibits indoors. If that cannot be guaranteed then at least a roof or a temporary cover should provide protection against humidity, as most of the industrial artefacts are made from metal and suffer badly from corrosion.

The enormous number of small objects in industrial collections should be sorted and separated according to the principles of preventive conservation. Paper should be separated from textiles, for instance; the former should be stored in a heated room at a humidity of 50 per cent to 55 per cent, while textiles are better deposited in cool rooms. Objects made from wood should be stored separately, especially if it is not known if they are infested. It is important to mark storage areas clearly, showing their function, and to fence outdoor depots to show that the objects stored there are not part of a freely-available hoard of spare parts, but are cultural goods and being protected.

Observation of these very simple standards leads in many cases to an improvement in the situation of collections and stores.

Over the last few years, many industrial museums have started to reconsider the value and the quality of their collections. Specifically, the question has been raised of whether mass-produced industrial objects should be collected so as not to take up too much valuable storage space. Standards have also changed the perception regarding conservation and restoration work. The old practice of polished restoration 'as new', carried over from historic technical collections, has usually been abandoned in favour of more moderate conservation which preserves the marks of usage and wear.

However, questions are increasingly asked regarding the adoption of the object worthy of conservation within the museum's operation. Taking a technical object into a museum collection generally implies the suspension of its evolution. Objects should exhibit all the traces of manufacturing and the marks of use and maintenance, repair and adaptation, which they acquired during their operational lives. If, however, the museum reactivates the objects and uses them for demonstrations, then additional objectives of conservation and maintenance are required. Furthermore, during the course of operation within the museum the object will be altered, so that after some time its original condition, as it was when introduced to the collection, may no longer be apparent.

This very brief insight into some of the problems regarding the management of collections in industrial museums already shows that a lot of retrospective collecting has to be done, because it has been neglected for years and even today comes second to many other tasks. At the same time, the continuing development of the industrial society leads to new challenges regarding future collection strategies.

Best practice for industrial collections

Ignoring the problems of financing and presentation, and just looking at the collections, it can be seen that because of the way in which the industrial society is changing, the work of collecting and the treatment of collected objects has to deal with new functions. The following recommendations are important preconditions for setting up and working with collections in industrial museums:

Collection policies

- Exemplary or reference collections are a major premise as the acceleration of product innovation, the shortening of product life cycles and the diversity of industrially produced objects results in ever-increasing numbers of new products, all available for collecting. The greater the dynamics of production the faster our present is filled with relics of the past.

- Collecting by industrial museums has been driven for many years by salvage actions, aimed to prevent objects from disappearing for ever. This cannot go on indefinitely. One of the essential tasks is to consolidate existing collections while optimising the use of resources.

- Collections are not rigid, and at times it may be necessary to eliminate parts of them. A certain adjustment to changing concepts must be possible. However, care has to be taken to guard against the dangers of fashionable scientific developments or the personal opinions of curators, both capable of destroying a collection which has been built up over many years. It is necessary to research thoroughly and to analyse the development history of collections.

- Mainly original objects should be collected based on a clear acquisition policy. This also provides the strategies for a possible release of objects – de-acquisition – to keep the collection within the limits of the museum.

- A careful inventory and scientific documentation of the objects is fundamental for the procedure for preserving and using the objects in exhibitions.

Treatment of collected objects

- The aim of conservation and restoration of installations and objects is to preserve them for future generations as significant carriers of information, with all the traces left by manufacturing and the marks acquired during their use. Through conservation, the effects of ageing of the object are reduced and the signs carrying information are preserved. Restoration is an attempt to safeguard the sum of information of an object and to retrieve lost information by means of restitution or supplementation. These objectives are incompatible with radical, and often irreversible, 'restoration as new'.

- Interventions to collections must respect the historic substance of both technical objects and historic buildings. They should not be sacrificed for short-term objectives of presentations, as was done in the 1990s to boost publicity effects in events and exhibitions. The possibility of reversing such interventions has to come first.

- Within the framework of the museum's conservation mandate, the public should be informed of necessary protective actions: some sections of authentic industrial sites are only open to visitors with limitations or restricted to special tours.

- In this context and especially in museums where live demonstrations of original machines are running, it is important to explain to visitors the problems related to the treatment of the collection. At demonstration sites, objects are undergoing wear. The museum is in breach of its mandate to maintain in an authentic state the objects of testimony of the historical development for the present and future. Many visitors are not aware of this conflict when viewing a panting steam engine or a rattling vehicle, and the

An Oberon class submarine HMAS *Ovens* at the Western Australian Maritime Museum straddles the line between object and built heritage. Too big to fit inside the museum building, it sits on the adjacent historic World War II submarine slipway, which provides great context and viewing opportunities, but is a highly corrosive environment. (Alison Wain)

fun of a public presentation easily lets us forget the conservation mandate of the museum.

Conclusion

To return to the question framed at the beginning: have industrial museum collections reached their final objectives, and can they now pursue purely cosmetic adjustments? The collections of objects of the twentieth century face enormous challenges. The size of the installations, the materials used in their manufacture, the amount of mass-produced articles and the loss of value of such products, as well as the correct conservation and restoration regarding manufacturing and function, all challenge the collections of industry museums. The future is not yet clear. A few years ago, some perspectives were shown by the discussion of slimming down and weeding the museums' stocks. But the collections in industrial museums definitely have not reached their ending.

Further reading:

FELDKAMP, J & LINDNER, R: *Industriekultur in Sachsen. Neue Wege im 21. Jahrhundert*. Chemnitz: 2010

INTERNATIONAL COUNCIL OF MUSEUMS: *ICOM Code of Ethics for Museums*, Chap. 4: Disposal of Collections. Paris: ICOM, 2002

JOHN, H and MAZZONI, I: *Industrie – und Technikmuseen im Wandel, Perspektiven und Standortbestimmungen*. Bielefeld: Transcript Verlag, 2005

PRYTULAK, G: *Outdoor Storage and Display: Basic Principles*. Canadian Conservation Institute (CCI), Notes 15/8 and 15/9, 2010

27

Conserving industrial artefacts

Eusebi Casanelles and James Douet

Introduction

This chapter deals with some of the practical and ethical issues relating to the conservation of technical objects in museum collections. There are many challenges surrounding the conservation of industrial artefacts. Industrial mass-production created identical products with interchangeable components; some are very large, sometimes rendering meaningless the distinction between a machine and a building. In many cases, too, *use* constitutes a large part of the special historical interest of an artefact and represents the reason why the decision was taken to take them into the care of a collection; this is frequently the case with tools, machines and engines, as well as transport vehicles such as cars and trains. These questions give a special interest to how technical and industrial collections are approached by conservators.

The Farga Palau, Ripoll, Spain. This small Catalan forge was built in the seventeenth century and abandoned in 1978. It was conserved as found, and is now a museum. Detailed archaeological study and documentation preceded the stabilisation of the objects. Though it is not used, visitors enter and touch the tilt hammers, tools, products and observe the trompe air blowing system which defines this ironworking technology. (MNACTEC)

Technical and industrial collections

The first museums collected works of art or objects that in some way qualified as curiosities, but today almost anything on earth might become part of the collection of a particular museum. The first technical collections were started by the Conservatoire d'Arts et Métiers in Paris in 1794, followed half a century later by the Science Museum in London. The museology represented by the great science museums such as Munich, Paris, London and Chicago began with the policy of taking technical objects into care and using them for instruction – a dichotomy that still affects how museums conserve and exploit their collections. Over time, these were grouped into assemblages that might illustrate the evolution of a single typology. They also preserved machines of certain manufacturing processes that were moved to the museum, such as textile production or gun manufacture. In contrast, from the 1960s many of the new industrial museums began to conserve production processes 'in situ'. Along with the machines and tools were items related to everyday work, aiming to capture the 'spirit of place' which is sacrificed when objects are transferred to a museum. An extreme example is the RIM Solingen in Germany, a nineteenth-century foundry and knife-grinding works that reopened as a museum the day after it closed as a factory, with all the original contents in their place.

What, however, is understood as a technical object? A first classification could separate man-made 'artefacts' from 'naturfacts', that is objects that are found in nature. The Latin word for 'art' means 'made by man' and has the same meaning as the Greek word τέχνη (tekhné) from which we get the word 'technique'. If historically the most common use in the West of the word 'art' was work made by 'artisans', from the seventeenth century this was monopolised by 'artists' who were in schools of 'fine arts'. The word 'technology' first appears in English in 1829. Among the objects made by humans, those that are aesthetically beautiful or those intended for worship are preserved in museums of art and ethnology. Technical objects, having a practical function, can be divided into those that are made with pre-industrial and industrial techniques. This chapter will refer to those machines and technical objects made within the *industriekultur*, the society created by the Industrial Revolution, and especially those of special technical interest such as tools, instruments, machines, engines and vehicles.

Industrial technical objects have characteristics that make them different from other man-made 'artefacts'. The first is that many of them and their components are manufactured in series. As a result they are not in any sense unique as would be the case with pre-industrial or artistic products. A second feature that emerges from the above is that component parts are frequently interchangeable. To create an industrial design, the prior involvement of an engineer is required (a third distinguishing attribute) which determines the pieces and the mechanisms, how they are put together in order to make the object function as it is intended. Therefore, plans are of great importance for the information they transmit. Innovation is the engine of technical evolution and is the distinctive value of technical objects conserved in science museums. In industrial museums, on the other hand, the value of technical objects tends to be their testimonial quality as representatives of a productive activity located in a particular place.

Documentation of technical objects

Heritage objects are not only witnesses to history but are also documents. Their structure, surfaces and materials give us an amount of information which has to be retrieved before undertaking any intervention aimed at preservation or restoration. On the other hand, the history of the object must also be studied to find as much as possible about how it was used and the alterations and modifications made to it since it left the factory. Information about its use is what converts a mass-produced object into a unique one, adding a social and historical context and therefore value to its technical interest. An object with a history acquires a life.

Established museum protocols for documenting artefacts use written inventory forms, photographs and increasingly digital processes such as three-dimensional modelling to identify the material, form and physical condition of the object, as well as information on how it functioned and was used. All of the documentation relevant to the object has to be included in the inventory form, including the identity of the maker, photographs of the piece in operation, ownership history, and so forth. Once the object has been given a code to identify it within the collection, photographed and placed in the store with the appropriate packaging, a protocol is chosen for handling and moving it. These reports will inform future use of the piece in exhibitions or display or, in the case of operating machinery, provide official documentation for safety inspections.

Going further, the functional state of working objects can be described using tribology, the emerging science of friction, lubrication and wear, to help the conservator express the state of technical parts in function and to understand and recognise degradation traces caused by their function.

This close study and investigation can be taken into the realms of archaeological analysis. The pioneering archaeological study of the *Rocket* locomotive by Bailey and Glithero in the London Science Museum in 2000, in which forensic techniques of archaeology were applied to analyse an historic piece of machinery, provided remarkable insights into the design and history of a key artefact from the Industrial Revolution. There is great potential for such analysis to be applied elsewhere within industrial collections.

The documentation process will help to establish the significance and importance of each artefact, reflecting its rarity, historical or technical value, authenticity and other attributes. Some repositories, such as the Henry Ford Museum in the United States, rank or score the significance of new acquisitions to their collections, giving them, for instance, a value between 1 and 4. This ranking then forms the basis for deciding on the subsequent approach to historical research, artefactual analysis, conservation treatment, storage, exhibition and interpretation, and even possible operation.

Authenticity

Both the Nizhny Tagil Charter and the 1994 Nara Document on Authenticity stress the importance of authenticity, the latter defining it as 'the essential qualifying factor concerning values':

> The understanding of authenticity plays a fundamental role in all scientific studies
> of the cultural heritage, in conservation and restoration planning, as well as

within the inscription procedures used for the World Heritage Convention and other cultural heritage inventories.

The problem of mass-produced objects is to define what is understood as authentic. The authentic object may be considered as one made from the original components it had as it left the factory, or one whose components correspond to the original model design. Alternatively it can be seen as the sum of all the changes that have caused it to become whatever it is. In most cases it is almost impossible to distinguish whether the parts are original or not, as the interchangeability of components is another of their intrinsic characteristics. As a general rule, the second assumption is accepted, that the authentic object has all the components of the original model. In everyday use, when an object breaks it is normal practice to replace the piece with another of the same series, as happens to a car or washing machine. Authenticity is most frequently compromised when damaged components are replacement by substitutes from a different brand or by copies. In this case it is very difficult to identify the genuine article.

However, the concept of authenticity of technical objects can be still more complicated. Until a few decades ago, machines were durable and mechanics not only repaired but also adapted them to new processes or technologies, making changes to improve their performance. With the change from steam to electrical power in the early twentieth century, for example, it was normal for electric motors to be incorporated into looms or lathes to replace the mechanism of pulleys and shafting that had previously transmitted movement from the prime mover. In this case we can ask what is understood as the genuine, the original, or the adapted condition.

Clearly, both options can be valid. The course of treatment will be determined according to the cultural value of the object and what the museum wants to explain and this depends on the criteria of the institution. In some cases it may be interesting to show the adaptations to explain changes in processes or work patterns. In periods of scarce resources such as during periods of austerity, for instance, the machine can manifest the limits as well as the ingenuity of the operators, as exemplified by the 1950s American cars kept on the road in post-revolutionary Cuba.

Moving parts: to use or not to use

Movement is an essential part of a great deal of technical heritage, especially machines and engines. For this reason there is a tendency for parts that are damaged or missing to be replaced so that the mechanism can be made to work. Moreover, the operation of any technical artefact is the assurance that it is complete. If that is not the case it is not possible to know if one or more of its components is missing.

The big problem is that operational use causes wear. Sooner or later some of the components must be mended or replaced, which is why some conservators are reluctant to put them in motion and thereby threaten their authenticity. This approach is justifiable if the object is unique and of considerable historical significance: some machines, such as a Newcomen engine, a 1908 Model-T Ford, or the first typewriter, should never be used. In the case of ordinary objects, of which there are others of the same type, components can be replaced so that the appliance can work. The authentic exemplar must be preserved and alterations indicated on the restoration document.

The interpretative impact of machinery is often transformed by working demonstrations. Many stationary steam engines are brought to life in museums, though not all under live steam. This horizontal mill engine, built in 1897, is turned by electric motor at the Museu de la Ciència i de la Tècnica de Catalunya, Terrassa, Spain. Its robust design backed by careful maintenance helps to limit losses through wear. (MNACTEC)

Big stuff: conservation of large technical objects

Industrial museums and industrial heritage preservation organisations often face the problem of restoring very large machines or gigantic industrial structures. These cannot be moved to a safe place with suitable controlled atmospheric conditions and have to be left where they stand. The problem comes when periodic restoration is prohibited by the costs. In these cases the preservation for future generations cannot be guaranteed and all that can be achieved is to prolong its existence. Natural heritage ends up overcoming cultural heritage. The priority for those responsible for the care of such heritage is to record the object in sufficient detail and to preserve the plans and drawings so that understanding its function and knowledge of its history are not lost.

Conclusions

Conservation work may be done by museum staff or contracted to external specialists but it is a complex task. Conservators of technical objects may have to deal with all manner of materials – metals and alloys, different woods and other organic substances such as ivory or bakelite, vegetable and mineral lubricants and fuels, electronic and digital components – combined in a wide variety of ways, not all of them compatible from a conservation standpoint. Objects may be unique, or so familiar that their historic value is not properly recognised. Throughout their useful lives they may have been repaired, modified and parts replaced so that they continue working, or adapted to meet new technologies. Once in captivity in a museum they may be required to operate, perform a process, move or even travel; operation is as much a part of their essence as the designer's original conception. The approach to the care and display of technical objects will depend on their cultural value, physical attributes and functional characteristics, the philosophy of the museum and the use to which they are to be put, provoking both ethical and practical reflection on the part of their custodians.

Further reading

BAILEY, M R and GLITHERO, J P: *The Engineering and History of Rocket: a survey.* Report. York: National Railway Musem, 2000

CANADIAN CONSERVATION INSTITUTE (CCI): *CCI Notes 15/2: Care of Machinery Artefacts Stored Outside.* Ottawa: Canadian Conservation Institute, 1993

ECCO: *Professional Guidelines (II): Code of Ethic.* Promoted by the European Confederation of Conservator-Restorers' Organisations and adopted by its General Assembly, (Brussels 7 March 2003)

ICOM: *Code of Ethics for Museums*, 2004

STORER, J D: *The Conservation of Industrial Collections – a survey.* Resource: The Council for Museums, Archives and Libraries, 1989

28

Industrial heritage tourism

Wolfgang Ebert

'We need to recognise that industry, with its huge buildings, is no longer a disturbing part in our town/cityscape and in the countryside, but a symbol of work, a monument of the city, which every citizen should show the stranger with at least the same amount of pride as their public buildings.'

Fritz Schupp, Architect, 1932

Introduction

The Industrial Revolution was a story of success, which also had its dark side. Economic and social changes were neither without rupture nor problems. Riches and poverty, land recovery and consumption of the countryside, town and country, work and unemployment, war and peace were all opposites which at the same time were inseparably linked to each other.

Now the opportunities and potential of so many industrial areas fallen to waste in former industrial regions have been available for thirty years. They are potentially a historically unique opportunity of meaningfully reorganising urban areas.

Therefore restoration, above all in the sense of clearance with subsequent new construction, ignores the potential that exists in historic industrial architecture. These resources must be handled carefully, not least in the interest of tourism.

Industrial monuments are no longer regarded 'merely' as cultural symbols but also as important parts of cultural landscapes. This implies pursuing a much more integrated approach that involves applying aspects of landscape conservation and urban development. Industrial monuments are now considered resources of urban development, to be enjoyed rather than shunned.

If new life is to return to old industrial regions, it will return not to newly rebuilt city centres alone but to historic focal points, to the monuments of industry. These monuments may be used not only for setting up museums but for living and working, just like any 'new' quarter.

Moreover, industrial monuments are highly interesting sites of cultural life, forming a novel and intriguing background and serving as highly individual locations for important branches of the cultural economy.

In business, industrial monuments may play an important role as destinations of a new branch of tourism that focuses on industrial heritage. We can see that tourism has become a success in many old industrial regions, thereby acquiring great importance for the future of these areas. The preservation of industrial monuments no longer appears as a cultural luxury but as a necessary expenditure that promises good economic returns.

Examples of success

There had been a number of projects starting with a focus on industrial heritage tourism, not only but mainly in Europe. Examples of best practice can be seen in Great Britain in the Castlefield district of Manchester and the re-use of the docks in Liverpool, the development of the harbour districts of Rotterdam and Amsterdam, in Holland, the change of the former Le Crachet mine in Mons in Belgium into a Scientific Adventure Park, the Völklingen ironworks World Heritage Site in Germany and in particular the 'Route of Industrial Heritage' in the Ruhr with its numerous sites.

Heritage and regeneration of the Ruhr

The Ruhr Basin is not among the world's oldest industrial agglomerations, for the traces of early industrialisation are most evident in the mother country of industrial development, Great Britain. It was only in 1848–49 that the first coke-fired blast furnace was commissioned in the Ruhr, 110 years after its invention in England. Leap-frogging over other industrial regions that developed more slowly, however, the coal-mining, steel-making, chemical, mechanical engineering, and electrical engineering industries created gigantic facilities at a furious rate – an industrial monoculture that characterises the Ruhr conurbation to this very day. These facilities formed the centres of newly created cities in the Ruhr Basin, while any historic town centres that existed here and there were simply swept away. And around this focus of pit-head towers and blast furnaces, gigantic workers' settlements arose, of which more than 3,500 can still be counted today. A gigantic urban machine was created, organised along the lines of labour division and subject exclusively to industrial interests.

It was only in the 1950s that dramatic changes began everywhere in the world, including the Ruhr Basin. More and more pits and foundries were closed down, leaving only a few units behind. At this time, however, it became clear that in the industrialised world, the end of the Industrial Era – as it was known – was approaching. The region's former image of itself as the industrial heart of Europe was wounded deeply, a state of affairs experienced as extremely hard by the local people. On the other hand, in the late 1980s a team of politicians of remarkable far-sightedness and integrity began considering another approach in the Lande of North Rhine-Westphalia. To repair industrial landscapes together with the industrial cities at their core on a sustainable basis was a task that will have positive economic consequences in the future. Based on these assumptions, a development agency for the Ruhr Basin was founded in North Rhine-Westphalia in 1988 called the Emscher Park International Building Exhibition (IBA) with excellent results.

The most important task of Emscher Park IBA was preserving and finding new uses for old industrial sites and the architectural monuments they contained. Since the 1950s

The former Zollverein XII colliery and coking plant, a World Heritage Site, in the Ruhr, Germany. The museum is one of the 'anchor points' of the European Route of Industrial Heritage. (Wolfgang Ebert)

more and more people living in Germany and in the Ruhr Basin had become interested in their industrial heritage. In consequence, a great number of industrial museums were created, and numerous industrial monuments were listed.

While a number of notable successes had been achieved by the early 1980s, it was only the creation of the IBA that finally ensured comprehensive public acceptance of the cultural witnesses of the industrial age, and of their significance in social history.

As one of the final projects, a network of industrial heritage tourism was developed for the Ruhr Basin, finally opening in 1999, the so-called 'Ruhr Industrial Heritage Route'. The system operates on two levels. The upper level is formed by so-called 'anchor points', consisting of the most significant (and handsome) industrial monuments in the region. Representing highlights and landmarks comparable to the Empire State Building or the Eiffel Tower, their brilliance serves as an advertisement for the entire system.

Besides these anchor points, however, there is much more to be discovered along the route. The second level is formed by so-called 'theme routes' that combine into one long journey of discovery and adventure, offering intriguing insights into specific subjects to those who are particularly interested. These 900-odd sites are aligned along a route of about 400 km, signposted in brown for tourists. A central visitor centre at the Zollverein World Heritage Site at Essen offers all manner of information as well as facilities for booking tours and events.

The aim for the future work in the area is to form a 'National Park of Industrial Heritage' where the preservation of the industrial landscape will have an even stronger link to the development of the future. An application to claim World Heritage inscription is on its way for the entire region.

The story of the 'Route Industriekultur' has become a big success, and numerous visitors from all over the world have discovered the area. The brand and the experience behind it have changed the image of the area completely. Based on its industrial heritage, the area was acclaimed as 'European Capital of Culture' in 2010.

ERIH – European Route of Industrial Heritage

'I see the Past, Present and Future existing all at once before me.'
(William Blake, 1757–1827, English poet)

From the beginning an important goal was to integrate the Ruhr Industrial Heritage Route into a wider European Industrial Heritage Route in order to demonstrate that industry is no purely national affair, and never has been, and the industrial division of labour has never stopped at national borders. To that extent, industrial heritage forms part of the joint European memory.

At this juncture permit me to point out by way of conclusion that there is another assumption of fundamental importance to our work. The most valuable resource of old industrial regions is the people who live there. Like industrial monuments, they should never be regarded as a social burden, a view which, although it is unfortunately often expressed, is highly reprehensible for political as well as ethical reasons. If the conversion of old industrial regions is to have any chance at all, it must rely on people. We must give these people the courage and the strength to sustain change, but this cannot be done if their pride is broken again and again. This is why it is of primary importance in this age of globalisation to preserve regional identity. Just as the pride and the life of a medieval city revolved around the palace and the church, so the pit-heads and blast furnaces formed the centre of the industrial city. Consequently, one of the purposes of preserving industrial monuments is to underpin regional identity. And the stories of the lives of people are what interests tourists most!

When thinking about ERIH we first had to learn about many European sites of industrial heritage tourism. And the question was how can all these sites become strong enough to be visible and successful in the tourism market? No individual sites have a chance, even the best ones, but together their potential is much bigger so the idea was to turn ERIH into a brand. From this base there was a good chance to compete in the tourism market.

The most important concept for the ERIH strategy, learned from its model route in the Ruhr, is Network Marketing. Classical methods of marketing have much less success than direct customer contact on site. To tell local visitors that there is more to see in the Regional or European Routes, by media on site and by the assistance of the counter personal, is the best way of marketing: one for all, all for one, is the idea. But in the tourist market a 'brand' must be a common 'seal of quality'. This means the visitors or customers expect something to be satisfied with their visit.

ERIH started with the creation of a master plan starting with a model region in north-west Europe. The first step was the definition of quality criteria for the selection of the Anchor Points. Then we developed a system very similar to the one at the Ruhr. Anchor Points and other sites are in the main route, but also form part of 'Transnational Theme Routes' and 'Regional Routes'. Promoting the network is most effective with the existence of a Regional Route and/or an Anchor Point. Both should be aware that their activities should always make their membership of the whole network as visible as possible. Only this guarantees the overall success of the entire system.

ERIH opened in 2004 and since then it has developed quickly and now stretches through twenty-four countries in Europe. Fortunately, it was accepted enthusiastically by the European institutions – and no wonder, it is by far the biggest of the continents' cultural networks.

ERIH is more than a marketing network. The ERIH network encourages the trans-national transfer of knowledge and the development of joint marketing strategies and cross-border initiatives. It is about exchanging experiences: there is no need to invent every new wheel. There are many solutions for good interpretation, preservation methods, effective marketing and so on which can be shared. This will save money and will raise quality. And you never walk alone: this is more important than you might believe. To feel not alone with the daily boring problems you are confronted with is of a great psychological value.

Therefore ERIH is a success for the members. Based on common experience and the reputation of the network, local sites and networks very often benefit, receive more support (and sometimes money) from their politicians, can upgrade their site interpretation and more. One of the best examples is the Regional Route of Upper Silesia in Poland, which is very impressive and attracts a lot of visitors.

Industrial heritage is a growing business, both in general but for ERIH especially. We have about 150 million visitors to industrial heritage sites in Europe; ERIH sites have about 24 million at the moment. For many of these sites visitor numbers have grown by a third since they had become a member. The best economic impact on the sites and the region is obviously the marketing of a 'Regional Route'.

These are examples of best practice from Europe only; many more could and should be mentioned. But its principles and basics are valuable and usable at other industrial heritage tourism sites all around the world.

Finally, 'Industrial Heritage Tourism' should not be understood as a commercial branch of the local activities of a heritage site. Its big importance for me is to serve as a tool to tell the story of the history of industry – and of the people who served it. Especially the transnational aspects and the story of the 'industrial landscapes' can be told ideally when we are able to make people travel through them. Let's network!

Further reading

ARWEL EDWARDS, J and LLURDÉS i COIT, Mines and Quarries. Industrial Heritage Tourism. *Annals of Tourism Research*, 1996, vol 23, No. 2, 341–63

CONLIN, M and JOLLIFFE, L (eds): *Mining Heritage and Tourism. A global synthesis.* London: Routledge, 2010

Industrial Tourism and Community Building, new directions in industrial tourism, Transactions, Nagoya/Aichi, 2005

OTGAAR, A H J, BERG, L van den, BERGER, C and XIANG FENG, R: *Industrial Tourism: opportunities for city and enterprise.* Aldershot: Ashgate, 2010

PARDO, C J: *Turismo y Patrimonio Industrial/Tourism and Industrial Heritage.* Madrid: Editorial Síntesis, 2008

www.erih.net

Part V

Teaching and learning

29

Teaching in schools

Gràcia Dorel-Ferré

Introduction

The teaching of industrial heritage in schools already has a long background. In the 1970s private initiatives and on-site or industrial museum learning centres provided the resources for a tuition that might not have been particularly ground-breaking but whose contents upset the balance of the traditional cultural order. Instead of focusing on a heritage founded on aesthetic values deriving from Antiquity, embedded in recognised and acclaimed artistic masterpieces, industrial heritage examined the legacy left behind by a production system, often unremarkable in itself, with few or no artistic attributes. In this case, the monument was a factory or a machine, and the artist was replaced by the engineer or mechanic. Its construction was not the result of work in a studio while the end product required the intervention of many actors.

In many parts of Europe and the United States the place of industrial heritage was soon recognised. But the position of industrial heritage in the school syllabus varies from country to country and needs to be painstakingly explained. The French case, with which the author has been most concerned, is a good example. After having attempts to introduce the teaching of industrial heritage in First Grade School, industrial heritage faded away in basic education and almost vanished from in-service training. As a result, even in the best cases it was postponed until the final years of university training as a specialist topic. In this course of events it is possible to emphasise the structural and institutional constraints which curtailed its impact.

Working definitions

Experience has allowed some progress in the epistemological field, resulting in ways of distinguishing the components of the notion of industrial heritage and of contemplating new contents.

Industrial heritage is the field of knowledge that combines the study of construction, the geographical milieu, the human environment, technological processes, work conditions, skills, social relations and cultural expressions. In short, this represents the study of manufacturing societies in time and space, since their inception, by the collation of material and non-material evidence. This definition requires the explanation of sub-concepts that underlie it: time, space, location and work organisation.

In relation to the notion of time, industrial heritage can be seen as originating in the farthest periods of human prehistory. The simplest examples would be the caches of flaky stone debris, as early as the Palaeolithic period, that testify to a production pattern, following appropriate techniques, for numbers of tools that appear to have been destined for distant markets. There are also many such examples from Antiquity and the Middle Ages, and the closer to the current period the more there are.

From a didactic point of view, sub-notions such as age, order and succession are gathered to construct the notion of time, but also that of modernity. Alongside the domestic production system, the seventeenth century witnessed the beginnings of what we might call the factory system, although it did not supersede the domestic system. Both have changed, one independently of the other.

One should make it clear that industrialisation was not a process that appeared all of a sudden, like Athena born fully armed from her father's forehead. Only a sequence of factors and historical coincidences made Britain's industrialisation possible, before the process spread to the European continent in the nineteenth century. In fact, northern Italy, Flanders, Catalonia, Alsace, were already industrialised in the late Middle Ages, and from that period have left a plentiful and magnificent heritage. There was, therefore, a 'time before' – of complex industrial heritage – that bears witness to divers fields of activity. At the other end of the timeline, the late twentieth century and the closing stages of Fordism in North America and Western Europe heralded the end of a specific period, having lasted three centuries and encompassing what is commonly termed the Industrial Revolution or the Industrial Era. Some of its elements have been relocated to Asian countries such as India and China, with similarities albeit with many differences.

The study of industrial heritage must be focused on chronology in its entirety, but also on its global distribution. Thanks to TICCIH's efforts, many Latin American and African countries have been brought into the process. There are many indications that China and India, cradles of technological inventions, were close to industrialisation in the eighteenth century. Colonisation and wars waged by the Great Powers held this trend back.

When industrialisation is a by-product of colonisation, other notions than those mentioned above come into light: issues of imitation or rejection, information networks and influences, assimilation, blending and syncretism. As long as colonisation lasted, the foreign power took care of this heritage. Once gone, this heritage becomes undecipherable and destined to quick oblivion. The issue of understanding heritage is critical, and this is one of the aims of education.

Teaching industrial heritage

In elementary, junior and senior or high schools, provided that progress is adjusted to different levels, students go from learning notions derived from direct observation (the local environment or field trips) to a more general outlook from examples chosen in a global context. With a coherent arrangement, children and students tackle the contents of industrial heritage through its three rationales; space, technology and society within global systems defined in particular by their chronological scope. The most useful tools for this approach are varied. The study of the landscape puts into place the key notions of site, infrastructure and functional architecture. The production space, the outlining of a technological processes, the social organisation of work that ensues, the life histories

A school group at the Museu-Molí Paperer de Capellades in Spain learns how rags were prepared for making paper. Industrial museums are an excellent resource for schools, providing direct contact with objects in a stimulating and secure environment, while for many industrial museums school groups are their major source of visitors. (Milena Rosés)

that can be reconstituted, the social context, the position in a larger timescale are other approaches.

To teach industrial heritage is also to take into account two dimensions of a subject unlike any other. On one side, the scientific aspect that has just been described, and on the other, the human aspect. Confronted with a testimony about industrial activity from past societies, the pupil must be able to reflect on its future: conservation, reuse, rehabilitation for other purposes, and so on. Students must learn to bring together memory and survival, to choose the most relevant traces from the past and to preserve their significance in a context, which does not always allow it.

This is also why industrial heritage is not a class-room subject. The students will only face this witness of the past outdoors, in the field. In such an approach, the preserved site museum or the collection museum plays a vital part. Intellectual tools must draw on experience and direct observation. Teaching methods in field trips must be scrupulously followed, whether the project is the first stage of learning how to collect data. Back in the classroom, the information collected during the trip is shared and processed, in order to discover, contextualise and put into perspective the main axes: space, technology and society. This is the whole essence of historical reasoning.

Translated by Denis McKee

Further reading

DOREL-FERRE, Gràcia: *Enseigner le patrimoine industriel, le cas de Saint-Dizier (Haute-Marne), collèges et lycées*, Chaumont, 1998

Investigating industrial sites: English Heritage teachers' kit, 2011, http://www.english-heritage.org.uk/publications/investigating-industrial-sites-tk/investigating-industrial-sites-tk-02.pdf

30

University training

Györgyi Németh

Introduction

Accommodating industrial heritage-related educational programmes in the university system is almost as challenging as finding a place for industrial archaeology among the academic disciplines. This is due, without doubt, to the multidisciplinary approach to the subject, as well as its primary interest in practical work. The main focus of industrial-heritage higher education is on providing a variety of skills and competences so that students can not only understand the surviving evidence of industrialisation but also promote its preservation and appreciation. In order to give industrial-heritage students insight into the nature of industrial development, including the transition from pre-industrial to industrial societies, introductory studies are needed to academic fields such as the history of technology, economic and social history, geography, urban planning and environmental sciences. Meanwhile, to equip them with professional skills regarding the conservation, interpretation and management of the significant material remains of past industrial activities, training is essential in the practical aspects of above- and below-ground archaeology, understanding artefactual evidence, the use of documentary and oral sources, recording and dating technologies, databases and spatial analysis, protective legislation and fund-raising, to list only the most obvious. Providing the breadth of capability and capacity that can be required of industrial-heritage professionals within a single curriculum is the challenge that educators face.

Courses of study

Developing several competences and a whole range of practical skills in future industrial archaeologists requires comprehensive higher educational programmes. Courses embedded in the curriculum of related academic disciplines usually transfer significant basic knowledge. However, more substantial expertise can only be obtained in specialist programmes focusing entirely on industrial heritage. Combining theoretical and practical training most effectively, these are typically organised at masters level, offering further education after completion of a first degree (graduate training in the US or post-graduate in Europe), leading to a research-based doctoral degree in the subject. These are provided at Michigan Technological University in the US and in the Erasmus Mundus programme entitled *Techniques, patrimoine, territoires de l'industrie* (Master

TPTI) operated jointly by the universities of Paris 1 Panthéon-Sorbonne (France), Evora (Portugal) and Padua (Italy). The Technical University and Mining Academy of Freiberg in Germany offers a masters programme following a bachelor programme in industrial archaeology. Nevertheless, individual university programmes not granting degrees in the subject but concentrating on specific problems, such as, for example, the Nordic courses or the Industrial Heritage Platform, both initiated by Marie Nisser in the northern European countries, also considerably enhanced proficiency regarding industrial heritage.

University programmes in industrial archaeology propose varied approaches according to their particular priorities, aims and available resources. The objective of this strategy is to form graduates with specified expert knowledge concerning the specialist spheres while initiating them into the complex domain of industrial heritage higher education.

Consistent with its title as well as its organisational structure, emphasis in the Erasmus Mundus programme headed by the University of Paris 1 has been placed on the technology, heritage and territorial issues of industrialisation in a transnational framework. They also investigate the evolution of industrial landscapes in an historical perspective as well as the impacts of industrial production on urban settings worldwide.

In Freiberg, the oldest institution of technical higher education, located within an important historic mining region of Germany, considerable attention has been given to industrial culture and society as well as to the history of science and technology. Having been acquainted with the basics of engineering and natural sciences, such as physics, chemistry, material and geosciences, students also analyse environmental problems provoked by industrial development.

Michigan Tech., situated in the centre of a once significant copper-mining area on the Upper Great Lakes, integrates practical courses in historical and industrial archaeology, as well as the history of technology, historic preservation and the documentation of historic structures, to produce a strong emphasis upon the material culture of industry. Consequently, participants in the programme receive substantial training in numerous techniques and methodologies such as site survey and testing, excavation and record-keeping, measured drawings and architectural photography. The prominent role in the curriculum of anthropological studies related to industrial communities has been due to the strong link at the university between industrial archaeological research and the social sciences.

In the case of the Nordic courses, which are no longer run, the training programme aimed fundamentally to increase collective knowledge of industrial history as well as the industrial heritage of northern Europe. To this end, a special theme was selected in each of the four participating countries, such as mining and iron-making in Sweden, wood industries in Finland, waterpower and electrical industries in Norway and urban and agricultural industries in Denmark. In another doctoral training project entitled *Industrial heritage and societies in transition*, coordinated by Sweden and Latvia, the focus has been on the past two or three decades, with special reference to the restructuring of industry and its impacts on heritage in the Nordic and Baltic countries.

In the current programme of the Ironbridge Institute in the United Kingdom, heritage management and historic environment conservation have been placed in the centre of post-graduate studies coordinated with the University of Birmingham. A successor to the pioneering Industrial Archaeology course developed by Michael Stratton and Barrie Trinder in 1981, and the Heritage Management course started in 1986, the main fields of instruction, such as the ethics and philosophy of conservation, the legislative background, project design, business management and finance, marketing and interpretation, are concerned with various types of cultural heritage and not exclusively the heritage of industrialisation. Making full use of the unique setting of the industrial monuments of the Ironbridge Gorge, museum and World Heritage site, the specialised programme puts stewardship, sustainability and economic viability at the heart of the training.

Practical training

'Activity is the only road to knowledge': George Bernard Shaw's fundamental principle of teaching is particularly relevant in industrial-heritage education. Indeed, regardless of familiarising students with theory or practice, each university course in industrial archaeology demands active participation in experiential learning processes. The most suitable terrain for involving industrial archaeology students actively in training is fieldwork. Having been introduced through field visits to industrial heritage problems on site, students are ordinarily requested to undertake the implementation of a field project of their own. Field projects may focus on industrial heritage sites maintained by the universities, such as the historic mine at Freiberg, or involve a large-scale university project such as the multi-year archaeological investigation carried out by Michigan Tech. at West Point Foundry in Cold Spring, New York. In Ironbridge the continuing investigation, conservation, interpretation and economic development of the World Heritage site and museum offers scope to expand practical experience.

To face the challenges of industrial-heritage preservation in a real-world environment, students often engage in internships with an external partner of the university. The range of partners consists of heritage organisations, museums, research institutions, professional associations as well as development agencies, business companies and departments of central and local administration. Depending on the educational programme there is a wide variety of internships, from part-time work during the university year, through summer field schools, to complete semesters devoted to full-time employment. Based on an original research plan or on internship, field projects are commonly developed into final dissertations, while their collective version can take the form of an online publication, as in the case of the TPTI programme. In addition to providing key expertise through direct student involvement in the practice of industrial heritage preservation, they raise awareness of the crucial role of networking and multidisciplinary co-operation among industrial archaeologists.

Professional knowledge regarding the industrial heritage should be transferred in a multinational context owing to the global traits of industrialisation over the past two centuries. Participating in partnership programmes operated by several foreign universities, students gain experience through studying in each semester in different countries. For example, in the pioneering joint masters programme of TPTI, the same route of mobility is followed by every student, spending the first semester in Paris, the second in Evora and the third in Padua, the fourth being retained for personal selection according to the final thesis. Similarly, training locations in Denmark, Finland, Norway and Sweden have been alternately changed during the Nordic courses, the week-long teaching periods focusing, four times a year, on diverse issues of industrial archaeology. Due to part-time training between the semesters in additional foreign

Students at the Technical University and Mining Academy at Freiberg investigating excavated industrial remains. (Helmuth Albrecht)

partner universities, preferably outside the developed countries of Europe, such as the National University of Mexico, the Federal University of Technology in Parana (Brazil) or the University of Ouagadougou (Burkina Faso), learning on the universal heritage of past industrial production is further raised for the masters students of TPTI. In Ironbridge and at Michigan Tech., global teaching has been mostly provided within the framework of international projects implemented with substantial student contribution in France, Italy, Germany, Greece, Spain, Colombia as well as at Svalbard in the Arctic, respectively.

Conclusion

Professional opportunities for graduates of industrial archaeology are, at the same time, narrow and broad. While employment in traditional fields such as heritage administration, archaeology, museums or academic research is small, an increasing number of jobs can be found in new working fields associated with sustainable building, urban and landscape planning, environmental management, economic development, tourism and education. This brief overview of the best practices current in industrial heritage higher education shows how the necessary knowledge and skills for industrial heritage professionals can be transmitted efficiently. Accommodating a multidisciplinary curriculum with emphasis on a specific field and concentrating on active student participation in various forms of teaching, first of all in fieldwork, university programmes convey complex knowledge regarding the matcrial evidence of industrialisation. A multinational approach must be prioritised, working in partnership with various institutions, to create an appropriate setting for training.

Nevertheless, despite the numerous accomplishments of these programmes, deficiencies can still be found in the education of industrial archaeologists. For example, although the discipline focuses mostly on the conservation and reuse of industrial buildings, architecture as well as town planning has been generally assigned a minor role among industrial heritage courses. Regrettably, little attention has been given to the industrial remains of significant geographical regions, such as eastern Europe and the whole Asian continent. These weaknesses should be corrected in future university programmes in industrial archaeology.

Further reading

GARÇON, A-F, CARDOSO DE MATOS, A, FONTANA, G L (eds): *Techniques, patrimoine, territoires de l'industrie: quel enseignement?* Lisbon: Ediçoes Colibri, 2010

GEIJERSTAM, J af (ed): Reports/Working Papers. The TICCIH Seminar on Training and Education within the Field of Industrial Heritage. Stockholm and Norberg, Sweden, June 8–11, 2008. See http://www.mnactec.cat/ticcih/documentation.php

NISSER, M: Our Industrial Past and Present. Challenges in Training and Education. *Patrimoine de l'industrie – Industrial Patrimony.* 2008, 20, 2, 27–32

PALMER, M: Archeology or Heritage Management: The Conflict of Objectives in the Training of Industrial Archeologists. *Industrial Archeology,* 2000, 26, 2, 49–54

SEELY, B E and MARTIN, P E: A Doctoral Program in Industrial Heritage and Archeology at Michigan. *CRM: The Journal of Heritage Stewardship,* 2006, 3, 1

31

Distance and on-line learning

Tuija Mikkonen

Introduction

The documentation of industrial sites and production processes must be done on site, but on-line methods and tools can be beneficially exploited in training and education when direct physical connection with the study object is not essential. The principal advantage of these methods is the saving of time and money, which is an important issue when teachers and students come from different parts of a country or even from different countries far away from each other. But on-line methods have many other advantages. This chapter outlines the structures and methods of using e-learning as complementary to face-to-face studies, deploying Finnish experience as an example of best practice.

What is e-learning?

Although e-learning usually comprises all forms of electronically supported learning and teaching, the term usually refers to a form of learning in which the teacher and student are separated by space and/or time, and the gap between the two is bridged through the use of on-line technologies. E-learning is one form of distance learning, which can refer to different kinds of tools, from regular postal mail to broadcast and mobile learning. E-learning can be used in conjunction with face-to-face teaching. Different pedagogical elements such as on-line lessons, assignments, multiple-choice questions, discussion groups or case studies, can all be used to build up a stimulating learning environment. E-learning lessons guide students through information and help them perform in specific tasks.

The communication technologies used in e-learning can be categorised as asynchronous or synchronous. The first one refers to the activities that participants may engage in to exchange ideas or information without depending on other participants' involvement at the same time. Wikis, discussion boards and electronic mail are examples of asynchronous communication. Synchronous activities involve the live exchange of ideas and information with one or more participants during the same period of time, such as face-to-face on-line discussion, chat sessions and virtual classrooms and meetings.

International education of industrial heritage is a challenging undertaking that requires adequate resources. Although the most important issue in the planning of international education is to build up a course with the content that satisfies the students' diverse needs, attention should be paid to learning methods. E-learning offers a useful learning method to complement traditional learning environments in on-campus lecture halls, classrooms, workshops and in the field. Different pedagogical elements can raise motivation of the students by building up a stimulating learning environment.

On-line education: best practice

The Finnish University Network for the History of Science and Technology – called Torus – was a joint effort of a number of Finnish universities to deliver education by e-learning methods. The goal of the network was to offer multidisciplinary academic education for graduate and post-graduate students independently of the geographical location or university affiliation of the student. The network was coordinated by the Department of History at the University of Oulu and financed by the Finnish Ministry of Education. Unfortunately, the network operated on a project basis and it was closed in 2007. The experience of the network was, however, encouraging and worth developing to meet international needs.

The programme offered by Torus consisted of about twenty different courses on the history of science and technology. The maximum number on any one course was between 15 to 30 students, depending on the contents and pedagogical methods that were being used. One of the courses was an introduction to industrial heritage studies, which was planned and conducted by the author.

The students of the network could take singular courses or, alternatively, a whole grade of 25 European Credit Transfer System (ECTS) credits. The courses that the student passed at Torus were included as a part of the degree at the student's own university, provided that the university was a member of the network or accepted Torus studies in its curriculum, through a separate agreement. Each course was the equivalent of two to five credits. The combination of courses could be selected according to the student's own interests.

The network was run by a small coordinating group working at the University of Oulu. The coordination staff took care of all practical arrangements, but they also supported the teachers with technical and pedagogical assistance. The courses were prepared by invited teachers with special knowledge on the subject concerned. The teachers represented different disciplines, universities and expertise. In that way, the highest possible competence could be gathered to benefit the network. Torus also collaborated with international networks of the history of technology such as Tensions of Europe and the European Society for the History of Science.

The studies were mainly carried out by e-learning methods, which was a clear advantage in a topic of relatively small interest in a geographically large country. The courses were organised in open learning environments, such as Optima, provided by the Finnish company Discendum, and by internationally well-known WebCT. Optima was regarded as more suitable and flexible for diversified interactive work, offering a wide range of tools for the support of on-line learning according to the teacher's own pedagogical methodology. The choice of learning environment is especially important in creating inspiring study experiences that support the pedagogical goals of the course in the best possible way.

On-line industrial heritage training

The industrial heritage course of the Torus network was carried out by a group of three teachers of which the leading teacher was responsible for the whole course, while the assisting teachers only for their own lectures. The course consisted of eight lectures and a voluntary excursion to an industrial heritage site in central Finland. Furthermore, the students could earn extra credits by writing an essay on an optional theme. At the end of the course, a final discussion was carried out at the electronic work space where both the contents of the course and the practical issues were aired.

All course materials were available at the work space to which the students had access through a user name and password. The material could be loaded on a personal computer, if needed. The course proceeded lecture by lecture during a period of about ten weeks. The lectures consisted of texts, illustrations, film clips, additional readings, links to external websites and on-line exhibitions and so forth. The students were also encouraged to take initiatives and actively search for additional material supporting their studies.

The students could study the materials of a lecture at the work space during seven or fourteen days, after which they had to make assignment(s) to deepen their knowledge and as a control to show that they really had absorbed the information given in the lecture. In order to keep up the students' interest, the assignments were of different characters, including materials to be analysed, a short essay on a given topic, reports and discussions at the work space on a specific topic or film, analysis of a book. After every on-line lecture and control assignment the teacher gave comments and feedback on all the assignments for the whole group collectively and/or for every student personally. This tutoring phase took many hours of the teacher's time, but it was highly appreciated by the students.

During the whole course, the teacher took part actively in tutoring the students at the work space. The students and the teachers could communicate at a friendly discussion forum, called the coffee room, which in Finland refers to a place where people used take a coffee and meet each other during a working day to discuss formal and informal issues – a kind of village pump. The forum was frequently visited by the students, and the conversation was lively even between the students without the teacher's involvement. Close and continuous connection between the teacher and the students was highly appreciated. This is usually not possible in the same way and at the same extension in traditional campus-based learning systems.

The interactive connection and a feeling that the teacher was always easily reachable clearly raised the motivation of the students. According to the feedback collected at the end of the course, the students put especially high value on interactive work, which was fruitful for the teachers, too.

As mentioned above, the independence of the space is one of the main advantages of e-learning. The students on the Torus network could participate in their studies at home, at the university campus or anywhere. The only technical requirements were to have access to an internet connection with relatively high speed and an email address. At some courses a meeting of teachers and the study group or an excursion to a stimulating place with a direct connection to the course topic was an integral start to the studies. The meeting was a practical way for students and teachers to meet, giving a face to the other people on the course. It was also regarded as valuable for the commitment of the students.

E-learning complements traditional learning methods

The experience acquired by the Finnish network Torus can be exploited in international industrial heritage education to collect expertise from different countries and to offer high-quality education for students scattered in different parts of the world. E-learning is an effective method to save financial resources and time. With industrial heritage studies, fieldwork and site visits are essential components which cannot be replaced by any other means. However, learning in classrooms can easily be adapted to be carried out in internet environments, which can offer diversified possibilities for using different kinds of materials and, at the same time, give plenty of opportunities for interactive connections between the participants of the study group.

In many countries, large photographic collections and databases on buildings and sites have been transformed into digital format and put on the internet, offering new information for researchers, heritage authorities, developers, architects and enthusiasts, regardless of their physical location. The TICCIH website offers a list of links to such inventories of industrial heritage. During the past ten years, the number of virtual publications has increased remarkably and the capacity of virtual libraries has grown. Today the on-line material to be utilised on e-learning environments is no longer an obstacle.

Conclusion

As is evident from the above, e-learning has all sorts of advantages. However, there are also many problems and critical points to be dealt with. The motivation and the preparedness of the participants should be high enough to overcome the absence of peer support and direct teacher contact. A physical meeting of the participants and the teachers is recommended at the beginning of the course to make the group-work and the interactive connection more natural and effective.

The commitment and active participation from the teacher's side is demanding, but especially important on an internet-based course. The full use of digital materials, databases, registers and other information, as well as adapting new learning methods, should be developed to give the best possible results.

Through international co-operation, putting together the experience and knowledge of individual experts and organisations, all sorts of interesting e-courses could be offered at graduate and post-graduate levels, as well as many other forms of training and education such as workshops for heritage professionals, collaborative research projects, site recording exercises or preparation of museum guides.

Further reading

BATES, A W: *Technology, e-Learning and Distance Education*. London: Routledge, 2012

DALY C and PACHLER, N: *Key Issues in e-Learning: Research and practice*. London: Continuum, 2011

Part VI

TICCIH

32

The work of TICCIH

Stuart B Smith

Introduction

Forty years ago, industrial archaeology was a newly founded subject with few adherents, and it had little influence on society at large. In the UK, it had grown out of the railway and canal preservation movements and the controversial destruction of the Euston Arch outside Euston station, London, in 1961. Modernism was supposed to supplant and improve on the old Victorian architecture.

How wrong they were – over the past 40 years public opinion has swung strongly in favour of industrial preservation, which is now seen as a mainstream activity. Textile mills which were being pulled down are now instead converted to fashionable apartments. The contribution of industry towards the development of twentieth-century society has been recognised, and increasingly is reflected by the number of industrial World Heritage Sites. There are industrial preservation organisations in most of Europe, America North, Central and South, Australasia and increasingly in Asia, most of which are affiliated to TICCIH and ICOMOS.

There are still some problem areas that need to be addressed. Probably the most important is that industrial sites particularly in Africa, Asia and the ex-Communist block can be seen as sites of colonial power subjugating a local population. Of course, these same powers also provided most of the infrastructure which these countries now enjoy.

The other problem is one of snobbery, where industrial sites are seen not to be designed by great architects or as just too modern to be deemed worthy of preservation. While the Industrial Revolution in Europe took place largely between 1750 and 1900, there has been a second industrial revolution from 1900 onwards, particularly in the fields of medicine, communications, food supply and transport, which has revolutionised everyone's lives. The rate of acceleration of new technology is increasing almost weekly and therefore the sites and processes associated with this change must still be recorded and on occasion preserved.

Finally, it has to be recognised that some industrial sites, although of great importance, are perceived as having been be places of great suffering and exploitation. This does not mean that they are not important in terms of world history. One can think of the site of the terrible chemical explosion in Bhopal, India, or the construction of the Burma railway during the Second World War. To remember, record and

The Iron Bridge, Telford, UK, (1779) is perhaps the primary global icon of industrial heritage. The opening international meeting of industrial archaeologists was organised at the nearby Ironbridge Gorge Museum in 1973. (Alistair Hodge)

possibly preserve these sites does not glorify the oppressor but helps to commemorate the oppressed.

These are some of the challenges which face TICCIH into the twenty-first century.

TICCIH, a short history

The credit for creating the only global organisation for the study, interpretation and preservation of our industrial heritage must go to Neil Cossons, who had the idea in 1973 of bringing together practitioners, both professional and amateur, from all over the world to hold a conference at the Ironbridge Gorge Museum, in England, where he had recently been appointed director, to discuss the preservation of industrial heritage.

At this first meeting of industrial archaeological experts most of the delegates came from Europe, particularly Germany and the UK, together with a few from the United States. Subsequent meetings in Bochum, Germany, in 1975 and in Sweden two years later saw an increase in the number of delegates from other parts of the world, including Japan and eastern Europe.

It was at this third meeting in Sweden that TICCIH was formally established as an international organisation. Congresses have since been held more or less every three years since then, in Grenoble, Lowell and Boston, Vienna and Vordernberg, Brussels, Barcelona and Madrid, Montreal and Ottawa, Thessalonica, the Millennium Congress in London, Moscow and Ekaterinburg in the Russian Federation in 2003, Terni, in Italy, and in Freiberg, Germany in 2009. The 2012 TICCIH Congress was in Taiwan, the first to be held in Asia.

TICCIH congresses normally stretch over five days with pre- and post-conference tours. The meetings are organised by the host country which is responsible for publishing the papers and national reports. The meeting normally starts with distinguished lecturers on the area and country, followed by several days of thematic meetings, visits and receptions.

Each country is urged to form a National Committee, and strong organisations exist in countries such as Spain, Greece, Mexico and the UK, for example. National Committees are encouraged to draw up a reciprocal agreement with TICCIH international. Where no National Committee exists and there are only a few members, TICCIH works through a National Correspondent who tries to build up an organisation in that country.

TICCIH is essentially a volunteer organisation with no paid officials or staff and no central headquarters. It exists largely on subscriptions from individual members and from National Committees. It is formally established as a charitable trust (not-for-profit-organisation) in England and is governed by a Board of Trustees, led by the president. All our presidents have been instrumental in developing the organisation. These include the late Professor John Harris (UK), the late Professor Marie Nisser (Sweden), Professor Louis Bergeron (France), Eusebi Casanelles (Spain) and currently Professor Patrick Martin (US). Each president has brought unique expertise to the organisation and developed new aspects to TICCIH's work. John Harris and Marie Nisser were particularly interested in education, Louis Bergeron was deeply committed to publication and still helps to produce *Industrial Patrimony*, Eusebi Casanelles developed interest in industrial archaeology in South America where there are now strong organisations in almost every country, and Patrick Martin, the president at the time of publication, is committed to increasing communication through modern media.

Almost certainly the most important thing to have kept the organisation together over so many years has been the publication of a newsletter on a regular basis. It first appeared as *Industrial Heritage Newsletter* for the conference in 1984 in the US but only ran for three issues. It was succeeded by *World Industrial History* from 1985–1992, published by the Association for Industrial Archaeology (UK) and edited by Dr Barrie Trinder at the Ironbridge Institute. A *TICCIH Bulletin* was produced from February 1988, once again edited by Dr Trinder but funded by the Ironbridge Gorge Museum. This *Bulletin* continued until 1997 but in 1998 its production and finance were taken over by the Museu de la Ciència i de la Tècnica de Catalunya in Terrassa, Spain. Initially still edited by Dr Trinder, editorship passed to James Douet in Terrassa, who continued to produce a *Bulletin* of increasing quality, scope and value. However, with increasing costs of publication, it was reluctantly agreed in 2011 that the *Bulletin* should be published entirely electronically. Still edited by James Douet, with a great deal of co-operation from the President's office in Michigan, US, a new *Bulletin* has been produced which even to sceptics is now much better than anything previously. This is the only official publication of TICCIH, which keeps our members and supporters aware of what is happening in the industrial heritage movement. Many thanks are due to James Douet for producing the *Bulletin* over so many years.

TICCIH has special sections which meet from time to time. These include Agriculture and Food Production, Bridges, Communications, Local and Global Issues, Hydroelectricity and Electrochemical industry, Metallurgy, Mining and Collieries, Mints, Polar Region, Railways, Textiles and Tourism. Sections occasionally organise conferences, and other intermediate conferences are arranged by individual countries or groups of countries. Full details are on the TICCIH website.

Special thematic reports by TICCIH have been used by ICOMOS when assessing potential new World Heritage Sites and include Canals, Bridges, Railways and Collieries. There is a great potential for expanding these specialised reports as one of the main benefits that TICCIH brings to any individual or country working in a specific field is the objectivity of an international approach. TICCIH has affiliations with other international bodies as well as with ICOMOS, and held a joint conference with the International Committee for the History of Technology (ICOHTEC) in 2010. It is also working with the modern Asian Architecture Network (mAAN) which in 2011 held a conference in South Korea. Although TICCIH endeavours to work largely with international bodies, it actively supports cross-border projects such as the European Route of Industrial Heritage (ERIH).

A formal agreement was signed between ICOMOS and TICCIH in 2000 at the Millennium Congress in London whereby ICOMOS recognised TICCIH as the Expert Committee on the industrial heritage. This has led to TICCIH being a special adviser to ICOMOS on potential industrial World Heritage Sites and assisting with the assessment and designation of these sites throughout the world. Although not a scientific committee, TICCIH attends these meetings in an advisory capacity.

At the Russia congress in 2003, TICCIH president Eusebi Casanelles signed the Nizhny Tagil Charter for the Industrial Heritage with the congress host, Eugene Logonov, and after numerous deliberations this approach was confirmed by ICOMOS in 2011 as the *ICOMOS-TICCIH Principles for the Conservation of Industrial Heritage Sites, Structures, Areas and Landscapes*. TICCIH hopes these principles will be widely accepted by national governments.

TICCIH is increasingly asked to support preservation attempts in countries throughout the world, and this role of advocacy is formalised so that TICCIH can continue to provide informed and international advice to people who feel that their industrial heritage is under threat.

TICCIH has been firmly established in Europe and North America for many years, but increasingly countries in South America as well as Mexico and Australia, have become active members. The Board of TICCIH now represents every continent, Africa, Australia, Asia, Europe and America.

TICCIH is proud of the fact that it attracts large numbers of young people to its general conferences, almost equally divided between male and female, which also reflects its general membership and Board. For an academic organisation, this is quite

Delegates at the 1973 First International Congress on the Conservation of Industrial Monuments (FICCIM) debate the birth of the industrial revolution in front of Abraham Darby's Old Furnace in Coalbrookdale, Ironbridge, England. Darby's name is cast on the furnace. From left: Neil Cossons, Director of the Ironbridge Gorge Museum; John Corby, Curator, Industrial Technology, National Museum of Science and Technology, Ottawa, Canada; with hand raised, Michael Dower of the Dartington Amenity Research Trust, Dartington Hall; with his back to the camera is Professor John Harris, Head of the Department of Economic and Social History at the University of Birmingham, England; Dr Wolfhard Weber, Ruhr-Universitat, Historisches Institut, Lehrstuhl fur Wirstschaft Technikgeschichte, Bochum, Germany; far right John G Waite, Senior Historical Architect, New York State Division for Historic Preservation, Parks and Recreation, Albany, New York, US. (Neil Cossons)

outstanding, and every effort needs to be made to increase the number of young female members of the Board to reflect the general make-up of society.

The collapse of the Soviet Union in the 1990s led to a spectacular growth in industrial preservation and interest in Hungary, Poland, Romania, Russia and the Czech Republic. Many of these countries are now coming to terms with their post-colonial experience, and are faced with the problems of what to preserve. Similarly, there has been a huge increase in interest in the work of industrial preservation in Asia, in particular in India, China including Taiwan, Japan, the Philippines and South Korea.

What have been the main achievements of TICCIH, and what are its new challenges? Probably its greatest achievement is that it has survived all this time as a voluntary organisation with no funding from government or international organisations such as UNESCO. Interest in industrial preservation and interpretation has spread to almost every country in the world, with university courses, postgraduate training programmes, and even acceptance by conventional archaeologists.

Global industrial heritage

There has also been a huge rise in the interest by national governments of designating industrial sites as World Heritage Sites. Since Ironbridge became one in 1986, eight more have been designated in the UK since 1999, and two are currently on the next UK tentative list. Similar interest in promoting industrial World Heritage Sites is seen all over the world, and now more than thirty have been inscribed and many more are on tentative lists in numerous countries. There are many challenges to be faced, in particular the problems of ex-colonial countries, whether they be in eastern Europe, Africa, South America or Asia, where industrial activity was not created by indigenous peoples but by colonising powers.

Traditional national cultural departments find it difficult to understand that their churches, temples or castles may not be the greatest contribution that they have made to world society. Designating large-scale industrial or even urban World Heritage Sites is a proper reflection of the importance of these sites to world history, but it is not as easy as designating a single monumental site. This is particularly difficult if the industry is still in existence, but surely these are the most exciting sites of all? A closed industrial site, even though perfectly preserved, is nowhere near as exciting or informative as one that is still in operation. For many years Japan has led the world in the designation as important historic sites not only of monuments but also people with skills and also activities such as theatre. A shift away from the pure consideration of monuments towards culturally important processes and activities is probably the greatest challenge for TICCIH, ICOMOS and UNESCO.

33

TICCIH's Charter for Industrial Heritage

Eusebi Casanelles

Introduction

Discussing the meaning of industrial heritage in the 1980s with people from the world of culture in Catalonia and later in other countries, it was apparent that there was a degree of confusion surrounding the concept. Some of those interested in industrial heritage had arrived through trying to save a particular local factory, steam engine, mine or whatever. But they had no clear references or theoretical 'corpus' on which to base the defence of these physical remains, to which mainstream society, especially those with the power to determine the policies governing the cultural heritage, attributed little value.

The big problem for industrial heritage was, and partly still is, the absence of an academic discipline to provide the theoretical foundation which would locate it within the cultural field. Without this support it was considered a lesser heritage. This was abnormal in that all the other specialized areas such as archaeology, art history or ethnology had their corresponding university departments. Nor were the architecture professionals very appreciative, a collective occupying key positions in heritage administration, because industrial buildings for them presented no singularity, constructive, aesthetic or structural. In this situation the priority was to raise popular awareness, especially among those involved with cultural heritage.

Raising awareness

My experience in Catalonia had been fairly successful. Apart from creating the network of industrial museums known as the mNACTEC, a series of exhibitions, publications, videos and programmes had an impact. In the 1990s there were a number of campaigns in defence of industrial heritage sites in many parts of the country, spurred on by local initiatives thanks to a new consciousness developed by the museum.

Internationally, spreading this awareness had to be done in some other way. My election as Executive President in 1996 led to contacts with people from all over the world, and it was clear that in many places the situation was similar to that which had existed in Catalonia. But despite publications and campaigns, there was a need for a simple text which laid out the fundamental values and importance of industrial heritage as a part of our cultural resources. This text needed to define the main lines governing interventions, and it had to give guidance for a form of conservation which was in many ways different to that practised at other heritage sites. The main purpose of this text was to become an instrument for the advocates of industrial heritage while at the same time influencing those with the power to decide issues of cultural policy. This text had to be prepared by TICCIH, already a well-respected international organization, or at least one which created a good impression when you spoke on its behalf. The fact that this organization had members from the countries with the most cultural influence in the world, with many well-known professionals and university academics, helped greatly to accomplish a task which in Christian terms we would call 'evangelical'. Those people who had worked in TICCIH since the late 1970s had already done a great job. The name of TICCIH was already used by individuals and groups fighting to preserve a historic site of industry, to contradict those who claimed it had no cultural value, or, worse, was just a nostalgic obsession for forgotten ways of working.

International doctrinal texts

It was through the relationship between TICCIH and ICOMOS, initiated by previous president Louis Bergeron, that I appreciated the importance of charters and international standard texts and became convinced that this was the type of document TICCIH needed. In studying the various well-known or ICOMOS-approved documents, starting in 1964 with the Venice Charter for the Conservation and Restoration of Monuments and Sites, or the 1994 Nara Document on Authenticity, I realised that there were also very specific texts. Some were designed to define and promote an aspect of cultural heritage which was apparently not clear to many people, such as the Florence Charter of Historic Gardens (1982) and the Washington Charter on the Conservation of Historic Towns and Urban Areas (1987), or UNESCO's Convention on the Protection of the Underwater Cultural Heritage (2001). But two were more generic, the Charter for the Protection and Management of the Archaeological Heritage (1990) and the Charter for the Built Vernacular Heritage (1999) which referred to ethnological constructions.

It was evident that if there were charters about some themes and not others it was because ICOMOS had found itself facing problems similar to ours and had felt the need for such a document expressing the fundamental principles of conserving those explicit aspects of cultural heritage. The industrial heritage also needed such a charter, to help clarify the core values of the field while laying out the best means of conserving the evidence. I have to thank James Douet, who was working with me at the museum, for making the comparisons with other charters and writing the text.

Drafting the charter

The first problem was to define the period of history that framed the industrial heritage. It was – and remains – a question on which there is no clear consensus. Kenneth Huston, for example, defined the object of study of industrial heritage as encompassing all the physical remains from the world of production throughout the history of humanity. In contrast, others adopted a more restricted viewpoint, focused on the birth of industrialisation and the Industrial Revolution.

The TICCIH charter wanted to make clear that the material goods that formed our industrial heritage were from the transformation which began in the second half of the eighteenth century with the introduction of a specific method of production that historians have called the factory system. It consciously associated industrialisation with the enormous social upheaval which was a consequence of this change and took it beyond the narrower advances of science and technology as witnessed in earlier times and by different civilisations such as the Islamic and Chinese, but which had no comparable large-scale and prolonged social consequences.

Not everyone agreed that the principal period for industrial heritage began with the final quarter of the eighteenth century. Many members of TICCIH in Europe believed that it had roots in the Middle Ages; Italians claimed that the birth of the factory system took place with the northern Italian silk mills instead of Lombe's mill in Derby, England, often celebrated as the world's first modern factory.

For this reason, the introduction to the TICCIH charter refers to these older precedents and 'pre-industrial' roots. The term proto-industrial was added, even though it is not one favoured by economic historians, but it was very appropriate for us to emphasise that what really mattered in the pre-industrial period were the years immediately prior to the Industrial Revolution. I had proposed that the pre-industrial processes of particular

The Rheinfelden hydroelectric power station on the river Rhine, Germany. After the construction of a new power plant alongside, demolition of the old power station was approved to create an appropriate ecological compensation area. A local citizens' group fought for the preservation of the power plant supported by strong advocacy from TICCIH and others, but nature trumped industrial heritage. This site could have become an outstanding industrial witness to green energy. It was demolished in 2011. (Norbert Tempel)

The 1908 woollen mill in Terrassa, Spain, narrowly avoided demolition, despite its extraordinary vaulted north-lit roof. It is now the headquarters of the Museu de la Ciència i de la Tècnica de Catalunya, the Catalan national museum of industry and technology, and an important regional centre for schools education, artefact conservation and the promotion of industrial heritage. (MNACTEC)

interest were those whose products were not intended for autarchic markets, but this was too complicated a concept for what was intended as a clear-cut document.

The text also proposed an end date to the period of interest of industrial heritage. Some authors identify this as the 1960s when society evolved toward the era that Althusser named *post-industrial* and which other historians have called the consumer society. By the time the TICCIH charter was drafted it was already the twenty-first century and technological change was so fast that production systems became obsolete very quickly. Material goods turned into heritage in an ever-shorter time, as if history itself was accelerating. I experienced this phenomenon a few years after the adoption of the charter, when a town north of Barcelona voted in a referendum to designate a power station, on the design of which I had contributed as a young engineer in the early 1970s, as part of their cultural heritage.

It was proposed to define the historical end-point of industrial heritage as productive sites which had ceased serving the function for which they had been designed. But one delegate pointed to active industries in his country still using techniques from before the 1960s (some were pre-industrial) and which were considered part of the industrial heritage. Finally it was decided that the onset of technical obsolescence should define the theoretical moment at which our interest begins.

To the definition of industrial heritage was added the further detail that it was composed specifically of remains with values from a variety of fields so as to highlight its interdisciplinary character, widening the scope of industrial heritage from productive sites to include 'warehouses and stores, places where energy is generated, transmitted and used, transport and all its infrastructure, as well as places used for social activities related to industry such as housing, education or religious worship'. While these buildings and structures are usually included in books on industrial heritage, not everyone is clear on the matter, and they are sometimes destroyed because their importance is not appreciated, even when actions are being taken with the aim of preserving some industrial component.

The charter text also attached different concepts to industrial archaeology and industrial heritage. Perhaps this was unnecessary for English-speakers but for others, and particularly in Latin-speaking regions, there was a degree of confusion. Industrial archaeology was defined as a method for studying history through a focus on its physical remains while industrial heritage deals with the care and interpretation of those remains of historical or cultural interest.

The charter tried to underline that the dominant value of the industrial heritage is as testimony to social and economic changes generated by the introduction of new production processes that changed and continue to change humanity's forms of living and working. This incorporates the values of ethnological heritage, even if industrial heritage gives more importance to technology and production methods than the protagonists of the great transformation of society worldwide, while traditional ethnology treats these as the material goods of a particular society.

TICCIH's charter also wanted to underline the documentary value of industrial heritage, whose study provides data on the ways of life and working customs of ordinary men and women. This was to emphasise these values alongside the more obvious intrinsic ones such as its rarity, age or aesthetic quality.

The separation of these two types of values, the testimonial and the intrinsic, was because failing to appreciate the evidential value of industrial heritage is one of the main reasons it is poorly understood in the wider cultural and political world. Cultural heritage managers habitually evaluate the built heritage on the basis of intrinsic structural but above all aesthetic qualities. This is why it is common in many countries for the administrations responsible for cultural heritage to be called Departments of Artistic Heritage or of Fine Arts. Age is another intrinsic value that traditionally defines heritage, one of the common conditions for forming part of the national heritage being that elements have to be more than a hundred years old.

Industrial heritage frequently lacks these characteristics. Its buildings are not aesthetically fine, its structures can be commonplace or poor, they are not especially old, nor have they witnessed the great moments or personalities of national history.

The sections of the charter directed to the administration of the industrial heritage pressed the importance of inventories, and that they should include all the available historical sources, from the textual or graphic to the personal memories of people who worked or lived there. While personal accounts may be subjective and not very reliable for historians, they are invaluable for understanding the world of work and everyday life, and are a fundamental resource for museums wanting to interpret the spirit of the place.

On the other hand, the charter recognises that not all the remains of industry have to be protected and conserved, only those whose significance has been demonstrated according to generally accepted criteria.

The discussion of criteria introduces two measures that are widely accepted throughout the world of cultural heritage but with a special relevance for that of industry, which are authenticity and integrity. The charter noted how the former can be severely harmed by the mere act of removing plant and machinery. Moreover, authenticity in industrial sites, as is reflected in the charter text, is not always easy to determine for places which have been adapted to new technologies and different uses during their working lives. Which is most authentic, the original form or the final condition, when both criteria are valid?

If the principle of authenticity is more conceptual, that of integrity presents major practical problems for conservators and restorers. In many cases the extent of an industrial site brings it into conflict with the urbanistic and constructional interests of owners and planners. A consensus is often reached to preserve only part of a site as evidence of the former productive activity. The problem is accentuated when the evidence for an industrial landscape or neighbourhood is involved, and in these cases the decision is often taken to preserve fragments or isolated elements from different industrial buildings. In the section on criteria of preservation there are several references to the re-use of buildings, since not everything of value can be saved in a museum and even less as a preserved historical monument.

The final theme to emphasise, and which recurs throughout the charter, is international collaboration. This has a special relevance for industrial heritage due to the transfers of technology, capital, knowledge and population which have accompanied industrialisation.

After a long process of consultation and discussion, the final text was presented to the TICCIH General Assembly at the 2003 Congress in Russia and signed jointly by me and the organiser of that congress, Eugene Logunov, and named after the great iron and steel-producing city in the Urals where the meeting was held, Nizhny Tagil.

In 2011 a shorter text inspired by the Charter was adopted by the 17th ICOMOS General Assembly in Paris as the Joint ICOMOS-TICCIH *Principles for the Conservation of Industrial Heritage Sites, Structures, Areas and Landscapes*, sometimes referred to as 'The Dublin Principles'.

Rereading the Charter some years after it was signed, some changes could be made and other concepts included, but the text remains very valid and has become a point of reference in many parts of the world. The publication here of the Nizhny Tagil Charter is a continuation of its work and an amplification of its ideas through the writings of international authors so that it may reach a broader and more universal public.

The Nizhny Tagil Charter for the Industrial Heritage

The International Committee for the Conservation of the Industrial Heritage (TICCIH) 17 July 2003

TICCIH is the world organisation representing industrial heritage and is special adviser to ICOMOS on industrial heritage. The text of this charter was passed by the assembled delegates at the triennial National Assembly of TICCIH held in Moscow on 17 July, 2003.

Preamble

The earliest periods of human history are defined by the archaeological evidence for fundamental changes in the ways in which people made objects, and the importance of conserving and studying the evidence of these changes is universally accepted.

From the Middle Ages, innovations in Europe in the use of energy and in trade and commerce led to a change towards the end of the 18th century just as profound as that between the Neolithic and Bronze Ages, with developments in the social, technical and economic circumstances of manufacturing sufficiently rapid and profound to be called a revolution. The Industrial Revolution was the beginning of a historical phenomenon that has affected an ever-greater part of the human population, as well as all the other forms of life on our planet, and that continues to the present day.

The material evidence of these profound changes is of universal human value, and the importance of the study and conservation of this evidence must be recognised.

The delegates assembled for the 2003 TICCIH Congress in Russia wish therefore to assert that the buildings and structures built for industrial activities, the processes and tools used within them and the towns and landscapes in which they are located, along with all their other tangible and intangible manifestations, are of fundamental importance. They should be studied, their history should be taught, their meaning and significance should be probed and made clear for everyone, and the most significant and characteristic examples should be identified, protected and maintained, in accordance with the spirit of the Venice Charter,[1] for the use and benefit of today and of the future.

---

[1] The ICOMOS 'Venice Charter for the Conservation and Restoration of Monuments and Sites', 1964.

1. Definition of industrial heritage

Industrial heritage consists of the remains of industrial culture which are of historical, technological, social, architectural or scientific value. These remains consist of buildings and machinery, workshops, mills and factories, mines and sites for processing and refining, warehouses and stores, places where energy is generated, transmitted and used, transport and all its infrastructure, as well as places used for social activities related to industry such as housing, religious worship or education.

Industrial archaeology is an interdisciplinary method of studying all the evidence, material and immaterial, of documents, artefacts, stratigraphy and structures, human settlements and natural and urban landscapes,[2] created for or by industrial processes. It makes use of those methods of investigation that are most suitable to increase understanding of the industrial past and present.

The *historical period* of principal interest extends forward from the beginning of the Industrial Revolution in the second half of the eighteenth century up to and including the present day, while also examining its earlier pre-industrial and proto-industrial roots. In addition it draws on the study of work and working techniques encompassed by the history of technology.

2. Values of industrial heritage

i. The industrial heritage is the evidence of activities which had and continue to have profound historical consequences. The motives for protecting the industrial heritage are based on the universal value of this evidence, rather than on the singularity of unique sites.

ii. The industrial heritage is of social value as part of the record of the lives of ordinary men and women, and as such it provides an important sense of identity. It is of technological and scientific value in the history of manufacturing, engineering, construction, and it may have considerable aesthetic value for the quality of its architecture, design or planning.

iii. These values are intrinsic to the site itself, its fabric, components, machinery and setting, in the industrial landscape, in written documentation, and also in the intangible records of industry contained in human memories and customs.

iv. Rarity, in terms of the survival of particular processes, site typologies or landscapes, adds particular value and should be carefully assessed. Early or pioneering examples are of especial value.

3. The importance of identification, recording and research

i. Every territory should identify, record and protect the industrial remains that it wants to preserve for future generations.

ii. Surveys of areas and of different industrial typologies should identify the extent of the industrial heritage. Using this information, inventories should

---

² For convenience, 'sites' will be taken to mean landscapes, complexes, buildings, structures and machines unless these terms are used in a more specific way.

be created of all the sites that have been identified. They should be devised to be easily searchable and should be freely accessible to the public. Computerisation and on-line access are valuable objectives.

iii. Recording is a fundamental part of the study of industrial heritage. A full record of the physical features and condition of a site should be made and placed in a public archive before any interventions are made. Much information can be gained if recording is carried out before a process or site has ceased operation. Records should include descriptions, drawings, photographs and video film of moving objects, with references to supporting documentation. Peoples' memories are a unique and irreplaceable resource which should also be recorded when they are available.

iv. Archaeological investigation of historic industrial sites is a fundamental technique for their study. It should be carried out to the same high standards as that of sites from other historical or cultural periods.

v. Programmes of historical research are needed to support policies for the protection of the industrial heritage. Because of the interdependency of many industrial activities, international studies can help identify sites and types of sites of world importance.

vi. The criteria for assessing industrial buildings should be defined and published so as to achieve general public acceptance of rational and consistent standards. On the basis of appropriate research, these criteria should be used to identify the most important surviving landscapes, settlements, sites, typologies, buildings, structures, machines and processes.

vii. Those sites and structures that are identified as important should be protected by legal measures that are sufficiently strong to ensure the conservation of their significance. The World Heritage List of UNESCO should give due recognition to the tremendous impact that industrialisation has had on human culture.

viii. The value of significant sites should be defined and guidelines for future interventions established. Any legal, administrative and financial measures that are necessary to maintain their value should be put in place.

ix. Sites that are at risk should be identified so that appropriate measures can be taken to reduce that risk and facilitate suitable schemes for repairing or re-using them.

x. International co-operation is a particularly appropriate approach to the conservation of the industrial heritage through co-ordinated initiatives and sharing resources. Compatible criteria should be developed to compile international inventories and databases.

4. Legal protection

I. The industrial heritage should be seen as an integral part of the cultural heritage in general. Nevertheless, its legal protection should take into account the special nature of the industrial heritage. It should be capable of protecting plant and machinery, below-ground elements, standing structures, complexes and ensembles of buildings, and industrial landscapes. Areas of industrial waste should be considered for their potential archaeological as well as ecological value.

II. Programmes for the conservation of the industrial heritage should be integrated into policies for economic development and into regional and national planning.

III. The most important sites should be fully protected and no interventions allowed that compromise their historical integrity or the authenticity of their fabric. Sympathetic adaptation and re-use may be an appropriate and a cost-effective way of ensuring the survival of industrial buildings, and should be encouraged by appropriate legal controls, technical advice, tax incentives and grants.

IV. Industrial communities which are threatened by rapid structural change should be supported by central and local government authorities. Potential threats to the industrial heritage from such changes should be anticipated and plans prepared to avoid the need for emergency actions.

V. Procedures should be established for responding quickly to the closure of important industrial sites to prevent the removal or destruction of significant elements. The competent authorities should have statutory powers to intervene when necessary to protect important threatened sites.

VI. Government should have specialist advisory bodies that can give independent advice on questions relating to the protection and conservation of industrial heritage, and their opinions should be sought on all important cases.

VII. Every effort should be made to ensure the consultation and participation of local communities in the protection and conservation of their local industrial heritage.

VIII. Associations and societies of volunteers have an important role in identifying sites, promoting public participation in industrial conservation and disseminating information and research, and as such are indispensable actors in the theatre of industrial heritage.

5. Maintenance and conservation

I. Conservation of the industrial heritage depends on preserving functional integrity, and interventions to an industrial site should therefore aim to maintain this as far as possible. The value and authenticity of an industrial site may be greatly reduced if machinery or components are removed, or if subsidiary elements which form part of a whole site are destroyed.

II. The conservation of industrial sites requires a thorough knowledge of the purpose or purposes to which they were put, and of the various industrial processes which may have taken place there. These may have changed over time, but all former uses should be examined and assessed.

III. Preservation *in situ* should always be given priority consideration. Dismantling and relocating a building or structure are only acceptable when the destruction of the site is required by overwhelming economic or social needs.

IV. The adaptation of an industrial site to a new use to ensure its conservation is usually acceptable except in the case of sites of especial historical significance. New uses should respect the significant material and maintain original patterns of circulation and activity, and should be compatible as much as possible with the original or principal use. An area that interprets the former use is recommended.

V. Continuing to adapt and use industrial buildings avoids wasting energy and contributes to sustainable development. Industrial heritage can have an important role in the economic regeneration of decayed or declining areas. The continuity that re-use implies may provide psychological stability for communities facing the sudden end a long-standing sources of employment.

VI. Interventions should be reversible and have a minimal impact. Any unavoidable changes should be documented and significant elements that are removed should be recorded and stored safely. Many industrial processes confer a patina that is integral to the integrity and interest of the site.

VII. Reconstruction, or returning to a previous known state, should be considered an exceptional intervention and one which is only appropriate if it benefits the integrity of the whole site, or in the case of the destruction of a major site by violence.

VIII. The human skills involved in many old or obsolete industrial processes are a critically important resource whose loss may be irreplaceable. They need to be carefully recorded and transmitted to younger generations.

IX. Preservation of documentary records, company archives, building plans, as well as sample specimens of industrial products should be encouraged.

6. Education and training

I. Specialist professional training in the methodological, theoretical and historical aspects of industrial heritage should be taught at technical and university levels.

II. Specific educational material about the industrial past and its heritage should be produced by and for students at primary and secondary level.

7. Presentation and interpretation

I. Public interest and affection for the industrial heritage and appreciation of its values are the surest ways to conserve it. Public authorities should actively explain the meaning and value of industrial sites through publications, exhibitions, television, the Internet and other media, by providing sustainable access to important sites and by promoting tourism in industrial areas.

II. Specialist industrial and technical museums and conserved industrial sites are both important means of protecting and interpreting the industrial heritage.

III. Regional and international routes of industrial heritage can highlight the continual transfer of industrial technology and the large-scale movement of people that can be caused by it.

Signed by Eusebi Casanelles, President TICCIH, and Eugene Logunov
TICCIH XII International Congress, Nizhny Tagil, 2003

Index of sites